EX·LIBRIS

ALICE KRINGSTEIN

THE COOPER UNION

BFA : 1953

# THE GREAT CENTURIES OF PAINTING

COLLECTION PLANNED AND DIRECTED BY

## ALBERT SKIRA

TRANSLATED BY STUART GILBERT

★

Library of Congress Catalog Card Number: 57-11641

© by Editions d'Art Albert Skira, 1957

THE GREAT CENTURIES OF PAINTING

# EARLY MEDIEVAL PAINTING

## FROM THE FOURTH TO THE ELEVENTH CENTURY

MOSAICS AND MURAL PAINTING BY ANDRÉ GRABAR

*Member of the Institut de France, Professor at the Collège de France*
*Member of the Board of Scholars, Dumbarton Oaks, Harvard University*

BOOK ILLUMINATION BY CARL NORDENFALK

*Chief Curator of Paintings and Sculpture at the National Museum, Stockholm*

At the request of Albert Skira we have undertaken the task of writing the text of the two volumes dealing with Early Medieval and Romanesque Painting respectively in his series: "The Great Centuries of Painting"; we concur with him in regarding these volumes, which will be published in succession, as two parts of a single work, and it is with this in mind that we have planned them. As in other volumes of the series, text and illustrations march side by side and complement each other in the creation of a book envisaged as a work of art in its own right. For this reason the selection of the color plates was determined largely in consultation with the publisher and we have also collaborated with the translators so as to ensure uniformity between editions of the work in different languages.

The subject of these volumes, whose first part covers the period termed, not without good reason, "the Dark Ages," has been seldom dealt with; indeed we would go so far as to say that the survey of pre-Romanesque and Romanesque painting given in these two volumes includes a far wider field and is completer than any previous book dealing with this period. Also we have taken into consideration the results of the latest research work in this domain, which has proved exceptionally fruitful.

The investigator of these subjects soon discovers that the further he presses his enquiries, the more works he comes on that have been neglected hitherto or lie outside the beaten track, and that to study them adequately and make the necessary photographs calls not only for a joint effort on the part of authors and publisher but also for the constant help of colleagues and public institutions. Only those who have engaged in an enterprise of this scope can know the number of persons whose aid, in different capacities, is indispensable.

For the chapters on mural painting we owe much to the generous assistance of the authorities in charge of Historical Monuments in Austria, France, Switzerland and the Vatican; also to the directorates of the Prado in Madrid, the Museum of Fine Arts at Barcelona and the Landesmuseum at Trier. Numerous curators of collections and directors of scientific institutions have done much to simplify the task of the author of the chapters concerned with frescos and several friends have kindly put their expert knowledge at his disposal. We have particularly in mind Mr Otto Demus, Dr and Mrs Walter Frodl, Dr Theodor Hoppe and Dr Wibiral in Austria; Mr Ejnar Dyggve in Denmark; Mr Francis Wormald in England; M. Paul Deschamps, Dom Dubois, Mlle Desfarges, Mme C. P. Duprat, Mme M. M. Gauthier, Mme Colette Lamy-Lassalle, M. André Lapeyre, Dom Lemarié and M. Jean Porcher in France; Messrs Tilman Buddensieg, Hans Eichler, Ludwig Heydenreich, Dr Florentine Mütterich, Mr Hermann Schnitzler and Dr Andreas Trapp in Germany; Messrs Giulio Ansaldi, W. Arslan, G.-B. Bognetti, Luigi Crema, Ferdinando Forlati, Mrs Bruna Forlati Tamaro, Miss Noemi Gabrielli, Messrs Mario Mirabella-Roberti, Ottavio Morisani, Michelangelo Muraro and Monsignor Zovatto in Italy; Messrs Hans L'Orange and Hjalmar Torp in Norway; Messrs J. Ainaud de Lasarte, Joaquin Manzarenes and Pablo de Palol in Spain.

In the chapters relating to the art of illumination we owe much to the good offices of individual experts and learned institutions. The National Museum of Stockholm and the Institute of Advanced Study at Princeton, N.J., have enabled the author of these chapters to work under exceptionally favorable conditions and the directors of the great libraries of Europe and the United States have given him free access to the treasures in their keeping. We would make special mention of the manuscript departments of the libraries of Brussels, Leyden, London, Munich, Oxford, Paris, Vienna and the Vatican, and, on the other side of the Atlantic, the Pierpont Morgan Library of New York and the Walters Art Gallery of Baltimore. Among the directors of these institutions we are particularly indebted to the Reverend Father van Lantschoot, Messrs Frederick B. Adams, Albert Boeckler, Julian Brown, Robert Delaissé, G. I. Lieftinck, François Masai, Jean Porcher, Franz Unterkircher and Mesdames Meta Harrsen and Dorothy Miner.

Many eminent specialists have generously placed their documentation and knowledge at our disposal, notably Bernhard Bischoff in Munich, Hugo Buchthal in London, E. B. Garrison in New York, Wilhelm Koehler at Cambridge, Mass., E. A. Lowe at Princeton, Dora and Erwin Panofsky at Princeton, Otto Pächt at Oxford, Meyer Schapiro in New York, Hanns Swarzenski in Boston, Karl Heinrich Usener at Marburg and Francis Wormald in London.

To all alike we tender our warmest thanks.

ANDRÉ GRABAR - CARL NORDENFALK.

# THE PRINCIPAL ART CENTERS OF THE EARLY MIDDLE AGES

# EARLY MEDIEVAL PAINTING

## FROM THE FOURTH TO THE ELEVENTH CENTURY

★

## INTRODUCTION
## TO EARLY MEDIEVAL PAINTING

# INTRODUCTION
## TO
# EARLY MEDIEVAL PAINTING

BY ANDRÉ GRABAR

ORANT. LATE THIRD CENTURY.
FRESCO, CRYPT OF "LA VELATA", CATACOMB OF PRISCILLA, ROME.

THIS volume is concerned with paintings which, over a long period, were accorded no more than casual and fleeting attention or, at best, an interest mainly due to their extreme antiquity or to the sanctity of the shrine or book containing them. The paintings in question are those of Western Europe dating to the period between the reign of Constantine the Great and the year 1000, six centuries singularly unproductive of world-famous works of art. For it cannot be denied that this transitional period failed to produce an aggregate of works comparable with those of the classical era or the Romanesque and Gothic periods. But the lack of a Europe-wide flowering of the arts did not by any means preclude some brilliant phases of art activity, if local and sporadic, nor individual successes equaling the masterworks of the great epochs.

This is demonstrated beyond all doubt by the works of western painters illustrated in this volume: the deeply moving frescos in the Catacombs of Rome; the mosaics and murals in the most ancient Roman churches and other paintings and mosaics, likewise in Rome, but dating to the reign of Charlemagne and the restoration of the Western Empire; also, outside Rome, the venerable mosaics in Milan, then a leading center of Christian art, and the church decorations and paintings of greatly varied types produced in the lands within the Carolingian Empire and its Germanic successor, the realm of the Ottonian emperors. To these can now be added a group of monumental paintings, some of which have only recently been brought to notice: the frescos in Asturian churches and also those in Catalonia. Interesting as are these masterworks of archaic European mural painting taken separately, they gain by being brought together and studied as an ensemble—as we plan to do in the present volume—when the rich diversity of their esthetic innovations can be seen to full advantage. Still more striking and no less instructive is the juxtaposition in the same volume of the murals in the Mediterranean tradition and the contemporary but often radically different paintings that had a sudden flowering on the pages of manuscripts in the lands of northwestern Europe. Whereas only relatively few frescos have survived, there is an abundance of illuminated manuscripts produced in the monastic scriptoria of Ireland, England, Gaul and Spain, and above all in the workshops of the Carolingian and Ottonian schools.

While geographically the mural paintings illustrated in this book belong to all the lands of Western Europe, they are not distributed between them equally. The greatest number come from Rome, the city where paintings of all the centuries with which we are concerned—from the 4th to the 11th—can still be seen. Rome is indeed the only city of Europe in which there is evidence that the craft of figurative painting was practised without a break throughout our period. In other cities—for example Milan, Trier and Ravenna—painters' ateliers existed during the early Christian era but these were forced to close down under the stress of the barbarian invasions, and the same fate befell artists in all the cities of the Western Empire. The Roman frescoists, however, continued to decorate the walls of churches with ornamental or iconographical paintings and thus maintained unbroken, from the earliest times up to the height of the Carolingian era, the craftsmanly traditions which were cut short, untimely, in other parts of Europe. Outside Rome few ateliers of lay artists can have survived in the cities of the West and art activity was almost wholly confined to the Benedictine monasteries. Little is known of the part played by monks in the decoration of the walls of churches, but there can be no doubt that the making of these and other works of art was for the most part left to them. Their speciality was illuminating manuscripts, and for this they had no occasion to leave the monasteries. These were often located at the gates of towns, sometimes within the walls; thus the fact that painting was now carried on almost exclusively by monks did not necessarily involve a displacement of the painters' workshops. These fall into two classes: the monastic workshops in Rome, Tours, Metz and Cologne; and those in establishments remote from towns, for example the workshops in Ireland, on the shores of the Lake of Constance or at Farfa (north of Rome). It would seem, in any case, that the transfer of the urban workshops into monasteries, though socially speaking it marked the end of the system that had obtained throughout Antiquity, did not have much effect on the general trends of art. Still it is a matter for regret that so little information is forthcoming on this point, and also as regards the general conditions under which the painters worked.

Historically speaking, the paintings we are to deal with fall into three periods: (1) the decline of the Roman Empire, (2) its division into separate kingdoms following the barbarian invasions, and (3) the revival of the Empire under Charlemagne. The earliest paintings were made during the last phase of the Roman Empire, then still Europe-wide, and under the Western Empire until 476, the year when it disintegrated. We have practically no painting dating to the age of Theodoric and the Ostrogothic kingdom he founded in 493, or produced in the other Germanic states that took form on the former territory of the Empire—with the exception of the illustrations in Merovingian and Visigothic (Mozarabian) manuscripts. The frescos at and in the neighborhood of Oviedo were directly sponsored by the Christian kings of the Asturias, whereas in Rome, however great the power wielded from time to time by Byzantine governors or high-born Roman families after the collapse of the Empire, the historian of early medieval art has to confine himself to recording the activities of popes and their foundations.

The vast changes that came over the map of Europe between the age of Constantine and the year 1000 contributed to a dispersion of art centers, following the creation of a number of new kingdoms and a redistribution of the wealth needed for financing works of art. Actually, however, the development of these local art centers did not have any noteworthy effect on the nature of the works turned out, the reason for this being the central control exercised by the Church and also perhaps the fact that the ambitions of the artists were limited in scope. None of the cities in the new kingdoms became the headquarters of a genuinely original school, and though the art practised in them usually took on a certain local color, the differences, by and large, were trifling.

It is only at the beginning and at the end of the period dealt with in this book that we find a given type of art exercising a more than local influence. During the 4th century, when tradition still held its own, a basically similar form of art prevailed throughout the Empire, which then included the British Isles, Spain and North Africa. Next, five centuries later, the Carolingian renaissance led to attempts to unify once more the modes of artistic expression within its borders. But this point does not lend itself to demonstration, for two reasons; firstly, because very few paintings of this period have survived, except in Rome, owing to the wholesale destruction of the works of art produced under the Late Empire; and, secondly, because the great diversity of styles and programs characteristic of the 4th century tends to obscure the underlying unity of its art. As for the Carolingian and Ottonian "renaissances," there can be no question that they made for unification, but—not to mention the forms of art prevailing at the time in lands outside the recreated Empire, such as the British Isles and Spain—their effects were limited. The fact that various ateliers were located in monasteries far distant from each other, the use of prototypes of different racial origins and esthetic tendencies (Irish, Roman, Byzantine and even Mohammedan) and, last but not least, the existence of indigenous traditions that had sprung up or gathered force during the preceding period, told against the development of a unified imperial art.

In Rome during the 4th century, and in Gaul as well during the 5th, there still were private persons, members of the senatorial aristocracy, able to commission the building and decoration of a palace, a church or an entire monastery. But soon the only people, apart from the ecclesiastical authorities, who could finance such large-scale undertakings were princes and noblemen. That this change took place so rapidly was due to the concentration of wealth in the hands of the government, attended, as so often happens in such cases, by the impoverishment of the populace at large. In Rome, however (anyhow between the 4th and 7th centuries), some private persons could still afford to pay for votive paintings. But the later Roman ex-votos are of small dimensions, few in number, rustic in style and for the most part the work of unknown artists. (Exceptionally, a Byzantine official was able to pay for the decoration of a whole chapel in Santa Maria Antiqua.) In countries remote from Rome, works of art—Asturian, Carolingian and Ottonian—were commissioned in all cases by members of princely houses or by the ecclesiastical authorities.

Despite the ravages of men and time, enough 4th-century painting remains to show how remarkably wide a field it covered and how great was the demand for it. Not only was it extensively used for the decoration of public and private buildings, but all the religions still flourishing side by side within the Roman Empire had recourse to it, notably in the domain of funerary art. There was also much demand for sumptuously illustrated books, and in particular for portraits. Besides these minor forms of art the painters of the age were given commissions for the decoration of Christian catacombs and, later, of the majestic churches which were being erected at the behest of emperors converted to the Christian faith. In executing these works artists were careful to keep to the taste of the period and Christian elements were freely mingled with survivals from the pagan age. Even in mausolea and private sanctuaries we find paintings of mixed pagan and Christian inspiration, corresponding doubtless to the somewhat ambivalent beliefs of those commissioning them, and these works go far to show how close were the links between Christian painting in its early phase and the climate of contemporary taste.

Meanwhile, thanks to an ever-increasing flow of orders from wealthy converts and from the Church itself, now generously endowed by the emperors, Christian painting made haste to break away from the invidious associations of heathendom and, after the official prohibition of idolatry, became (round about the year 400) the sole form of religious art current within the Empire. For while, as a result of the ban on "idols," statuary tended to die out, painting remained in favor on condition that it dealt exclusively with Christian subjects, though these, through various channels, inherited and assimilated a considerable number of the pagan traditions of Roman art. By the beginning of the 5th century painters had come to regard the ecclesiastical power as their chief patron. The Church continued to hold this privileged position, and even reinforced it, during the succeeding centuries, and by the same token secular painting gradually declined into a purely aulic art. In Western Europe from the 5th century onward, the Church had to all intents and purposes a monopoly of painting dealing with religious subjects; the Palace, a monopoly of non-religious painting. Both treated art as a means of acting on the masses, subjects or believers as the case might be, and deliberately shaped it to their ends, with the result that whatever did not fit into their programs atrophied and was forgotten—pending its rediscovery under the auspices of a subsequent renaissance.

As regards the themes employed in the painted murals of palaces in Western Europe we have relatively little knowledge. Besides sumptuous decorations making frequent use of polychrome marble revetments and the costliest pictorial technique—that of the mosaic—the walls of palaces were adorned with scenes of the "triumphal" cycle comprising both historical and allegorical themes and a great number of figures and likenesses of monarchs and their friends or foes. We find similar subjects in illustrated books, such as chronicles and astrological almanacs made for the use of princes. Other books dealing with literary and scientific subjects were provided with illustrations of a secular character; these were intended for members of the royal courts, including poets, philosophers and physicians. That stock repertories of themes for such secular works existed is proved by illustrated books produced in the 4th, 5th and 6th centuries at Rome, Trier, Milan and Ravenna. At Trier some fragments have recently been discovered of a figured ceiling painting which adorned a room in the Imperial Palace at the beginning of the 4th century. Elements of these programs seem to have found their way during this period to the palaces of the Germanic kings at Pavia, Toledo and Toulouse.

Charlemagne and his successors—first the Carolingian, then the Ottonian emperors—sought to revive the tradition of aulic art in all its pristine splendor and succeeded in enlarging both its repertory and its field of action. Unfortunately, as regards the paintings in the Carolingian residences at Aachen, Ingelheim and Germigny (near Orléans), we have only written descriptions to go on, since none of these works has survived. But the records make it clear that pride of place was given to mythological, historical and even "scientific" subjects (e.g. representations of the Cosmos). The function of these images, when figuring in an Imperial Palace (at Ingelheim and Aachen, for instance), was to extol the person and prerogatives of the ruling monarch. The depictions of the liberal arts and capital cities of the ancient Empire which figured at Germigny, the country residence of a dignitary of the Church, merely testify to the high esteem in which were held, in such circles, the literature and lore of classical antiquity. Of no less interest is the fact that this sequence of non-religious paintings was commissioned not by a ruling prince, but by a cultured bishop. Still there is no knowing if his example was often followed in his own time or subsequently—until the end of the Middle Ages—though the designs of Romanesque embroidery and their imitations in paintings, sculpture and mosaic pavements prove that this tradition was still alive in the 11th and 12th centuries. We find other reminiscences of this secular art, in the form of certain type themes, in the paintings on the dedication pages of some Carolingian and Ottonian manuscripts.

However, from the end of the 4th century onward, ecclesiastical painting predominated both in Rome itself and in the provinces where, in the nature of things, there was less use for "profane" painting. And since the conception of the church as a building to be given the utmost possible magnificence had no Christian antecedents but resulted from Constantine's conversion to the faith, a great creative effort was called for on the part of architects and artists. Doubtless there had been religious painters before the *pax ecclesiae*. But, looked askance at by the more enlightened early Christians, art found its way into the Christian community chiefly at its lowest level, in association with customs stemming from Roman tradition and for special purposes such as the decoration of burial chambers. Thus the earliest Christian painting conformed for a large part to the programs of the funerary art found in the Catacombs; little concerned with esthetic or doctrinal considerations, it employed figures and symbols tantamount to prayers for the salvation of the deceased. The subjects of this catacomb art were sometimes Old Testament scenes, probably deriving in part from Jewish paintings of biblical themes (e.g. those in the synagogue of Dura-Europos, on the Euphrates).

Once Christianity became the state religion and Constantine decided to provide believers with appropriately grandiose places of worship, new problems arose which the painters called in to decorate the interiors of the great churches built by the Emperor and his sons tackled with remarkable success. In view of the magnificence of these foundations and the interest taken in them by the rulers, there can be little doubt that the best artists of the day were employed, working in consultation with the bishops.

The range of subjects in church painting was steadily enlarged from the 4th century on and (probably at the instance of Pope Leo I) given a deeper theological purport in the course of the 5th century. Thus finally the paintings in a church came to provide a sort of résumé of the chief events of sacred history, as seen through Christian eyes. On the walls of the naves were depicted, in chronological sequence, events that had taken place on earth, grouped in such a way as to show the concordances between the Old Testament and the New, with an emphasis on the part played by the founders of the Church of Rome, Sts Peter and Paul. When the worshiper gazed up at the apse, at the far end of the church, he saw a "theophany": God investing princes and apostles with tokens of the authority delegated to them, St Peter with the keys, St Paul with a muniment. Finally, portraits of the bishops—successors of the apostles—were aligned along the walls of their cathedrals, in the same way as portraits of high Roman officials were displayed in government basilicas.

As regards these early periods all we have to go on, for the most part, are large sanctuaries whose painters kept as a rule to the programs outlined above. However there are other edifices of a less official nature in which early paintings have survived, and in these attempts to vary the program can be seen. Here (as in the catacombs) the paintings are an expression of personal piety or imagings of specific prayers whose content is sometimes clearly indicated. We find votive paintings of this type on the walls of mausolea and oratories, ancient sacristies and the shrines erected in memory of saintly martyrs, constantly recurring figures being the Mother of God or the individual saint to whom the *votum* is addressed.

During the 7th, 8th and 9th centuries the chief decorations of a sacred edifice were often a long series of portraits of saints; in Rome especially the number of saints was being constantly added to, and their likenesses were often supplemented by scenes descriptive of a life spent in the service of the Master. One of the results of the widespread cult of the "holy places" and relics was the importation of a considerable number of pictures and images made in Palestine and elsewhere in the East. Such was the prestige of the places of pilgrimage from which they emanated that they were freely imitated in the West, and had a lasting effect on the standard imagery of Christian painting. This applies chiefly to certain key themes of the Gospels, crosses of traditional forms and depictions of Christ and the Virgin. Once the Oecumenical Council of 787 had approved of the use of sacred images, successive popes made a point of encouraging their production in ever greater numbers, thereby stressing their divergence from the iconophobic Franks. In this respect the mosaics of Pope Paschal I in Santa Prassede and Santa Maria in Domnica are particularly revealing. But the sole channels through which iconographic works of art reached a wide public were frescos, pictures on articles of furniture, vases, liturgical drapery and probably paintings on portable wood panels (none have survived). The return to "imaging" at Byzantium, while restoring for a while the œcumenical entente between East and West, also favored the introduction of Byzantine elements into Roman and Italian painting at the end of the 8th century and in the 9th; just as in the period of Byzantine iconoclasm they had found favor with the popes, whose policy it then was to patronize and befriend the iconodule Greek refugees, adversaries of the heretical emperors at Constantinople.

But the erudite theologians who sponsored the Carolingian renaissance do not seem to have approved of the wide diffusion of iconographical programs glorifying saints and relics, or indeed pious imagery of any kind. Unlike the Greeks and Italians, Northerners had little relish for such forms of art and the hagiographical themes dear to the populace at large did not reappear until the Romanesque period. Meanwhile the art patronized by the Carolingian nobility centered on representations of Christ and His life on earth, on visions of celestial beings and demonstrations of the Christian verities by means of symbols, allegories and the like. Attempts were made to revive the theological picture cycles of the 5th century, which still possessed the glamour of all that tended to a *renovatio* of the lost glories of ancient Rome. In the 10th century the Ottonians continued to give prominence to iconographical themes of this order, primarily that of "Christ in Majesty," which a century earlier had figured even in descriptive paintings illustrating the Psalms of David. Hostile to the cult of images and keeping in this respect to Byzantine and even Italian practice, the Frankish and after them the German clergy made much of the pedagogic value of moral paintings and illustrations of the Scriptures. The first full-length cycles of paintings of subjects from the Old and New Testaments date to the end of the first millennium of our era.

In 9th-century Rome, as a result of the stabilization of the Lombard kingdom, now converted to Catholicism, and the hopes of a revival of the Roman Empire, the iconographical programs of 4th- and 5th-century churches returned to favor. Pope Formosus (891-896) restored the frescos in St Peter's and Sergius III (904-911) those in the Lateran basilica. In St Paul's, too, the walls were painted prior to the 11th century. Even in the Asturias, when after the Moslem invasion there came a revival of art activity, painters made attempts to resume contact with the Christian art tradition of Visigothic Spain. In all these works of the end of the first thousand years of our era we find a desire to revert to the archetypes and programs of antiquity. Hence the various "renaissances" of more or less limited scope and of brief duration that characterize the age.

Particularly striking is the variety of esthetic trends revealed in the works illustrated in this volume, not only during the renaissance that took place shortly before the year 1000 but throughout the period. From the very start—in the 4th and 5th centuries—there was a florescence of styles and techniques whose wonderful diversity is only now receiving the attention it deserves. For in those centuries there were still many ateliers catering to an élite of wealthy connoisseurs. Trained in very different ways, these craftsmen turned out works at every level, both of cost and quality, and it is a mistake to regard their productions as being all of a kind or following the same line of evolution. Rather, in such works of art as have survived, we find the *disjecta membra* of a complex of various traditions and new, divergent trends. Nevertheless all alike can be situated in the main stream of that classical painting which, perpetuating the Greek art of the Hellenistic age, had flourished within the Empire for several centuries. Far from having spent its force, this form of art was enjoying a new lease of life at the time when Christian art came on the scene.

There is no need to dwell on all the various aspects of this Roman painting, since of its manifold achievements only a few were taken over in the Middle Ages and it is with these alone that we are here concerned. All the same we would draw attention to two main tendencies that were operative in such works of the close of the imperial era as have survived, for they throw much light on the subsequent course of painting. True, they reveal a great variety of nuances in their interpretations of classical forms, but on a general—if deliberately simplified—view of the data available, we can discern two quite distinct categories: on the one hand, the sophisticated productions of talented professional artists who perpetuate traditions stemming from Hellenistic and Roman painting of the great epoch, and, at the opposite extreme, paintings of a more rustic order which (like all arts linking up with folklore) develop a stability of forms and techniques, leading inevitably, if unwittingly, to the establishment of new esthetic values. And it is the oscillations between these two extremes that account for many of the most striking characteristics of the paintings of the late Roman period: for example, certain specific, often conventional methods of rendering space, plastic volumes, figures in movement; or, again, a frequent tendency to linearism combined with the use of flat tints bound with strongly marked contour lines. The view that these characteristics necessarily derive from Egyptian or Syrian sources is erroneous. Doubtless we find similar tendencies at work in Syrian and Egyptian art at a quite early date, but there too they should be ascribed to the same cause: the adaptation of classical esthetic to demotic tastes and practices. Less permeated with Greco-Latin culture and concerned with producing pictures in large numbers for a wider public, the Near-Eastern artists were perhaps the first to manifest such tendencies, approximating in some respects to the indigenous art of earlier times. It seems likely that, under the Empire, western Christendom became acquainted with this oriental art by way of works imported from the Holy Land or made by Orientals practising in the West. But I am also inclined to think that this type of art had a more immediate appeal because its methods were so well suited to the depiction of the supernatural, owing to the more abstract way of seeing characteristic of eastern art and the exotic glamour of its other-worldly evocations.

Thus all revealed religions and Christianity in particular found an ally in this art and from the 4th century on it continued to be in high favor with the Church. But since what it stood for, in the last analysis, was little more than a re-interpretation of classical forms, this somewhat "primitive," abstract style never made a clean-cut break with the sophisticated classical tradition—and in fact harked back to it time and again. Always potentially feasible, these returns to the sources gained momentum when one of the full-fledged classical renaissances was under way, as in the Carolingian and Ottonian periods, and on several later occasions.

I think the views set forth above as regards the origins of the flat, schematic, rigid yet expressive style characteristic of the period we are dealing with are the most satisfactory. They explain why sporadic manifestations of it occur in different epochs, and also why we find, simultaneously or alternating with it, paintings conforming to traditional classical esthetic. From the 6th century on Roman painters increasingly favored the more abstract, rudimentary style and such brief accesses of classicism, spaced out at ever lengthening intervals, as took place in the Eternal City owed their origin to Greco-oriental sources. For there is no question that it was Byzantine painters who made known to the Romans in the 7th and 8th centuries the all but lost tradition of classical painting. In the frescos of Santa Maria Antiqua and at Castelseprio (near Milan)—whatever was their immediate source and the nationality of their makers—this lesson was turned to good account; we have here the achievements of artists exceptionally responsive to the forms and beauty of ancient art and technicians all the more remarkable considering how rare in their days were such highly successful imitations of the art of classical antiquity.

In a Carolingian or an Ottonian atelier it was all the more natural to imitate a given Early Christian, classical model, since all employed in it were committed to the *renovatio*. The problem for the art historian is that of determining, firstly, which ancient models (they were not always the same) were imitated in these workshops and, secondly, how close the artists kept to them; in other words, to what extent the painter "put himself" into his work. In the case of the Carolingians, anyhow those who worked in Germany in the Ottonian epoch, a special aspect of this problem has to be considered: how far the borrowings from antiquity in their art derived, not at first hand from classical prototypes, but from Byzantine painting of the day.

It was under the Roman Empire, in the first centuries of our era, that the art of the illuminated book took its rise, and once the *codex*, the book-form still in use, superseded the roll *(volumen)*, this type of art made rapid headway. All these manuscripts link up with each other and have a family likeness. In every region of the Mediterranean littoral, both East and West, there was an intensive production of illustrated books, including copies of the Bible and the like which missionaries carried with them to the northwest confines of Europe, into Ireland. Their illustrations resembled the paintings made by Greek and Roman artists at the dawn of the Christian era, but were scaled down to the size of the manuscript page and sometimes enclosed in a simulated frame painted on the vellum. These early illuminations of the 4th and 5th centuries were imitated in all the Christian countries.

Such revivals of cycles of painting of this kind in the illuminations produced under the Carolingian and above all the Ottonian emperors did much to shape the course of art during this period. No less effectual was the dispatch of works of art from Italy to England (in 684). But before inaugurating new pictorial cycles, western painting was enriched by another type of art, hitherto quite unknown. In Ireland, Northumbria on the west coast of England and also on the Continent—in the Alps, in Gaul and in Spain—it became the practice to adorn with decorative paintings the frontispieces and initial letters of manuscripts. Above all in the British Isles this form of ornamental painting was carried to a high pitch of perfection by artists gifted with exceptional technical proficiency and inventiveness. Whereas in the Mediterranean area all that was done was to transpose mural or easel paintings, without stylistic modification, on to the pages of the manuscript, the northern artists composed decorations closely associated with the script and the pages serving as their support—works of art in their own right, not mere adaptations of Mediterranean paintings.

The origins of this art will be discussed by Carl Nordenfalk in the second part of this volume; meanwhile, however, we would draw attention to the fact that these northern artists drew inspiration not only from the illuminations in Mediterranean manuscripts and other works of similar provenance, but also from the ornamental metalwork in which the Celtic and Germanic craftsmen excelled. The objects thus produced and their motifs were of local, non-Christian inspiration, but when during the 7th and 8th centuries Christian art made a fresh start, it took them as its starting-point, and the decorations in manuscripts of this period reveal a wholly new and original form of ornament. Building up richly colorful patterns of geometric and grotesque motifs, these artists sometimes integrated into their abstract imagery figures and animals, after converting them into schematic ideograms. Brilliantly successful first in the islands of the north, then on the continent of Europe, this painting had nothing in common, esthetically, with Mediterranean art. Not that artists of other schools (the Copts for example) did not, apparently at this same time, strike out in a similar direction and try to elicit from the traditional Greek forms bequeathed them by their predecessors the elements of an abstract art. But in the East these tentatives (which certainly came to the notice of the artists of the British Isles and Merovingian Gaul) were never pressed to a conclusion or systematized; whereas abstract painting in the West was fostered by indigenous traditions and techniques that, though stemming from a remote past, were still very much alive at the time when the makers of illuminated manuscripts had the idea of utilizing them. This direct transmission of Nordic practices and idioms accounts for the promptitude with which western illumination made good; just as familiarity with the Mediterranean tradition explains the facility with which in the 3rd and 4th centuries the Christian art of the South came into its own in mural paintings.

Thus while Mediterranean artists tended to concentrate on murals and, in the field of portable works, on illustrative painting in the strict sense of the term—more or less conforming in both cases to classical tradition—the Northerners tended to specialize in the decorative painting of books and in so doing created a new art of wholly autochthonous inspiration whose esthetic was at a relatively far remove from Greco-Latin practice. Our knowledge of this very special art is almost wholly derived from illuminated manuscripts. But, judging by such sidelights on it as are given by certain archaizing frescos in Spain and the Tyrol, the esthetic and technique of northern, non-classical painting sometimes ranged beyond the confines of the illuminated book.

*Part One*

# MOSAICS AND MURAL PAINTING

### TEXT BY ANDRÉ GRABAR

★

MILAN AND ROME
SAN VINCENZO AT THE SOURCE OF THE VOLTURNO
MÜSTAIR - MALLES - NATURNO
TARRASA - OVIEDO
GERMIGNY-DES-PRÉS - SAINT-GERMAIN, AUXERRE
ST MAXIMIN'S, TRIER - LORSCH
OBERZELL, REICHENAU - GOLDBACH - FULDA

ANGEL. NINTH CENTURY. MOSAIC. VAULT DECORATION, CAPPELLA SAN ZENONE.
SANTA PRASSEDE, ROME.

*Part One*


# MOSAICS AND MURAL PAINTING


UNDER the Empire the Romans constantly used paintings for the decoration of the inner walls of buildings of all kinds, from the vast halls of palaces, public baths and government offices to private houses and tombs. These decorations varied greatly, according to the kind of edifice in which they figured and also to the taste and means of the persons commissioning them and the proficiency of the artists employed. We also find variations of style, technique and subject matter that differentiate the works produced in successive periods and the expert eye of the archeologist enables him to fix, within a margin of fifty years or so, the date of any given mural. Nevertheless, the stability of this art and its esthetic is one of its most striking characteristics; indeed it is amazing how many of its forms, motifs and techniques persisted from the age of Augustus down to that of Constantine. True, taste changed, fashions arose and passed away from one reign to another and from one generation to the next, yet these were only ripples on the surface, without effect on the basic traditions and esthetic of Roman mural painting, of which Christian art in its early days was but a humble offshoot, giving no promise of the splendid flowering it was destined to achieve with the Europe-wide triumph of the Church.

There is evidence that as far back as the 2nd and 3rd centuries, during periods of peace, the Christians made some attempt at decorating their places of worship with pictures of an edifying order. What may be traces of Christian painting of this kind, mixed with pagan elements, can be seen on the wall of a 3rd-century Roman tomb under the Viale Manzoni. The Christian tombs in the catacombs of Rome were often adorned with paintings in which the methods of decoration employed in Roman mausolea of the period were adapted to the tenets of the new religion. Actually, however, the purely Christian element is inconsiderable, being usually limited to the themes: symbols and depictions of biblical incidents that had a bearing on the dead man's or woman's Christian virtues and the hopes of an afterlife these warranted. The characteristics of this art, as apart from its content, were the same as those in pagan burial chambers; it aspired to gaiety and eye-pleasing effects—which is why white backgrounds, flowers and elegant delineations of the human form prevailed over so long a period. Keeping to the fashion of the day, the Christian artists had no qualms about depicting in a style of smiling grace even the most serious subjects: original sin, the rite of baptism, the Eucharist, the raising of Lazarus, the sacrifice of Isaac.

Towards the middle of the 3rd century, however, there came a change; the moral earnestness of the new religion imbued this light-hearted pagan style with something of its gravity and after the Peace of the Church those who commissioned frescos for the tombs of kinsmen and fellow Christians insisted on the use of larger, sedater figures, depictions of episodes of the Old and New Testaments and portraits of the deceased. There was now a tendency to widen the scope of Christian art, to employ a wider range of subjects and to stress their psychological content. The effect was a new emphasis on the moral significance of concrete historical events and also on the individuality of the figures represented. God himself makes his appearance in mid-4th century art, for example on a ceiling in the Catacomb of Commodilla, and is shown as a specific personage with distinctive features. In the 4th century the spiritualization of certain pagan cults (those of Hercules and Orpheus for example) was bringing about a similar modification in some of the pagan funerary paintings. And Christian art, so long as other forms of religious art held their own beside it, was never able wholly to detach itself from its environment. Actually, however, very few pagan 4th-century paintings are extant; whereas Christian works are, even at this early stage, more frequent—for example in an hypogeum recently discovered near the Porta Latina, all the more revealing in this respect since it contains a large number of tombs built by well-to-do families. Indeed I am inclined to think that in point of fact the ultimate development of pagan art, then *in extremis*, was conditioned by the new trends of Christian painting, not vice versa. One thing is certain: though the earliest Christian paintings in the catacombs—from the 4th century on—may foreshadow later Christian art, the essential creative impulse of the period after Constantine is to be sought for not in catacomb paintings but in the decorations of the new churches built above ground.

The vast interiors of these basilicas called for a monumental type of painting, and this was doubtless inspired by the interior decorations of Roman palaces. The female figures handling jewels and the *putti* in the 4th-century paintings at Trier (cf. page 14) give an idea of the aulic decoration in vogue during the Constantinian epoch: a strictly conservative type of art, pedestrian, ponderously ornate. And this is also the style reflected in the later catacomb paintings. It should here be noted that the iconographical decorations in basilicas were confined to the apse and the extremity of the nave and that in consequence the number of themes available to the artist was limited (see below). But from the 4th century on there were paintings in other sacred edifices above ground —mausolea, martyries, private chapels—and these provided opportunities for whole cycles of commemorative historical paintings or sequences of portraits of martyrs and bishops, together with scenes of incidents in their lives. No decorations of this class prior to the 7th and 8th centuries (chapel of Santi Quirico e Giulitta at Santa Maria Antiqua) have survived, but it is clear that the decorations in a 4th-century cubiculum discovered in 1953 in the Catacomb of Commodilla are copies of murals then existing in a private chapel. This is borne out by the fact that in the same catacomb imitations were still being made as late as the 7th century of paintings dedicated to the same saints and in the style of the decorations figuring in churches.

Of the latter two kinds, more or less independent of each other, can be seen in Roman churches. To one class belong the mosaics in the apses and triumphal arches in basilicas; to the other the frescos in less lavishly decorated edifices. The former certainly derive from the mosaics in St Peter's and St Paul's (San Paolo fuori le mura), which were made in the Constantinian era and the mid-5th century by artists commissioned by the emperors and popes and doubtless capable of producing original works. Though the prototypes are lost we can get a good idea of what they were like from copies in two apses dating to the 6th and 9th century respectively. For one of the most striking features of Christian art in Rome, until the age of Cimabue and Cavallini, was the tenacity with which Roman artists kept to the style of apsidal decoration inaugurated by the mosaics in St Peter's and St Paul's. It was there that for the first time the joyous visions of a pagan paradise which had figured in the hypogea were replaced by large-scale works instinct with Christian gravity, obviously inspired by the mosaics in the Palace and Lawcourts and their grandiose depictions of the reigning emperor and his dignitaries. Thus Christ is shown as a monarch surrounded by a "Court" of saints and angels. These mosaics made a deep and durable impression on the art of Rome; as late as the 9th century Pope Paschal I had their themes reproduced in all the churches that he founded, these decorations being the supreme expression of the Roman "renaissance" contemporary with that promoted by Charlemagne.

But neither Paschal I in the 9th century nor Felix IV (responsible for the mosaics in Sts Cosmas and Damian at Rome) in the 6th, any more than the first decorators of the apses of churches in the period of Constantine, ever thought of extending the pictorial decorations to other parts of the basilica.

This was in accordance with a Roman tradition (followed up later in Romanesque church painting) of limiting the pictures to the apse. Nevertheless at the end of the 4th century and in the 5th, in the basilicas of St Peter and St Paul (as in Sant'Ambrogio at Milan and also Santa Maria Maggiore) frescos or mosaics of Old Testament or Gospel scenes figured on the walls of the nave as well. And finally, in the 9th and 10th centuries and also in the 12th and thereafter (see our volume on *Romanesque Painting*), this precedent was followed in a great many churches in Rome, Northern Italy and transalpine Europe. Of Early Christian productions the only surviving example is the mosaic cycle in Santa Maria Maggiore, which, despite its high esthetic qualities, was not esteemed as highly as the others. One reason for this was the smallness of the figures, originally placed in "tabernacles," and the fact that their illusionist style did not commend them to the makers of church decorations; another reason, that their thematic material was limited to the stories of Abraham, Moses and Joshua. We shall find echoes of the same style in the mosaics in the chapel of Sant'Aquilino at San Lorenzo, Milan. Illustration page 27 In the series of mosaics depicting Gospel scenes in the nave of Sant'Apollinare Nuovo at Ravenna, Byzantine elements bulk large; this cycle, like the still more typically Byzantine mosaics in San Vitale, was dealt with in our volume on *Byzantine Painting*.

Meanwhile, however, as already mentioned, paintings of a different nature were being made in small shrines whose religious functions were of a specialized order. To this class belong the mosaics in baptisteries, notably those at Naples and Ravenna. However, we have not thought it necessary to reproduce these since their art conforms in the main to the tradition discussed at length in our *Byzantine Painting*. The same applies to the mosaics in the oratory known as the Mausoleum of Galla Placidia in Ravenna, and also to the later (7th century) mosaics in the chapel of San Venanzio in the baptistery of St John Lateran. These relatively modest edifices illustrate an aspect of Christian mural art, between Antiquity and the Middle Ages, to which we shall revert later.

But before dealing with some examples of this art in Rome, we would draw attention to the traces of 5th-century decorations that have survived in certain sanctuaries at Milan. The importance of Milan as a cradle of Christian art in the 4th and 5th centuries has been confirmed by recent research work. The city's geographical position, the presence of the Emperor's Court and such eminent prelates as St Ambrose and St Augustine and the wealth of this great commercial center did much to foster exemplary achievements in the realm of art, several of which have recently been brought to light.

Illustrations pages 27-28 The mosaic ensembles that can still be seen in Milan figure in two small edifices: a *martyrium* and a baptistery with a vestibule annexed. As elsewhere, the themes of these decorations relate to their religious functions, but the Milanese interpreted them in a manner of their own, differing in some ways from that obtaining in Rome, Naples and Ravenna, and their handling of their medium, too, is somewhat different. True, the effects these artists aimed at were, generally speaking, the same as those of frescos in other cities: richness of color, hieratic dignity in the attitudes of figures, intense expression in faces, fully plastic forms in certain cases, an emphasis on contour lines in others. All the same, the methods by which the Milanese secured these effects were original; whether, as in the chapel of Sant'Aquilino at San Lorenzo, they relied purely on color values, or whether they resorted to an expressive line that in its fashion linked up with the "popular" tradition of Roman painting as exemplified in the San Vittore chapel of the basilica of Sant'Ambrogio.

At Milan none of the smaller, unpretentious shrines adorned with frescos instead of mosaics has survived. It is in Rome only that we find examples of this style of decoration, sometimes of a more moving quality than the big mosaics in the basilicas. Made by artists in the direct line of the painters of the catacombs, these pictures show us martyrs and their sufferings, or donors of votive paintings paying homage to the saint whose aid they have successfully invoked. Unmistakably present in these more intimate compositions are recalls of the religious imagery of the East, examples of which had been brought to Rome from Syria, Egypt and above all the Holy Land by pilgrims and immigrants. Many such works can be seen in Santa Maria Antiqua and San Saba. But it was above all in smaller churches and chapels—for example at San Crisogono, Santa Maria in Via Lata in the 6th century and, later, in the 9th-century chapel under the bell tower of Santa Prassede—that this distinctive feature of Roman painting was in high favor. For as a result of the vast number of holy relics imported from the East, there was a steady output in Rome of hagiographical paintings which, it seems, were used as models throughout Western Europe.

AN ANCESTOR OF CHRIST. FIFTH CENTURY. MOSAIC, CAPPELLA SANT'AQUILINO.
SAN LORENZO, MILAN.

ST AMBROSE. CA. 470. MOSAIC, CAPPELLA
SAN VITTORE. SANT'AMBROGIO, MILAN.

It is the frescos in these smaller Roman edifices that throw most light on the evolution of painting between the 6th and 10th centuries. True, all we now have to go on in most cases are not the vestiges of ancient churches uncovered by excavation but fragments that have survived underneath some relatively modern churches, the only exception being the makeshift places of worship installed by early Christians amid the ruins of the Forum. None of the buildings in question has survived in its entirety and often we have to content ourselves with such remnants as can still be seen in a sacristy. Moreover, all these wall paintings quickly lose their color when exposed to light and will soon have disintegrated altogether, except in the catacombs where darkness and an even temperature preserve them indefinitely—as is proved by the fact that they are in exactly the same condition today as when they were described and illustrated over three hundred years ago by that pioneer archeologist Antonio Bosio. The frescos in Santa Maria Antiqua on the Forum (discovered about 1900) will soon be no more than a memory.

These paintings which, as regards their date, have practically no equivalent outside Rome are of great interest to the art historian. No doubt they do not take us very far since they are limited to fragments; for the most part, effigies of saints. Yet, thanks to the large number of these extant fragments covering four successive centuries, they have much to tell us about the way the painters of the time handled faces, hands and drapery; the palette at their disposal and their techniques.

There is a family likeness in all these works and what is individual in any given one of them depends less on its date than on the tradition prevailing in the atelier concerned. Thus throughout the period we find painters who kept to the methods of the more rustic, least sophisticated artists of the imperial age; like them the men who painted the 6th-century frescos in Santa Maria Antiqua, those of the 8th century in San Crisogono, Santa Maria in Via Lata and elsewhere, and all 9th-century painters, used emphatic contour lines, made practically no attempt to suggest depth or volume, and fell back on decorative patterns in flat tints and expressive renderings of faces and gestures. But there were other artists who, likewise carrying on a tradition of imperial Rome, made a cult of classical beauty and kept to the ancient technique, with its insistence on plastic values, spatial gradation and the use of color as a means of producing the illusion of reality. This applies to the maker of the mosaics in Sts Cosmas and Damian, and to another artist in the next century—as the frescos in Santa Maria Antiqua demonstrate—who practised the same form of art with remarkable ability. Some of the other painters of Santa Maria Antiqua, and those of San Crisogono and the Catacomb of Callista, fall more or less into this class. The reader may remember that in our Introduction we drew attention to the co-existence of these two tendencies from the period of the Empire until well into the Middle Ages. So when we find them in Rome between the 6th and 10th centuries, there is no need to infer a conflict between local tradition and importations from the East; what we have are two separate but equally persistent currents of Roman pictorial art. This view is supported by the fact that the proportions of classical and non-classical elements during this period vary from one work to another and also that those who claim to see Eastern influences gaining ground in the 7th century are led to attribute to them the more classical paintings, whereas, under other circumstances, they hold these selfsame influences responsible for the precisely opposite tendency. There are better reasons, in our opinion, for believing that in Roman paintings of this period we find as in the past—and as in other Mediterranean regions—differing interpretations of the classical tradition, though since academic art was alien to the spirit of the time, schematic and "popular" versions tended to predominate.

In much 9th-century painting, on the other hand, we can see a deliberate return to classicism. Thus the Roman mosaicists who worked for Paschal I reverted to the technique of rendering faces in terms of color, as also to the themes of the early Christian apses. Meanwhile fresco painting, practised without a break in the intervening centuries, had made more rapid progress thanks to its suppler technique. This is evidenced by the San Clemente frescos, notably in the attention paid to color and the modeling of bodies and garments, in the boldness of the drawing and the painter's feeling for dramatic effect. The same qualities can be seen in the frescos of San Vincenzo (at the source of the Volturno, some 70 miles southeast of Rome), where we also find reminiscences of the more popular type of Roman painting, but esthetically and technically refreshed by contacts with more classical works.

If the art of the mosaic in 9th-century Rome entered on a new lease of life, this was certainly due to the support—especially on the financial side—given by the Franks to the Popes. Likewise the decorations of the Scala Santa in the Lateran testify to the influence of the political situation on the mosaics then being made in Rome; the restoration of the Empire under Charlemagne revived memories of the great age of Constantine and led to imitations of the art of the Late Empire. And I think it likely that the 9th-century mural paintings in the vicinity of Rome—like those at San Vincenzo—reflect a movement whose fountainhead, so to speak, was the Papal Court.

In no other part of Italy are there so many frescos dating to the Carolingian era as in the North—a circumstance which in itself has a certain significance. For it seems to tell in favor of the theory that these paintings, many of which are extant, were associated in some way with the renaissance of art within the Carolingian Empire, of which this region formed a part. But it must not be forgotten that northern Italy had already an abundance of works of art; mention has been made in an earlier page of the flowering of Christian art that took place in the North during the 4th and 5th centuries. Under the Lombard kings Pavia replaced Milan as the art center of the North and fragments still exist of three mural decorations prior to the Carolingian era which give us an idea of the fresco painting in northern Italy during the transition period between the Early Christian and Carolingian eras. Like the Romans, the artists of the North of Italy, unaffected by the art of the Franks, took as their starting-off point an indigenous tradition which may well have been handed down, unbroken, from very early times.

The oldest painting of this North Italian group figures in the central apse of a highly archaic triconchial chapel at Castelseprio, some twelve miles from Milan. Here the sequence of paintings, in superimposed tiers, illustrating the life of the Virgin and Christ's childhood, is clearly the work of a very fine artist with an exceptional feeling for classical form and at the same time a gift for striking a new, quite personal note in the look of intense spirituality he imparts to faces. The obvious kinship between these frescos and the most classical Byzantine paintings of the 9th and 10th centuries led us to include these Castelseprio frescos in our earlier volume on *Byzantine Painting*, to which the reader is referred. But, on the other hand, as then pointed out, these frescos had many distinctive features suggesting that they were the work of Italic artists and should be dated to the period just before the Carolingian renaissance. I am still of the opinion that here we have a pre-Carolingian work which, by reviving classical tradition with exceptional comprehension and success, did much to shape the course of 9th-century art.

Greatly damaged though they are, the frescos in San Salvatore, Brescia, made in the reign of Desiderius, last Lombard king, who was dethroned in 774, vouch for the continuity of the art of monumental painting in the pre-Carolingian period. The walls of this basilica were frescoed from end to end and we can still see, aligned in three tiers, busts framed in medallions, Gospel scenes placed side by side, and big isolated figures between the windows. Judging by what little has survived intact, the art of San Salvatore seems to point the way to that of Müstair.

Agreeing with Hans L'Orange and Hjalmar Torp, I am inclined to date the old frescos at Cividale to a little before 800; in them, however, the Byzantine strain is more pronounced, perhaps owing to the nature and arrangement of the subject (Christ and the saints disposed in a straight line), to the location of the town (in Friuli, on the eastern fringe of Venetia) and to the fact that they were commissioned by a Lombard prince. On the other hand, the paintings dating to the 9th century situated in the region between Milan and the Tyrol are both Carolingian in inspiration and owe more to the contemporary art of Rome. In Milan itself, in the church of San Satiro, are some figures of saints and decorative motifs belonging to the same period. The largest extant group of Carolingian frescos is at Müstair (or Münster) in the Grisons (Switzerland), and similar mural paintings, perhaps slightly later in date, can be seen not far away in San Benedetto at Malles (or Mals) in the Italian Tyrol.

Though no documentary evidence is available as to the precise dates of these 8th- and 9th-century works, I have little doubt that both are later than the Castelseprio frescos. But the interval of time between them is quite inadequate to account for the total dissimilarity of their general conception and it is obvious that they stem from very different traditions. This goes to show that in northern Italy, at short distances from each other and at approximately the same period, mural paintings of a very diverse nature were being produced; indeed this diversity was even greater than a comparison of the works at Castelseprio on the one hand and those at Müstair and Malles, Cividale, Brescia and Milan on the other might lead us to suppose. For at Naturno, in the Italian Tyrol not far from Müstair and Malles, there is a small church containing 9th-century paintings that have nothing in common with either the Castelseprio frescos or any of the 8th- and 9th-century works we have mentioned, and unmistakably derive (though unfortunately there is no way of knowing how this came about) from the illuminated books then being produced in the islands of the North, or from imitations of these made on the Continent. Thus at the foot of the Alps there existed almost contemporaneously three quite distinct types of mural painting and the differences between them were infinitely greater than those between the two types of fresco—those with a classicizing tendency and those of a more "popular" or schematic order—that prevailed in Rome between the 6th and 9th centuries.

This was due partly to the many varieties of ancient painting that the North Italian painters could see around them. Another reason was that during the 8th and 9th centuries several parallel but independent art trends, each with distinctive traits of its own, were making good and becoming known in Europe—we need only recall the differences between 9th-century Byzantine, Carolingian and Irish painting—whereas during the 6th and 7th centuries the idioms of these various forms of art had not yet crystallized and so far there was no possibility, in Italy for instance, of confronting and comparing these very different types of painting.

Finally, a tendency was developing to search for new forms of expression in painting in general and particularly in fresco painting, and this atmosphere of experimentalism was another reason why the practices of the North Italian painting we have been discussing differed so widely. The same factors evidently operated north of the Alps, where we find a like diversity in the mural paintings of the 9th century. However we must beware of over-emphasizing these divergencies, since the number of edifices that have survived is too small to provide a general view of the work of the Carolingian frescoists and such few widely scattered decorations as have survived figure in edifices having quite different purposes: three crypts, three churches, a baptistery and a public hall. Nor is it surprising that there is relatively little in common between paintings far distant from each other; between those in the Asturias (at Oviedo) and those in Germany (at Lorsch, Regensburg, Trier), and even between those at Germigny-des-Prés and Auxerre in central France. Such few decorations as are located near each other, for example those in and around Oviedo, have a family likeness. So there is no reason to suppose it was a principle of Carolingian fresco painting never to repeat itself.

One of its characteristics is a practice of drawing inspiration from ancient sources—sources, however, of rather different kinds. Thus the decorations at Lorsch stem from a pagan, classical model, while the mosaics (now destroyed) in the dome of Aachen Cathedral probably derived from a Roman absidal decoration; their theme, the twenty-four Elders of the Apocalypse in God's presence, had figured in mosaics dating to the mid-5th century on the façade of Old St Peter's and in the apse of St Paul's in Rome. And as we shall see, the mosaics in Oviedo are decorative compositions in the *opus sectile* technique, whose prototypes probably were the Visigothic works then to be seen in Spain. We have reasons for suspecting the influence of local Roman mosaics—particularly tessellated pavements—in the frescos with white backgrounds and heavily marked outlines at Tarrasa in Catalonia and, perhaps, those at Naturno in the Tyrol. Influences of contemporary Mohammedan art are evident in the ornamental mosaics at Germigny (though their Christian thematic material and technique affiliate them to the Italian schools), while the way figures are presented—in niches under an arcade—makes it clear that this tradition must have been transmitted by way of works of monumental art and not by way of fabrics or other portable objects.

At first sight we are tempted to detect in these murals of the Carolingian period a penchant for anti-iconic decoration, a reflection of the ambiguous attitude adopted by the Frankish clergy and Charlemagne himself towards "imaging." But though this may hold good for the church of Germigny, founded by Bishop Theodulf, one of Charlemagne's close associates, it cannot apply to the decorations in the churches of the Asturias (though here we find the largest ensembles without figures) since this region lay outside the frontiers of the Carolingian empire. This avoidance of the human figure had a different origin. And there is yet another explanation for the paintings of architecture without figures at Lorsch—the fact that this is a non-religious decoration.

Most, however, of the paintings that have come down to us have religious themes, and the choice of subjects, their number and location correspond to the functions of the buildings where they figure. Thus in the crypts of San Vincenzo (Volturno) and Auxerre stress is laid on the sufferings of the martyrs and in some 9th-century martyry chapels—e.g. the Tempietto at Cividale (Venetia), San Satiro (Milan), the chapel of San Zeno in Santa Prassede (Rome) and the convent chapel at Malles (Tyrol)—we still find portraits of martyrs and illustrations of their lives, following the earlier practice exemplified, notably, in Rome (cf. page 16). In the crypt of San Vincenzo, at Malles and in St Maximin's at Trier, the themes used in the apses are borrowed from paintings in full-size churches: the Crucifixion, Christ in Majesty, processions of saints and allusions to the liturgy. We find these also, but treated on a larger scale, at Müstair in the Grisons; this is the only Carolingian church in which all walls are decorated and the decorations are practically intact, the three walls of the nave displaying a full-length Gospel cycle culminating in a Last Judgment and preceded by a sequence of Old Testament scenes. There is every reason to believe that narrative painting like that at Müstair (and in San Salvatore at Brescia) played a much larger part in shaping the course of Carolingian monumental decoration than one might suppose judging by what has survived. From the literature of the time it would seem that similar large-scale decorations figured in palaces of the day—at Aachen and Ingelheim— as well as in the naves of churches. And there can be no doubt it was from these Carolingian narrative cycles that the frescos, made shortly before the year 1000 (they no longer exist), in San Bastianello on the Palatine and those at Oberzell and Goldbach on the Lake of Constance in South Germany derived.

The two German churches took over, though diminishing its scope, the iconographic program employed at Müstair, and in the representations of apostles in the choir (at Goldbach), scenes from the Gospels in the nave and a Last Judgment (at Oberzell, following that at Müstair) we find a group of themes which Romanesque art was later to disseminate throughout western Europe. A noteworthy feature of this tradition of church painting which originated in the 9th and 10th centuries at Müstair, Oberzell and elsewhere is its rejection of the practice of including the long series of portraits of saints which remained in vogue in Rome until the Carolingian ascendancy.

Another interesting fact brought out by this volume, in which the reader can see mural paintings and book illuminations placed side by side, is that though these two branches of the same art technique were constantly in contact during the Carolingian period, they never overlapped. It is in St Maximin's (Trier) and the crypt of St Emmeram's at Regensburg that an affinity between the murals and certain Carolingian miniatures is most apparent, while the narrative frescos at Auxerre and Müstair have obvious counterparts in Bible illustrations made by painters of the school of Tours. But whereas there seem to be no positive grounds for holding that miniatures of this kind exercised any direct influence on the frescos of the period (though this possibility cannot be ruled out), there can be little doubt, as Mr Nordenfalk points out, that some Carolingian illuminators took a lead from monumental painting. This applies chiefly to the illustrations of "theophanies" (appearances of Christ after the Resurrection) which recall the Majestas (scenes of Christ in Glory) figuring in the apses of churches. In a general way, the cleavage between mural paintings and book illuminations is most clearly indicated by the practically total absence of Irish influences in Carolingian frescos, though they played a leading part in most contemporary scriptoria. Only at Naturno in the Tyrol is Irish influence apparent, acting doubtless through the intermediary of miniatures of the Salzburg school. The interlace ornaments in St Maximin's at Trier and at Regensburg have perhaps the same origin—but this is a moot point. In connection with this question of Irish influences it may here be pointed out on the one hand that the art of painting in Ireland was wholly confined to book illumination, and also that each species of painting kept, with rare exceptions, to its chosen path and to its own traditions. This holds good, if in a less degree, for painting of the Ottonian epoch in general. Even allowing for the great number of murals of this period which have perished, we cannot fail to be

MELCHIZEDEK OFFERING BREAD AND WINE TO ABRAHAM. 432-440.
MOSAIC IN THE NAVE, SANTA MARIA MAGGIORE, ROME.

struck by the narrow range of Ottonian monumental painting as against the prodigious variety of paintings in books, their high esthetic value and their brilliant innovations.

A knowledge of Early Christian, Carolingian and Ottonian mural paintings helps to an understanding of Romanesque frescos. There is no break in continuity between them, as will be seen when our next volume dealing with Romanesque works follows up this survey of pre-Romanesque art. No clean-cut dividing line can be drawn between the two periods and the evolution of mural painting proceeded on different lines in different parts of Europe. Thus the 11th-century frescos in Germany deviated but little from those preceding them, which is why they figure in the present volume. In Italy, on the other hand, the paintings of around the year 1000 already belong effectively to the art of the Romanesque period and therefore have their proper place in our second volume.

## The Mosaics in Rome

Like Ravenna, Rome is so to speak the *locus classicus* of Christian mosaic art and many visitors to the city make a point of seeing these works in their entirety. Obviously there can be no question here of following in their footsteps, but the specimens we reproduce of this profoundly moving art show it under two characteristic aspects.

Let us begin with the biblical scenes in the nave of Santa Maria Maggiore. Made in the time of Sixtus III (432-440), they should not be differentiated chronologically, as once was done, from the mosaics on the wall of the apse. They form a sequence of independent pictures (there were originally forty-four) which, isolated under tabernacles, depicted the "life stories" of Abraham, Jacob, Moses and Joshua under the aspect of an heroic saga, in which figured generals, great ladies, crowds and armies treated in the iconographic tradition of imperial Rome. Thus Abraham is shown on horseback greeting Melchizedek in the manner of a Roman chieftain greeting an allied king who has come to present a gift in token of his friendship.

Illustrations pages 34, 37-39

Illustration page 34

But by placing in front of Melchizedek an enormous chalice the 5th-century artist has stressed the symbolic significance of the Old Testament scene as a prefiguration of the Eucharist. There are other modifications in a Christian sense. Thus in these scenes we find celestial beings, Christ and the angels, actively intervening in the affairs of men; blessing the Elect or sending down a hail of stones on their adversaries. This method of bringing home to the beholder the reality of divine intervention in the course of historical events was not unknown to classical antiquity, but it was left to Christian iconography to exploit it systematically, as in these mosaics.

It is in Santa Maria Maggiore that we see for the first time depictions of the blaze of celestial light accompanying a "theophany"—for example in Abraham's vision of the Trinity—and the no less miraculous cloud sheltering Aaron and his two companions from their enemies' attack. In other respects, however, these mosaics do not depart from the norm of Roman paintings of the imperial epoch—a practice which for obvious reasons makes the imaginary elements carry all the more conviction; their authenticity seems guaranteed by the realism of the setting.

Illustration page 37

Illustration page 38

The art of Santa Maria Maggiore is an art of transition, which in its style as well as in its subject matter forms a link between the ancient and the new esthetic. On the one hand we have fully plastic forms indicated by juxtaposed touches of different, often vivid colors; correctly rendered aerial perspective; landscapes of green hills, houses and fortified cities under a sky dappled with colored clouds; and, finally, figures, groups and even crowds moving with ease in skillfully suggested space. In some scenes, however

Illustration page 34

(that of Melchizedek for instance), a uniform gold ground takes the place of real sky, and spatial unity is disregarded, as when the procession of bearers of the Ark of the

Illustration page 39

Covenant and trumpeters is separated from the city of Jericho around whose walls it is supposed to be marching. Every scene indeed rings the changes on traditional arrangements of the thematic material and esthetic *trouvailles*. But this variety of techniques does not impair the artistic unity of the picture sequences in Santa Maria Maggiore, though it brings out the notable difference between the mosaics of the nave and those in the apse. In the latter a Gospel cycle (the Infancy of Christ or "theophany of the coming of Christ the King"), consummation as it were of the Old Testament scenes in the nave, fills the arch, and the system of separate panels in modeled frames is replaced by continuous pictorial friezes placed one above the other as in the reliefs on Late Antique triumphal arches: for instance that of Septimus Severus in Rome and, notably, that of Galerius at Salonica.

Contemporary with Justinian, the decorations in the apse of Sts Cosmas and Damian, commissioned by Pope Felix IV (526-530), are the most typically Roman of all the mosaics in Rome. Yet the general aspect and arrangement of the scene and the gorgeous costumes of the Greek saint Theodore are reminiscent of the splendors of the Byzantine court and of the mosaics at San Vitale, Ravenna, discussed at length in our previous volume in this series, *Byzantine Painting*. Thus, after drawing attention to the very special style of this Roman mosaic and the efforts of its makers to combine sophisticated color effects with an emphasis on sculpturesque plasticity, we shall now proceed to a study of the Roman mosaics of the 9th century.

Illustrations pages 40-43

Those in the apse of Santa Prassede are exceptional in size and quality; commissioned by Pope Paschal I (817-824), they are the largest of the many church decorations we owe to him. For though no other Roman pope installed so many mosaics in Roman churches, he evidently took a special interest in those of Santa Prassede, and it was in the tiny chapel of San Zenone (also adorned with mosaics) in this church that he had his mother's tomb erected. The apse of the basilica, the wall preceding it and the triumphal arch are covered with mosaics. Though the theophany on the arch, with its vision of the Elders of the Apocalypse, reproduces a theme first used (in the 5th century) in St Paul's (San Paolo fuori le mura) and though the apsidal mosaic reverts to the composition in Sts Cosmas and Damian, the decoration of the wall preceding it—a representation of Christ in the Celestial City welcoming the Saints and the Blessed—is something wholly new. These apsidal mosaics are an admirable introduction to the resplendent images of the Roman 9th-century mosaicists: figures as rigid as the gold backgrounds encircling them, from which they are differentiated only by dark, emphatic contour

ABRAHAM'S VISION IN THE PLAINS OF MAMRE AND ABRAHAM ENTERTAINING THE ANGELS. 432-440.
MOSAIC IN THE NAVE, SANTA MARIA MAGGIORE, ROME.

THE RETURN OF THE MEN SENT TO SPY OUT THE LAND OF CANAAN AND THE STONING OF AARON,
JOSHUA AND CALEB. 432-440. MOSAIC IN THE NAVE, SANTA MARIA MAGGIORE, ROME.

THE TAKING OF JERICHO: TRUMPETERS AND PRIESTS BEARING THE ARK. 432-440.
MOSAIC IN THE NAVE, SANTA MARIA MAGGIORE, ROME.

POPE PASCHAL I, ST PRAXEDIS AND AN APOSTLE. NINTH CENTURY.
MOSAIC IN THE APSE, SANTA PRASSEDE, ROME.

lines; and, on the other hand, the bright, pure colors used for faces and, here and there, for highlighting clothes and objects. As things now are, distance and the constant dimness of the light in the apses prevent the visitor from appreciating the wonderfully resonant colors of these 9th-century Roman mosaics. Recently, however, attention was drawn to their exceptional beauty, when measures were taken to protect them from possible bombardments and Dr Guglielmo Matthiae was enabled to get a close-up view of the heads of the figures.

Our color reproductions of these mosaics will, we believe, justify the opinion expressed above and prove that the Santa Prassede mosaics rank among the finest specimens of this form of art. The caryatid-angel (see page 22) in the adjoining chapel of

AN APOSTLE, ST PUDENTIANA AND ST ZENO. NINTH CENTURY.
MOSAIC IN THE APSE, SANTA PRASSEDE, ROME.

San Zenone was drawn by another hand, but this figure, which so well conveys the intimate union between mosaic and its structural support, is a no less striking testimony to the skill of the Roman mosaicists of the Carolingian epoch.

It was in San Zenone that they carried to the highest pitch their tendency to schematic abstraction in design and to the exclusion of all plastic volumes. Here the unity of effect is not merely decorative; all these strictly ordered images combine to evoke the World of Light over which Christ reigns. In San Zenone we have a preliminary version of those decorations of cube-shaped churches with a central dome which flourished at Byzantium in the Middle Ages (e.g. Daphni and St Luke's in Phocis) and in which profound mystic emotion is so tellingly allied with perfect harmony of forms.

POPE PASCHAL I, ST PRAXEDIS AND AN APOSTLE, DETAIL: POPE PASCHAL I.
NINTH CENTURY. MOSAIC IN THE APSE, SANTA PRASSEDE, ROME.

AN APOSTLE, ST PUDENTIANA AND ST ZENO, DETAIL: ST ZENO.
NINTH CENTURY. MOSAIC IN THE APSE, SANTA PRASSEDE, ROME.

# Mural Paintings in Rome

Given the dimensions of this book, there can be no question of describing or analysing at length the many frescos belonging to our period that still exist in Rome. All we propose to do here is to give some information which may prove helpful regarding the ensembles we have drawn on for our reproductions.

Among the various paintings adorning the Catacomb of Priscilla we have selected the figure of a woman with her arms and gaze uplifted heavenwards in an attitude of passionate invocation. Nothing could evoke more poignantly the yearning of a soul on the brink of the hereafter for divine compassion. While as regards style and execution it conforms in all respects to the antique pagan tradition, this is one of the most dramatic Illustration page 10 figures in the orans attitude depicted in the Catacombs, and we have thought fit to place it in the forefront of the series of reproductions comprised in the present volume. Dating to the end of the 3rd century of our era, there is nothing essentially Christian about it save the faith it so eloquently expresses in a resurrection of the body; indeed the art language employed by this unknown painter is pagan through and through. This fragment gives an excellent idea of the type of painting basic to the most classical realizations of early medieval art.

We regret that we have not been authorized to reproduce the large head of Christ (wearing a beard) in a medallion which figures in the center of the ceiling of a 4th-century sepulchral chamber in the Catacomb of Commodilla. The decoration of this cubiculum, discovered in 1953, is at once pleasing to the eye and of much interest to students of the period. These frescos were certainly the work of excellent artists who here (the same is true of contemporary works in other places) drew their inspiration from above-ground sanctuaries, copying their themes and monumental style, and using extremely vivid colors (red, black and brown) laid on in a rich impasto. This applies also to the façade of the cubiculum with its row of doves along the arch leading into the tomb, and to the two martyrs figuring first in front of the entrance, then in the interior, on either side of Christ. It seems probable that the head of Christ was inspired by some monumental work; indeed, like that in the chapel of San Venanzio in the baptistery of St John Lateran, this bearded Christ may well be a reproduction of the (reconstructed) mosaic in the apse of the great basilica of St John Lateran. The special cult of the two saintly martyrs, Felix and Adauctus, in this cubiculum led many Christians to have Illustrations pages 45-47 votive pictures painted on its walls. The two examples illustrated here testify to the high excellence of Roman painting in the 6th and 7th centuries.

Illustrations pages 48-49 In the ruins of the diaconicum of Santa Maria Antiqua in the Roman Forum are a great number of frescos of various periods (6th-9th centuries and even—in the vestibule—11th century) which are justly famous, some of them being of exceptional beauty. It is sad to see how rapidly these frescos, discovered some fifty years ago, are losing their colors now that they are exposed to light. But enough survives to show the great variety of styles and techniques employed in these pictures, set side by side or one above the other. Particularly striking is the cleavage between the works

VIRGIN AND CHILD WITH ST FELIX, ST ADAUCTUS AND THE DONATRIX TURTURA, DETAIL. 528.
FRESCO, CATACOMB OF COMMODILLA, ROME.

VIRGIN AND CHILD WITH ST FELIX, ST ADAUCTUS AND THE DONATRIX TURTURA. 528.
FRESCO, CATACOMB OF COMMODILLA, ROME.

ST LUKE. SEVENTH CENTURY. FRESCO,
CATACOMB OF COMMODILLA, ROME.

CHRIST IN MAJESTY WITH SAINTS, DETAIL. SEVENTH CENTURY (?).
FRESCO, SANTA MARIA ANTIQUA, ROME.

(less numerous) which faithfully keep to the classical tradition and those (the majority) in which classical form and procedures are modified and stylized (see pages 28-29 for a discussion of both tendencies). Noteworthy among the paintings in Santa Maria Antiqua which fall into the former category is a charming angel's head, gently drooping, pensive and, though a little ponderous, of a typically classical grace; the colors too are admirably handled. It is clear that this Roman 7th-century painter was versed in the most classical methods of rendering the plastic values of a face, and plied his brush with natural facility. A little above this head on the same wall of the apse we see a group of angels, treated in the same classical spirit, bending reverently before the Cross.

SCENE OF MARTYRDOM. EARLY SEVENTH CENTURY. FRESCO, SANTA MARIA ANTIQUA, ROME.

The excavations which brought to light the remains of the old parish church of San Crisogono in Trastevere have also uncovered some extremely interesting fragments of the 7th- and 8th-century frescos which adorned the walls from end to end. Though no large surfaces remain intact, some fragments of picture sequences can still be seen in two places. One of these (running along the wall at ground level) pictures a "Life of St Benedict" in several episodes, and includes a portrait of the saint which is remarkable for its lifelike effect. Another set of frescos figures in the corridor of an ancient crypt; here we see saints marshaled in a row between spiral columns and it is from these Illustration page 52 that the fragment we reproduce is taken. In it a standing woman saint is depicted in a strongly frontal, statuesque pose, and an interesting point about this figure is that though the artist kept wholeheartedly to the ancient model in his vigorous use of color he no less wholly disregarded the antique canon of beauty. The expressive power of the face owes nothing to classical models, whereas the brushwork owes much to them. Indeed we find in every picture of this period a different interpretation of forms and procedures inherited from the past.

Illustration page 51 In a famous fresco at San Clemente depicting the *Ascension*, we have a striking illustration of this form of Roman art. Like the other San Clemente frescos it is located in the Early Christian basilica underneath the modern church. The walls of the lower church were covered with frescos, not necessarily forming coherent cycles, since they were votive pictures made in different periods sometimes with the donor's portrait added, as in Santa Maria Antiqua and in many medieval Italian churches.

Under these circumstances it was only to be expected that the style of painting should vary from panel to panel even when the dates tally more or less. The 9th century is represented in San Clemente by a *Harrowing of Hell*, a *Deësis* and a *Madonna*, in addition to the *Ascension*. The first-named fresco suffers from an over-schematic layout, and the effect of so many recurring passages of blue and green drapery is monotonous. Faces, on the other hand, are treated in an original manner, prefiguring, at several centuries' remove, the idiom of Romanesque. Thus the panel has an interest of its own, despite the absence of any conspicuous artistic merit. This is not lacking in the more or less contemporary *Deësis*, in which along with the usual saints surrounding Christ we see St Cyril, apostle of the Slavs. In this second ex-voto picture the style is more elegant, the color scheme too is different, warmer, and the artist shows much skill in bringing out the modeling of faces by a painterly handling of color.

To another, roughly contemporary atelier we owe an interesting painting of the Virgin placed in a niche (resembling in this the Madonnas in niches at Santa Maria Antiqua). Posed frontally, she is wearing a crown and necklace which form a frame of glittering goldsmiths' work around the face, and with her large dark eyes and dalmatic of an intense blue this Virgin has the exotic glamour of an icon.

The *Ascension*, which has as its pendant a portrait of Pope Leo IV (847-855), is a painting of dimensions surprisingly large for the period, and inset in the wall in the center of the scene is a sacred relic, a stone said to have come from the actual site of the Ascension. The violent movements of the Apostles are accounted for by the fact that

THE ASCENSION, LOWER PART. NINTH CENTURY.
FRESCO, LOWER CHURCH OF SAN CLEMENTE, ROME.

ST ANASTASIA, DETAIL. SEVENTH-EIGHTH CENTURY.
FRESCO, CRYPT OF THE LOWER CHURCH OF SAN CRISOGONO IN TRASTEVERE, ROME.

the San Clemente painter deliberately adopted the Palestinian iconography and mode of presentation, and must not be regarded as characteristic of the Roman art of this period. On the contrary, the general practice was to stabilize the representation on a single plane, the picture surface, defining forms with well-marked contour lines and employing large tracts of local color. Another distinctive feature of this remarkable piece of painting is the brightness of the colors and their purity; ranking beside the mosaics commissioned by Pope Paschal I, it is unquestionably the finest extant specimen of 9th-century Roman painting.

When at a later page, with reference to frescos in Latium and the Abruzzi—and even paintings in the lands of the new Carolingian empire—we speak of Roman influence, it is the frescos in San Clemente and Santa Maria Antiqua, their style and their technique, that we have in mind, as well as the 8th- and 9th-century Roman mosaics. Limited as is our knowledge of Roman monumental painting in this epoch, we know enough to realize that it may well have exercised an influence outside the capital.

## San Vincenzo at the source of the Volturno

Some thirty miles from Isernia, at the source of the river Volturno in the Abruzzi, there once existed a large Benedictine abbey, a younger brother so to speak of Monte Cassino. Nothing now remains of the conventual buildings except an oratory half sunken in the earth. Cruciform in shape, it is dedicated to St Lawrence, and has all the walls and vaults adorned with frescos whose date is fixed approximately by the portrait of Epiphanius, abbot of the monastery from 826 to 843.

The advantage of having a relatively precise date is all the more appreciable since these frescos are of high quality[1]. Following the example of the Roman mosaicists and painters of the time, the artists responsible for the frescos in this chapel depicted a company of women saints, bearing crowns and advancing in slow procession towards the apse, where they are welcomed by the Virgin enthroned and surrounded by angels. Owing to limitations of space, the "Christ in Majesty" one would expect to see above the Virgin (as in San Bastianello on the Palatine and in Sant'Elia at Nepi) is placed in the vault opposite the apse. On each side of the figure of Christ are representations of the Annunciation, Baptism, Crucifixion and Resurrection (the Holy Women at the sepulchre), that is to say a brief sequence of Gospel scenes, Byzantine in conception, which had been already employed in some slightly earlier Roman edifices: the Oratory of John VII in the Vatican and the church of Santi Nereo ed Achilleo. Finally, on the side containing the procession of women saints, the cycle is completed by two scenes of martyrdom, St Stephen's and St Lawrence's, likewise a typically Roman theme. Facing this we see a Virgin arrayed as a Queen (a feature of Roman iconography) listening to the prayers of Abbot Epiphanius, who is humbly prostrate at her feet.

[1] Unfortunately, for purely technical reasons, it has proved impossible to include them among our color reproductions. However, given the exceptional interest of these pictures, we have decided to include photographs in black-and-white of two details of the San Vincenzo decorations; they will be found at the end of this volume.

For all these reasons we are justified in regarding the San Vincenzo frescos as a work of the Roman school. Nor is this belied by the dynamic renderings of some figures in the scenes of martyrdom and, above all, the Annunciation; for in the San Clemente *Ascension* in Rome we already find the same emphasis on violent movement. I am all the less disposed to see any need for speaking of Carolingian influence since in the paintings at Castelseprio near Milan (cf. page 30) we see gestures equally abrupt. Another notable feature of these frescos is the bold modeling of the faces, whose plastic vigor is quite exceptional. Formerly, like the iconography of the "Bathing of the Child Jesus," this was attributed to Byzantine influences. But it is safe to say that the style and iconography of Byzantine models were never directly copied, while a similar emphasis on plastic effects can be found in many 9th-century frescos both in Rome and in the North (Müstair, Malles).

During the 9th century the revival of mural painting was accompanied (as invariably happened) by a reversion to the procedures of classical painting, notably as regards the modeling of bodies and garments. But while taking the lessons of antiquity as their starting-off point the San Vincenzo artists struck out on their own lines and created some quite original works, ranking among the masterpieces of medieval Italian art.

## Johanneskirche, Müstair

The abbey of Müstair (or Münster) lies in the Münstertal, a high valley of the Grisons (Switzerland) not far from the Italian frontier. The first mention of this monastery is found in a document dated 805. It is thought to have been founded in the decade 780-790 and its church, dedicated to St John the Baptist and decorated with Carolingian frescos, may safely be ascribed to the same date. The interior of this church is a plain rectangle without any separations and with three apses in a line abutting on the nave. It had originally a flat wooden roof; the present vaulted ceiling was made later and dates to the Gothic period.

Illustrations pages 55-56

In Müstair we have the only painted decoration of a Carolingian *church* that has survived as an ensemble. Even so, some parts must have perished in the intervening centuries and the absidal frescos, most of which were repainted in the 12th century, are definitely Romanesque. Unfortunately, after the recent discovery (in 1947) of these paintings, they underwent a "restoration" quite regardless of the canons of ancient art. Though there is no documentary evidence indicating or even suggesting the date of the Müstair frescos, their style shows them to be 9th-century works. Personally I would ascribe them to the end rather than to the beginning of the century (as some have done), since they have certain peculiarities foreshadowing the painting of a later date.

The whole interior was frescoed, the eastern wall being occupied by an *Ascension* extending over the full width of the edifice above the triple apse; now detached, this fresco is preserved in the Schweizerisches Landesmuseum, Zurich. Each of the three vaults of the apses contains a representation of Christ: Christ with angels in the center, Christ investing Sts Peter and Paul with their missions in the northern apse and Christ

FIGURE OF AN APOSTLE. LATE NINTH CENTURY.
FRESCO, JOHANNESKIRCHE, MÜSTAIR.

in a medallion in the center of a cross with saints and the symbols of the Evangelists in the southern apse. Also in the apses, aligned in three registers, are scenes of the lives of St John the Baptist, St Peter, St Paul and St Stephen. The decorations of the nave originally comprised eighty-two scenes laid out in five tiers. The topmost register deals with Old Testament incidents (a cycle of scenes depicting the life of David); on the others, which contain no less than sixty-two New Testament scenes, we see one of the most detailed Gospel cycles known to art. Nowhere else, whether in this period or later in the High Middle Ages, were the Gospels illustrated so fully and meticulously

THE HEALING OF THE DEAF AND DUMB MAN. LATE NINTH CENTURY. FRESCO, JOHANNESKIRCHE, MÜSTAIR.

and it must indeed be admitted that, as regards their decorative qualities, this plethora of identical rectangular panels and the mass of small scenes figuring on the walls at Müstair hardly invited imitation. Obviously the provincial artists employed on these paintings had had little or no experience in the handling of big decorative ensembles, and a comparison of the Müstair frescos with the decorations of Roman or Byzantine churches is revealing. Nor did the Romanesque painters of a later date fall into this error of sacrificing harmonious layout and general effect to a desire to "tell the whole story"; on the contrary, they often showed much skill in adjusting their representations to the dimensions of the edifices they decorated and safeguarding the esthetic balance of the ensemble. The frescos on the west wall above the entrance, now in very poor condition, depict a huge Last Judgment of an archaic type and must have been very effective in their original state. We shall find the same arrangement at Oberzell, but this is the earliest Last Judgment thus located.

While of exceptional interest for the light they throw on Carolingian art, the Müstair paintings have little artistic merit, except for their luminous over-all tonality of pink and white, due chiefly to the local colors that have stood up best. In them pride of place is given to an array of rather stereotyped figures; thick-set, gesticulating, clad in flowing garments. The heads are often ungainly, widening out towards the top, with flat hair, low foreheads and an air of melancholy. Much concerned with plasticity, these painters tried to render volumes in the antique manner, by means of colored planes; but the tracery of white lines proliferating over drapery and even faces is excessively schematic and the same is true of the drawing of features, hands and feet, beards and hair. We have here the beginnings of a stylization pointing the way to the Ottonian frescos.

Backgrounds are filled with elaborately treated decorative architecture, the walls of buildings being opened out in a curious manner so as to show what is happening indoors. This procedure probably derived from the Roman workshops where, as at Oberzell, we find it being employed in frescos dating as late as the 11th century. Several other peculiarities of the art of Müstair show that the local artists were in touch with Roman traditions and even the hints of Byzantinism we find in it seem also to have found their way to Müstair *via* Rome. The 9th-century paintings in the neighboring church at Malles have obvious affinities with the Müstair frescos and we can also detect faint echoes of the latter in the 10th-century decorations in Santi Nazaro e Celso at Verona (996?), and even as late as the early 11th century at Galliano in Lombardy. Thus it would seem that Carolingian painting of this type flourished to some extent throughout the region of the Italian Alps. The discovery of the Müstair frescos has proved that the beginnings of this style of painting date to the 9th century and that there is no need for the art historian to regard it as derivative from Nordic art. Indeed we should go even further back, in view of the fact that the murals in San Salvatore, Brescia, were made before 774, the year in which Desiderius, king of the Lombards and founder of that church, was dethroned by Charlemagne. For in San Salvatore we find a Gospel cycle clearly prefiguring that of Müstair, and the chronological importance of these Brescia frescos should not be overlooked despite their very poor condition.

# San Benedetto, Malles

Some interesting 9th-century mural paintings have survived in San Benedetto, a small single-chamber oratory with three apses at Malles (known before the First World War as Mals) in the Italian Tyrol, near Bolzano. This chapel was once a dependency of the monastery of Müstair, near which it lies, and this as well as its proximity accounts for the similarity between the Malles and the Müstair frescos. There is no record of the date when the former were made. In the only monograph devoted to them, that of Garber, they are tentatively assigned to the 9th century, some time previous to 881, and if (as I believe) the Müstair frescos belong to the end of the 9th century, it would follow that the paintings at Malles should be dated a few years at most before that date.

Despite the small size of the building much attention was given to its adornment. The wall of the main apse, which as at Cividale is beside the entrance, was decorated with stuccowork forming a sort of iconostasis abutting on the side apses, and all the walls were painted. Though only a few of these decorations—those on the east wall and a nearby section of the north wall—have survived, they are in far better condition than any to be seen at Müstair. In the three apses are depicted a standing Christ (as at Müstair), St Stephen and St Gregory the Great; on the north wall are scenes of the lives of St Gregory and several martyrs which merit more attention than they have hitherto received. Of greatest interest, however, are two portraits on the narrow panels between the apses, those of the (unknown) donors: a nobleman and a priest holding a model of the chapel. They are placed alongside the apsidal figure of Christ but outside the recess formed by the apse, on either side of it, following a practice current in Rome, inaugurated by the Constantinian mosaics in St Peter's and followed in the arrangement of the figures of Constantine, Charlemagne and popes in the apse of the Scala Santa. Roman, too, as at Müstair is the iconography: Christ's standing figure in the apse and a scene of martyrdom in which the saint gives the effect of floating in the air among his executioners (cf. chapel of Santi Quirico e Giulitta at Santa Maria Antiqua and San Vincenzo at the source of the Volturno).

Illustration page 59 The frescos at Malles recall those of Müstair; in them, too, we find narrative scenes crowded with buildings, figures with big heads and heavily marked profiles. The faces, however, come nearer those in the illuminated manuscripts of the period; the artists employed at Malles gave more prominence to outlines and thus diverged more widely than those at Müstair from the norm of classical art. The portrait of the priestly donor is far and away the best piece in the ensemble and indeed one of the key works of 9th-century monumental painting. His square nimbus reminds us of the links that still existed between the art of portraiture and the ancient, presumably Roman tradition whose influence is also to be seen in the more detailed modeling of the face. But what above all commands our admiration is the skill with which this unknown artist has given a head composed according to a workshop formula the qualities of an authentic portrait. We have here in fact the finest portrait of the Carolingian era: richer in nuances than the mosaic portraits and completer than the small portraits in miniatures.

PRIESTLY DONOR. BEFORE 881. FRESCO,
SAN BENEDETTO, MALLES.

ST PAUL ESCAPING FROM DAMASCUS, DETAIL. NINTH CENTURY (?).
FRESCO, SAN PROCOLO, NATURNO.

ST PAUL ESCAPING FROM DAMASCUS, DETAIL. NINTH CENTURY (?).
FRESCO, SAN PROCOLO, NATURNO.

# San Procolo, Naturno

Naturno (formerly Naturns) lies in the Valley of Venosta, near Merano, in the Italian Tyrol. Some portions of the frescos in the small local church of San Procolo have survived and these deserve special mention for the originality of their style. On the triumphal arch we see an angel holding a cross and on the south wall of the nave three fragments of painting belonging to the same cycle (or perhaps a single picture). While it is difficult to make out anything of the subject of the other two, that of the central fragment is obvious: St Paul's escape from Damascus (Acts IX, 25). The apostle is shown being lowered on a rope slung over the city wall. Illustrations pages 60-61

Esthetically speaking, this fresco stands in a class apart. Painted in bright colors—black, red, blue—the figures tell out against the whiteness of the wall, while the drawing seems to owe nothing to classical tradition and is more akin to that of Ireland.

Indeed some have thought to see a family likeness between the Naturno St Paul and certain figures in the Book of Durrow and the Cutbercht Gospels (Salzburg, ca. 800). Be this as it may, we would draw attention to the fact that very similar figures can be found in the mosaic pavements (usually Romanesque) of North Italy and also that there are some affinities between the Naturno frescos and those of Tarrasa in Catalonia (9th century). The relationship between these paintings—at the furthest remove from the classical norm, with their white grounds and emphasis on line—and the art of the mosaic pavements will be discussed at a later page. The Naturno frescos are usually assigned to the 9th century, but their exact dating is still an open question.

## The Sanctuaries of Tarrasa

At Egara (now named Tarrasa) in the neighborhood of Barcelona, three sanctuaries dating to the early Middle Ages constitute a picturesque and striking group of buildings. Santa Maria and San Pedro are basilicas; between them lies the baptistery of San Miguel. Their dating is uncertain but Santa Maria is known to have replaced an Early Christian basilica and baptistery, and there is evidence that the other two edifices were built at the same time as Santa Maria. This was, according to some historians, the 6th century; on another view, the 9th. But what concerns us here is the fact that all three contain mural paintings and these were made at approximately the same time. Walter Cook and José Gudiol attribute them to the 10th or even the beginning of the 11th century, since they believe that the paintings in all three churches were made simultaneously and the frescos in San Pedro cannot belong to the period when the church was built— according to them the 9th century. Personally, after first endorsing the views of José Puig y Cadafalch who assigned both buildings and frescos at Tarrasa to the 6th century, I am now inclined to date the paintings to about the year 900, on the strength of their resemblances to certain mural paintings of this period outside Catalonia. It is however possible that in Catalonia, lying as it did on the outskirts of Carolingian culture, artists continued longer than elsewhere to practise a style of painting that had reached its climactic point towards the close of the 9th century. I also think the San Pedro frescos must have been made rather later than the others, whose freshness and distinctive charm they lack; moreover, they have undergone retouchings. Only one fragment of these frescos calls for mention; it is a sort of mural retable with angels and cherubim surrounding the chief apostles and symbols of the Evangelists placed in small niches. It would seem that other iconographic motifs, notably a Christ in Glory, completed the group of figures which, in their present state, have no artistic interest.

On the other hand, fragmentary though they are, the paintings in San Miguel (the baptistery) and Santa Maria have much to commend them. Those in Santa Maria occupy the apsidal vault, which forms an almost complete cupola. Their arrangement, in circular tiers around a central medallion, reminds us of the disposition of the 4th-century mosaics in an Early Christian mausoleum at Centcellas near Tarragona, not far that is to say from Tarrasa; also of the decorations in the cupolas of a mausoleum

THE ELECT. CA. 900. FRESCO. DETAIL OF THE VAULT DECORATION.
BAPTISTERY OF SAN MIGUEL, TARRASA.

at Bagawat in Egypt, in the baptisteries of Ravenna and in St George's, Salonica. Thus in the general layout of the Tarrasa vault this painter kept to an Early Christian tradition. This is no less apparent in the garland of laurels, complemented by a motif of intertwined peacock feathers, that acts as a ground to the octagonal star in the center. In such fragments of 9th-century frescos as have survived in the Asturias we find similar revivals of the arrangements and motifs of Early Christian art. The subjects of the scenes on the two superimposed circular friezes in the Tarrasa cupola are difficult to identify, but evidently they relate to Gospel incidents, since Christ's nimbus with a cross enclosed can be clearly seen on each. Whatever were the incidents depicted, it is clear that the scenes formed a continuous cycle without any "artificial" separations (i.e. vertical lines or frames) between them. In the decorations of the cupola of Centcellas, near Tarragona, this method of presentation had already been applied to hunting scenes —which goes to show that cupola painters of Late Antiquity were familiar with it. In any case the frescoist employed at Tarrasa, judging by what remains of his work, was hardly capable of inventing this rare and original type of decoration; he probably had recourse to a model of that earlier period.

It is chiefly in the unusual technique and style of these frescos that their interest lies. Upon a ground originally white, the figures, the trees and buildings surrounding them and even the objects they are holding are defined by thick, brick-red lines. Features and folds of drapery are similarly rendered, while the cross within Christ's nimbus, the clothing of some figures and their hair are done in patches of the same color. I see reason to believe that originally some faces and cloaks were picked out with touches of yellow ochre that have faded, but even so this cannot have altered the general near-monochrome effect, more akin to the pictures in illuminated manuscripts than to any other mural paintings. Here outline plays the leading part, as sometimes in Early Christian mosaic pavements (which the Tarrasa painter may have seen) or, much later, in the decoration of Gothic vaults or, yet again, in the illustrations of 11th-century English manuscripts. Unfortunately the Tarrasa decorations lack the elegance of these later works; the artist had little skill in the handling of drapery, while the figures produce an effect of heaviness despite their elongation. These curious bell-shaped silhouettes and even the drawing of the folds of garments remind us of the paintings in St Maximin's at Trier. Here we have perhaps a clue to the possible date of the Tarrasa frescos: somewhere around the year 900.

Judging by the style of drawing, technique and colors, the apse in the baptistery of San Miguel de Tarrasa, must have been painted at about the same time; thus here, too, we have a late Carolingian work. Though the central portion is obliterated, it is evident that the scene on the apsidal vault was a Christ in Glory placed against a luminous mandorla upheld by four flying angels. Below are kneeling figures, the twelve apostles, arrayed on either side of five medallions. The central medallion bears Christ's monogram; the others, now empty, may have contained symbols of the four Evangelists or "zodia" (images of animals figuring in the prophetic books). The bottom edge consists of a band of chevrons in perspective. The background of the theophany and the ground under the apostles' feet is studded with small disks, each with a little spike in it, linked Illustration page 63 together by thin lines. Other examples of this peculiar type of stylized flowers (the disks) and grass (the little spikes) can be found in the contemporary 10th-century art of the Christian East, whence no doubt it made its way to Spain. Also oriental, in my opinion (cf. Coptic frescos), is the gesture of the apostles lifting their hands to their mouths. This suggestion of the awestruck silence befitting a theophany—or appearances of the Emperor—had its parallel in the symbolic use of curtains. For we often find curtains drawn back to reveal images of the godhead in sacred buildings or the Emperor sitting in state in the throne-room of the palace. It would seem that 9th-century painting took over this "curtain motif" from Early Christian art, local examples being the Visigothic sarcophagi found in the neighborhood of Tarrasa.

As already mentioned, the decoration of the baptistery has much in common with that of the apsidal cupola in the nearby cathedral of Santa Maria. There, too, the general effect is that of a monumentalized miniature and line is the predominant means of expression—a boldly drawn, rather broad contour line telling out on a white ground. Here, however, it is usually brown, sometimes greenish-grey, and in some garments accented by brighter streaks of ochre. The schematic design of the faces seems reminiscent of the art of Naturno, though it is quite possible that the style of these frescos derived from those in St Maximin's at Trier.

We have reason to think that the craftsmen employed at Tarrasa made mural decorations in other parts of Catalonia. Thus in the 12th-century frescos of a Catalan church at Tahul we find recalls of the Tarrasa style, such as the white ground—exceptional during this period in Catalonia—and figures (Adam and Eve) in a setting of no less schematic vegetation. Here, too, we have an art of a rudimentary nature, essentially linear in conception and keeping to the technique of the illuminators, with the result that its general effect resembles that of the mosaic pavements.

## The Churches of Oviedo and the Asturias

The invasion of the Iberian Peninsula by the Moslems was halted by the Cantabrian Mountains, sheltered behind which the Christian kingdom of the Asturias succeeded in preserving its independence. In this region there developed in the 9th century a type of mural painting contemporary with Carolingian art but different in inspiration.

At Germigny, in France, and at Lorsch, in Germany, iconographic scenes (when not omitted altogether) played a very small part in mural painting. The aversion for such pictorial elements was even more marked in the Asturias and its effects can be seen in several more or less contemporary edifices, one of these being the large church of Santullano at Oviedo, capital of the kingdom. Probably the presence of the Moslem conquerors just across the border had something to do with this aversion, but it must not be forgotten that at the Synod of Elvira (ca. 300) Christian Spain had decided against the presence of cult-images in places of worship. Though the human figure was not systematically excluded—the church of San Miguel de Lillo, as we shall

DETAIL OF THE VAULT DECORATION IN THE CHOIR. FRESCO, NINTH CENTURY.
CHURCH OF SANTULLANO (SAN JULIÁN DE LOS PRADOS), OVIEDO.

66

CROSS-SECTION SHOWING THE INTERIOR OF THE CHURCH OF SANTULLANO
(SAN JULIÁN DE LOS PRADOS), OVIEDO. (AFTER F. DE SELGAS)

The drawing by Fortunato de Selgas reproduced above is not altogether satisfactory but it gives an adequate idea of the general nature of the decorations and their distribution on the walls of the church. Noteworthy is the alternation, in the upper register, of panels and pictures of buildings and, in the register below, a sequence of similar tripartite edifices. In the choir vault and on the walls of the side-aisles are simulated sunk panels. A row of circles runs along the arches, while the plinths are decorated with imitations of intarsia in polychrome marbles.

see, has figures dating to the first half of the 9th century—preference was given to decorations devoid of "imaging," in which the artist made known the Christian implications of his theme solely by representations of the Cross. However, the motifs of these works were rarely borrowed from the Islamic art of Cordoba and Saragossa, and the artists' most frequent source of inspiration was Roman monumental art of the late period. In this respect the Spaniards working in the independent kingdom of the Asturias fall in line with the artists of the Carolingian Empire and of Rome. It would even seem that 9th-century Asturian artists followed the example of the Carolingians in taking for models not the works of pagan antiquity but those of the Early Christian era. Thus in Oviedo, the city which in the 9th century claimed to be the capital of Christian Spain, we may well have deliberate imitations of the sanctuaries at Toledo which had filled the same role before the Moslem conquest.

Illustration page 66    The paintings in San Julián de los Prados (Santullano) have lost most of their color and some parts are almost obliterated. But though their esthetic appeal has suffered greatly by these changes, the decorative layout as a whole and all its vital elements can still be made out fairly well. In the half-cupolas of the apses are sunken panels decorated with motifs of various kinds; in the nave and transept, sequences of ornamental patterns on several registers: a plinth with simulated inlays of colored stone, and two or sometimes three rows of panels in which "Pompeian" architecture alternates with painted veils and crosses under arches.

These paintings in the upper registers seem to me—like the plinth—inspired by the inlays of polychrome marble which were in vogue from the 4th to the 6th century and in which abstract, floral, architectural and other motifs were juxtaposed, famous examples being the basilica of Junius Bassus (317) and Santa Sabina in Rome, and St Sophia in Constantinople. That this type of decoration was popular in Spain as well is evidenced by the ruins of two Early Christian churches, San Fructuoso at Tarragona and La Virgen del Mar at Malaga. Moreover such themes as miniature temples inset among other, still smaller motifs (tiny houses, vases, articles of furniture and so forth) had famous precedents in the Christian 5th-century mosaics in St George's, Salonica, and the Orthodox Baptistery at Ravenna. Similar architectural elements were frequently included in the designs of *opus sectile* (pavements made of slices of colored marble fitted into patterns). When imitated in painting these motifs lose much of their effect; necessarily the small scale of the painted edifices causes them to be dwarfed by the vastness of the church in which they figure, and there is no denying that these decorations (datable to the first quarter of the 9th century) are, esthetically speaking, a failure. None the less there is no question of their originality, and it is in this that their interest lies.

Paintings of the same kind, but in an even more fragmentary state, can be seen in some other Asturian churches of the same period: Santa Maria de Oviedo, 792-842; San Miguel de Lillo (Oviedo), 842-850; San Adriano de Tuñón, 891; San Salvador de Valdediós (Villaviciosa), 893; San Salvador de Priesca (Villaviciosa). But at Valdediós and Tuñón the decorative program of classical provenance basic to the art of Santullano is enriched with ornamental motifs of Moorish origin. It was towards the end of the 9th century that the painters of the Asturian churches began to develop an interest in the art of their Moslem neighbors and owing to the long-standing prejudice against imaging they had no difficulty in assimilating these exotic elements.

True, the human figure makes its appearance as early as the first half of the 9th century at Lillo (where we see a man seated on a throne with another man standing before him), but its use became generalized only in the Romanesque epoch. Though contemporary with the new art of the Carolingians, Asturian painting was in no sense progressive; it cultivated legacies of the past within the framework of Spanish Christian art traditions, while letting itself—involuntarily perhaps—be "contaminated" by the practices of the nearby Moslem art which, reciprocally, took over some local Spanish idioms. Thus the peculiarities of Asturian painting can be accounted for to a great extent by historical and topographical conditions.

THE ARK OF THE COVENANT. 799-818. MOSAIC, ORATORY OF THEODULF, GERMIGNY-DES-PRÉS.

# The Oratory of Theodulf at Germigny-des-Prés

Theodulf, one of the leading figures of Charlemagne's court and bishop of Orléans from 799 to 818, had a sumptuous country residence with a private oratory built for himself some nine miles from Orléans, near the great monastery of Saint-Benoît-sur-Loire of which he was the abbot. Nothing remains of the purely residential building and its famous "gallery" of paintings. Theodulf, the records tell us, commissioned not only murals depicting the seven liberal arts and four seasons, but also mosaic pavements, and some day, perhaps, excavations will bring these latter to light. Meanwhile all that Germigny has to show us is a mosaic decoration in the apse of the chapel. It seems certain that these mosaics date to the time when the house and oratory were built.

THE ARK OF THE COVENANT, DETAIL. 799-818. MOSAIC,
ORATORY OF THEODULF, GERMIGNY-DES-PRÉS.

In 1869 an ill-advised restoration of the chapel led to the disappearance of many highly interesting portions of the mosaic. As far as can be judged, these were confined to the apse and were originally located in the half-cupola, on the surfaces behind the arches decorating the inner wall of the apse, on the lunette above it and in the barrel vault linking it with the central tower of the oratory. All the mosaics outside the conch represented leaves and scrollwork with two (?) cherubim and a Hand of God holding a crown figuring in the center. Nothing remains today of this ensemble save fragments of big, stiffly rendered palmettes under the arches and—what interests us most—the mosaic decoration of the conch, where we see, above a versified dedicatory inscription in typically Carolingian style, a superb theophany: the Ark of the Covenant guarded by two cherubim Illustrations pages 69-70 and two angelic figures in adoration before it. When complete, this mosaic evidently represented Paradise, with the Ark placed in the center of the garden and ringed round with angels. Thus the general conception, while resembling that of a Majesta, was of a more abstract order, ruling out any anthropomorphic depiction of God and perhaps reflecting the Frankish clergy's distaste for images during the reign of Charlemagne.

Of the various Carolingian churches known to have been adorned with mosaics only that at Germigny has survived. Most famous of these decorations was the one in the dome of the Aachen round-chapel, a dependency of Charlemagne's palace as the Germigny chapel was of Theodulf's country residence. The mosaics in the Aachen dome represented the twenty-four Elders of the Apocalypse grouped around Christ Enthroned. These artists probably copied a Roman model and it is possible that the Germigny mosaics derive from a similar source. The iconography of the Ark may well be Roman; the drawing and execution of the angels' faces and draperies, as well as the "acromegaly" of the bodies (the unnatural largeness of extremities such as hands and feet) assimilate Germigny to certain frescos that were being made at the same time in Roman churches.

However, in the decorations at Germigny we can discern two varieties of motifs. One of these stemmed from more or less obviously ancient sources and the stock repertory of the decorative artists (makers of miniatures and reliefs) of the Carolingian period. Good examples of this type of decoration can be seen in Gaul, in Northern and Central Italy, and in Rome itself (Santa Maria in Cosmedin). But there are other motifs—notably the tall, angular palmettes behind the arches of the apse—which remind us, rather, of the floral ornaments of Omayyad art, slightly previous to Germigny or, in Spain, contemporary with it. It was probably by way of Spain, a country with which Theodulf was familiar, that the Germigny mosaicists became acquainted with these motifs and the practice of filling niches placed side by side with tall palmettes. These appear in France only two centuries later, in the representations of Mozarabic façades that figure in the Saint-Sever *Apocalypse* (Paris, Bibl. Nat.).

But from the 8th century on the paintings in illuminated manuscripts seem to show occasional borrowings from contemporary Asiatic art in their ornamental decorations, though it is impossible to say if the Carolingian illustrators derived their knowledge of it directly from Moslem sources or indirectly, by way of Byzantine works inspired by the sumptuary arts of Islam.

THE STONING OF ST STEPHEN. BEFORE 859. FRESCO, CHAPELLE SAINT-ETIENNE,
SAINT-GERMAIN, AUXERRE.

## Saint-Germain, Auxerre

Auxerre *(Autessiodurum)* became a Roman civitas and the seat of a bishop in the 3rd century. Under the Merovingian kings the abbey of St Germain, named after the great saint of Auxerre and its sixth bishop, was founded; some Carolingian frescos can still be seen in the crypt of the martyry church, most of whose nave has disappeared. These were made between 841, the year the crypt was built, and 859 when the ceremonial transfer of the saint's body to its new abode took place. It is also possible that, though they have much in common, not all the surviving paintings were made at the same time. Nor do they extend to all the crypts; some (seemingly earlier than 859) figure in a small Illustration page 72 side chapel dedicated to St Stephen, and others in the ambulatory east of the sepulchral chamber containing St Germain's remains, in which subsequently (ca. 862) those of several bishops of Auxerre were also interred.

Three frescos in St Stephen's chapel illustrate incidents in the life of the first martyr, as described in the Acts of the Apostles. In the ambulatory two symmetrical panels depict two canonized bishops standing on small pedestals. There are no inscriptions and, whereas this does not apply to the scenes of St Stephen's life, which are easily identifiable, it is highly unlikely that we shall ever discover who were the bishops represented on the outer wall of the tomb chamber. Perhaps these are portraits of bishops of Auxerre who were canonized and buried in the crypt; this seems to me the most likely explanation of their presence here. But we must not forget that other sainted ecclesiastics—for example Popes Gregory and Gelasius—often figured in Carolingian imagery. Posted on separate pedestals, the bishops in the Auxerre frescos remind us of the funerary portraits of the close of antiquity (those, for instance, which figure in the Spanish mausoleum at Merida); in the Middle Ages, however, motifs of this kind were also employed in paintings unconcerned with tombs.

The portraits of bishops aligned side by side have much in common with the ones found in Roman churches and the sequences of portraits of popes that were sometimes included in the decorations of naves from the 6th and 7th centuries on. The style of the Auxerre portraits, however, has no direct affinities with any Roman wall painting and more in common with the representations of bishops in Carolingian and even Ottonian illuminated manuscripts. It does not, however, follow that the Auxerre frescoist copied miniatures; on the contrary everything here points to the existence of a local and independent tradition of mural painting, distinct from that of Rome. This is borne out by the frescos in St Stephen's chapel, where the artist shows a real sense of the need to relate mural paintings to their architectural context. A handsome painted capital forms part of the setting he gives his pictures, each scene occupies a separate lunette and the images are presented with an eye to the concave surfaces of the semi-domes. Moreover the technique is skillfully adapted to the requirements of mural painting; clean-cut linear composition, "projection" of each scene on to the wall surface with only the shallowest of modeling, giving the effect of bas-relief. The Auxerre painter employs both thick contour lines and planes of color for giving a three-dimensional effect to his figures. His art links up with antiquity, but without any direct affiliation to any of the known 8th- and 9th-century schools of Italy and Germany. In France, too (so far as our present knowledge goes), the Auxerre frescos stand in a class apart—but this is doubtless due to the wholesale destruction of pre-Romanesque mural paintings.

## St Maximin, Trier

The Carolingian paintings in St Maximin's figure in the crypt of a sanctuary whose origins go back to a very early age. Administered by Benedictines, this church lay just outside the city walls. When, after being wrecked by the Northmen in 882, it was rebuilt in 935, the crypt was left untouched and even partially walled in, and it is due to this fortunate chance that the frescos have survived. They probably date to the close of the 9th century and mostly to the years immediately following the Norse raid. This dating is borne out by their style and iconography. (There had previously existed older paintings in the crypt when they were made.)

Rectangular in form, the crypt is roofed with a large barrel vault. Abutting on the back wall is an altar in stonework and on the wall above a monumental Crucifixion

PROCESSION OF MARTYRS. LATE NINTH CENTURY. FRESCO FROM THE CRYPT OF ST MAXIMIN'S.
LANDESMUSEUM, TRIER.

whose liturgical and eucharistic significance is stressed by a depiction of the blood from the Savior's side collected in a vase and of a serpent coiled around the foot of the Cross.

Illustrations pages 74-75 On the wall facing the altar are two lines of men and women saints (the women preceding the men), carrying palms and walking under a colonnade. The paintings in the vault are of a slightly different nature; alongside less identifiable figures we see a standing prophet, two seated Evangelists and an inscription FORTITUDO—but without a personification of that virtue. The figures are set off by decorative motifs, chiefly cable moldings. Though some parts of this fresco no longer exist, enough is left to show how harmoniously balanced was the layout of the various elements: a Crucifixion and a procession of saints grouped around the altar; Evangelists, prophets, decorative patterns (and names of virtues) in the vault.

Of all Carolingian monumental paintings this comes closest to the contemporary miniatures; in it we find the same subjects and a similar juxtaposition of images separated by ornamental frames and accompanied by explanatory inscriptions. Likewise the linear treatment of figures and drapery and also a special way of drawing faces have marked analogies with the paintings in illuminated manuscripts.

PROCESSION OF MARTYRS, DETAIL. LATE NINTH CENTURY. FRESCO FROM THE CRYPT OF ST MAXIMIN'S.
LANDESMUSEUM, TRIER.

# The Solarium of Lorsch

At Lorsch, not far from Worms, an oddly shaped little building, practically intact, stands on the site of the great Carolingian monastery of which only a few fragments have survived. Formerly this building occupied the center of a courtyard surrounded on all sides by porticos. It was recently restored to its original state as an independent building and the restorations brought to light some interesting 9th-century murals. I am unable to assign a more precise date to these paintings, which may not have been made at the same time as the edifice was built (traces have been found of earlier paintings); all that can be positively said is that they are not later than the 9th century.

It is an oblong building 31 feet by 22 containing a single upper room which was obviously intended to be entirely secluded from the outside world. The space below, at ground level, is open to the air, and access to the upper room is had by two spiral staircases clamped to the short sides of the rectangle. In the Bayeux tapestry we see an almost identical building: the "pavilion" in which Harold and his men are feasting before crossing the Channel. This, too, consists of a loft-like room supported on three arches, access to which is had by an outside staircase (only one in this case). The advantage of rooms built on these lines was that their occupants were safe from prying eyes and protected from intruders; which doubtless explains the popularity of this rather curious type of structure. Princes and abbots often had what were known as *solaria* in Roman times built in their palaces and monasteries—there is one at Saint-Wandrille, a 9th-century Benedictine abbey near Rouen—and I think the nature of the mural paintings at Lorsch justifies the identification of the room in which they figure as a *solarium*.

The foundation of the abbey at Lorsch goes back to the reign of Charlemagne (774), but no record exists suggesting that he was responsible for this peculiar edifice or explaining the purpose it was meant to serve when it was built, probably around the year 800. Though later in the Middle Ages the upper room was converted into a chapel dedicated to St Michael, the mural paintings, all of which have secular subjects, prove that it was not originally intended to serve as a place of worship; a fact that is borne out by the façades on the two longer sides of the edifice, where the rows of small pediments extending the full length of the upper storey are such as regularly figured on palaces and city gates. This type of architectural decoration seems to have come into vogue during the last period of the Roman Empire and was employed—for palaces—during the early Middle Ages in all the lands where Mediterranean traditions still prevailed. Thus both the structure and the decorations of the edifice at Lorsch belong to a tradition stemming from classical antiquity that had survived into the Carolingian era.

These paintings have a remarkable sobriety and, but for some precisely rendered details, the general effect is monumental, classical in spirit and, so far as 9th-century art is concerned, paralleled only by the frames of certain Gospel canon pages. But the Lorsch frescos rank above these other paintings in the classical manner in so far as they not only employ motifs drawn from ancient architecture but impart to them a

SOLARIUM OF LORSCH. DIAGRAM OF THE DECORATIVE PAINTINGS IN THE UPPER ROOM. (AFTER F. BEHN)

The above plan shows the general arrangement of the simulated architecture. As it is in such poor condition, a diagrammatic reconstitution gives a better idea of its original appearance than a photograph.

monumental aspect, likewise inspired by the art of antiquity. One of the features of this decoration is a simulated balustrade of large square slabs of stone in three alternating colors topped by a narrow monochrome ledge on which stand pillars white and red alternately. Finally, upon these pillars rests an elaborate architrave done in trompe-l'œil. Above the architrave and between the pillars lies the white ground of the wall.

What the painter was aiming at is evident: he wished the closed room to give the illusion of an open terrace at the top of a building, in the manner of the belvederes, surrounded by slender pillars with architraves above them, known in modern Italy as *altane* (equivalents of the above-mentioned Roman *solaria*). There can be no doubt that the artist who worked at Lorsch had this in mind when he planned these frescos and it goes to confirm what was said above: that this building and its decoration keep strictly to a specific tradition deriving from antiquity.

All the same we cannot fail to notice some instances of flagrant clumsiness in the artist's handling of classical motifs, as also the presence of elements deriving from some other source, and for both reasons we are justified in regarding these paintings as a typically Carolingian work. Among the instances of clumsiness are: the over-wide spacing of the pillars, the exaggerated slenderness of their shafts, the plethora of ornamentation on the architrave and, lastly, the polychrome checkerwork of the balustrade. We find the same polychromy—effected here with real colored stone—on the façades of the building, where however the chess-board pattern is combined with allied but different motifs: octagons and lozenges aligned and overlapping. On the façades all surfaces available between the structural elements are patterned with these many-colored motifs, whereas in the paintings inside the building they are used more sparingly, being limited to the pseudo-balustrade. In short, the ornamentation of the interior is far more classical than that on the outside of the building, despite the fact that we find a chess-board pattern which obviously derives from the same tradition as the polychrome motifs on the façades recurring also in the interior decorations. The historical antecedents of these motifs have not yet been definitely ascertained, but the most numerous and, chronologically, the nearest analogies are the depictions of buildings found in Mozarabian miniatures: representations of the Moorish or Christian edifices then existing in Spain. Charlemagne's followers may well have seen them during the anti-Saracen "crusades." Even in Spain, in the Asturias, 11th-century mural paintings, contemporary with those at Lorsch, combine classical with Mozarabic motifs, while in France, at Germigny, in paintings of the same period we find Omayyad decorative patterns intermingled with others in the Early Christian tradition. But it was only at Lorsch that painters took for their models not works of late antiquity, but those of the earliest, authentically classical age. The reason for this is probably that, whereas all other paintings of the time dealt with religious subjects and had recourse to Christian prototypes, the themes of those at Lorsch were uniformly secular. In any case there is no question that in the Lorsch frescos we have the finest flower of Carolingian art monumentally conceived and classical in spirit.

## Oberzell, Reichenau

During the early Middle Ages several large communities of monks dwelt on the island of Reichenau at the western end of the Lake of Constance. In the various monasteries were installed large scriptoria with ateliers for illuminators, and the manuscripts illuminated on the island rank among the masterworks of Carolingian and Ottonian art in Germany. While there is no doubt that all the churches in these monasteries were *Illustration page 79* adorned with frescos, only in one of them, that of St George at Oberzell, have they survived. All the paintings in the nave can still be seen and we reproduce a fragment from one of those which have suffered least from the well-intentioned but regrettable "restoration" that took place in 1880. In the course of it these 10th-century paintings were excessively retouched and the line, especially, has all too often lost its pristine crispness. Unquestionably ancient, however, are the iconography, the general disposition

THE HEALING OF THE LEPER. SECOND HALF OF THE TENTH CENTURY. FRESCO IN THE NAVE.
GEORGSKIRCHE, OBERZELL (REICHENAU).

of figures and architectural elements and the basic color schemes. On the other hand the original contour lines and modeling (indicated by streaks of white) are intact only here and there. These paintings are thought to have been made during the second half of the 10th century.

The artist responsible for the decorations in the nave deliberately confined himself to a small range of subjects. On either side of the apse (where the original paintings have disappeared) is an ecclesiastic under an arch, while on the side walls are scenes of Christ's miracles on eight large panels, with figures of prophets above them and, below them in medallions, portraits of priests. Since the wall surface available was too large for so small a number of subjects, the remaining space is filled with horizontal and vertical decorative patterns. There is a striking contrast between the sobriety of this ensemble—in which more attention has been given to the harmonious arrangement of the picture elements than to their didactic efficacy—and the Müstair paintings, which set out to illustrate as many Gospel episodes as possible. The priority thus given to decorative values foreshadows the Romanesque paintings in which, as we shall see, small groups of themes culled from a far wider cycle are used as the basic elements of church decoration; the eight miracles of Christ depicted at Oberzell have their Romanesque parallel in the scenes from Genesis in Saint-Savin near Poitiers. In both cases a relatively limited sequence of biblical scenes extends the full length of the nave. The view which has been put forward that in the choice of Christ's miracles as the leading theme at Oberzell we have an expression of a specifically Germanic type of Christianity seems uncalled for; we find the same theme persistently recurring in the Early Christian cycles on Roman sarcophagi. These, however, are primarily matters for the archeologist; more to our point are certain evident analogies between the color schemes at Oberzell and Müstair: notably the predominance of pink and white with a liberal use of ochre. But at Oberzell, besides the use of light blue grounds and a variety of colors for the folds of drapery, we find a monumental dignity and a refinement that are far to seek at Müstair. As they moved in the direction of Romanesque, painters began to elongate figures, to stress linear effects and to indulge in graceful curves; also they tended towards a more abstract and rhythmical design, more dignified and balanced renderings of movements. Though, given their limited scope, these Oberzell frescos can hardly rank beside the vast contemporary florescence of German miniatures, they nevertheless reflect an esthetic and a mental outlook owing much, like the illuminations, to the influence of the Emperor's court, which had taken over many of the practices of Byzantine palace art. The strongly eurhythmic composition of the Oberzell frescos may well have been inspired by that of contemporary Byzantine churches, where, however, it extended also to the carefully balanced iconographic programs which it implemented. No mention need be made here of the big *Last Judgment* on the outer wall of the west apse, since it is a purely Romanesque creation.

## St Sylvester's Chapel, Goldbach

The St Sylvester Chapel at Goldbach, near Überlingen, on the German shore of the Lake of Constance, is not far from the island of Reichenau. Like the Oberzell frescos, which probably inspired them, the paintings in this chapel date to the 10th century. But though clearly emanating from the ateliers of Reichenau, the Goldbach frescos represent a slightly later variant of this art, and we would date them accordingly to the end of the 10th century.

The interior of the Goldbach church is a plain rectangle. On its east wall, in front of the choir, are two portraits (rather indistinct) of the founders, husband and wife, escorted by their patron saints. It will be remembered that in the Lateran and at Malles portraits of the founders were given the same position; were placed, that is to say, on either side of the altar. Of the two fresco sequences on the side walls only fragments have survived; nevertheless one can still distinguish—though less clearly than in the past—portions of scenes of miracles, the same in parts as those at nearby Oberzell, and there are vestiges of other Gospel scenes, in particular one of the prayer in Gethsemane. But it is in the apse that we have the best preserved paintings: a row of big figures

FIGURE OF AN APOSTLE. LATE TENTH CENTURY.
FRESCO, ST SYLVESTER'S CHAPEL, GOLDBACH.

FIGURE OF A VIRTUE IN A MEDALLION. BEFORE 1023. CEILING FRESCO.
CRYPT, ANDREASKIRCHE AM NEUENBERG, FULDA.

of seated apostles (as in the mosaic decorations of 5th-century apses), relieved against Illustration page 81 a white background. Tall and narrow as statues interposed between the pillars of a portico and grouped in pairs, they have the air of persons engaged in a *sacra conversazione*. It is here that we can get the best idea of the Goldbach style, which carries the idioms of the art of Oberzell a stage further and in so doing approximates more closely to that of Romanesque frescos. Indeed the general tendency to bring out the decorative values of forms, as well as the means employed—elongated proportions, fine-spun, fluent line and bright, pure colors—points the way to the art of the Saint-Savin gallery, discussed in our companion volume, *Romanesque Painting*.

## Andreaskirche am Neuenberg, Fulda

None of the Carolingian paintings have survived in the ancient town of Fulda (some 70 miles northeast of Frankfort-on-Main) where St Boniface, missionary to the Germans, founded a famous abbey. But besides a few traces of decoration in the small, round church of St Michael, some Ottonian frescos are still to be seen in the crypts of two suburban churches. In the Petersberg church these are only fragments, mostly in very poor condition, but in St Andrew's at Neuenberg, consecrated in 1023, all essential parts of the painting are quite recognizable and some have kept their pristine freshness.

The layout of these murals is happily conceived, with a Christ in Majesty above the axial window dominating the ensemble and on either side some figures of the Eucharistic cycle (Melchizedek, Cain and Abel). On the vaults, groined in the Byzantine manner, are medallions containing half-length depictions of Christ and personifications of Virtues, Illustration page 82 while all around the crypt the walls are adorned with representations of angels, all very much alike. Though the ornamentation with its large floral motifs has a certain heaviness, the general arrangement was evidently the work of an expert in the decoration of vaulted rooms, who had probably seen Byzantine frescos. In his depictions of the long line of angels this artist was particularly successful. We reproduce two of these Illustrations pages 84-85 figures, which are oddly cut short at the knees by the clouds encircling them. Noticeable, too, are the disproportionately narrow wings, the heavy contour lines around the heads, the small straight noses, round chins and the drapery with long, infrequent folds indicated by rapidly brushed-in lines and dabs of color. Despite the ravages of time we can still appreciate this artist's fine feeling for color both in the angelic figures and in the paintings on the vaults: half-length personifications enclosed in medallions.

★

In the foregoing pages our color plates and the text accompanying them have combined, we hope, to throw light on the qualities to which individual pre-Romanesque paintings and groups of paintings—and the art in general of the Early Middle Ages— owe their intrinsic appeal: originality of techniques and forms, a lively sense of color and (in many cases) executive virtuosity of a high order. These works have been studied

ANGEL. BEFORE 1023. FRESCO.
CRYPT, ANDREASKIRCHE AM NEUENBERG, FULDA.

ANGEL. BEFORE 1023. FRESCO.
CRYPT, ANDREASKIRCHE AM NEUENBERG, FULDA.

both in the light of their relations *inter se* and with regard to the part they played in the overall development of European art through the ages. While some of the innovations distinctive of this art may be ascribed to the creative talent of individual artists, most of its idiosyncrasies reflect the historical context in which it took its rise.

Nevertheless those who study pre-Romanesque paintings through the eyes of the art historian or connoisseur familiar with the antecedent works of the Late Roman Empire and the subsequent creations of Romanesque, cannot fail to observe how frequent and how unmistakable are the links between the frescos, miniatures and mosaics dealt with in this volume, their Roman predecessors and their Romanesque successors. Indeed there can be no question that we have here one and the same art current, taken at successive stages of its long course. The art of the Early Middle Ages started out from traditional usages basically the same as those of Romanesque. For both alike claimed descent from the same ancestor, the art of the last centuries of the Roman Empire.

Thus the tendencies displayed by the early medieval artists whose work we have been examining did not die out in or about the year 1000. They were taken over or carried a stage further in the next period, which will form the subject of our forthcoming *Romanesque Painting*, sequel to the present volume. Together, these two books will give a panoramic view of the great art movement which, beginning at the close of classical antiquity, lasted until the Europe-wide triumph of the Gothic style.

In many respects Romanesque was a direct continuation of the art preceding it; it incorporated both the Celtic and insular elements which, as has been shown in this volume, had been grafted on to the Mediterranean tradition, and also many of the practices of Byzantium and the East. But, though they did not reject the lessons of the past, the Romanesque artists covered a much wider field, striking out in new directions and on original lines, while by the same token they embarked on more elastic programs and their art took effect at deeper social levels and in lands untouched by their precursors. In short, the Romanesque works to be discussed and illustrated in our second volume were an esthetic expression of the first collective cultural movement since the great age of classical antiquity to carry all before it in the Western World.

*Part Two*

# BOOK ILLUMINATION

TEXT BY CARL NORDENFALK

LATE ROMAN ILLUMINATION

IRELAND AND ENGLAND

MEROVINGIAN ILLUMINATION

CAROLINGIAN ILLUMINATION

MOZARABIC ILLUMINATION

ANGLO-SAXON ILLUMINATION
IN THE 10TH AND 11TH CENTURIES

OTTONIAN ILLUMINATION

*Part Two*

# LATE ROMAN ILLUMINATION

I T was in the Middle Ages that the illuminated manuscript had its finest flowering and this period provides the richest and in a sense the purest field of art available to the student of medieval painting. Basic to all pictorial art of the Middle Ages was illustration, and this applies *a fortiori* to the illuminated book. The practice of illumination was conditioned by the close connection necessarily existing between text, picture and ornament; a relationship that varied through the ages and assumed an immense diversity of forms.

But though the art of the illuminated manuscript is typically medieval, it was not, like the stained-glass window for example, invented in the Middle Ages. Long before this, in ancient Egypt, the papyrus rolls placed beside the dead to act as passports on their journey to the netherworld, were supplied with colored illustrations. And though, like the Romans, the Greeks of the Hellenistic age did not give illumination a leading place in their artistic output, there can be no doubt, despite the paucity of examples that have come down to us, that illustrations often figured in their books, especially those concerned with science. In purely literary works the illustrations seem to have been originally intended to serve as guide marks for the reader, and these were all the more useful since in early manuscripts the columns of writing were not numbered and therefore no system of numerical references or index could be provided.

During the second, third and fourth centuries of our era, the papyrus roll was gradually supplanted by the vellum codex (or leaved book), which furnished a new support for the illustrations and had the advantage of supplying artists with pages of a standard size to work on. Nevertheless they were slow to turn this to account except for portraits of authors. As in the papyrus rolls the form given the illustrations still depended more on the layout of the writing than on the format of the page, and they were inserted as before in the columns of text, usually without frames or backgrounds. Such was the arrangement of the illustrations in the 5th- and 6th-century Annals of Ravenna which have come down to us in the form of fragmentary copies made in the early Middle Ages.

The oldest extant miniatures in painted frames date without exception to the 4th century A.D. Thus the first efflorescence of the art of illumination took place about the time when the culture of classical antiquity was beginning to decline. But though illumination was late in winning for itself an honorable place in the lineage of art, it arrived in time to transmit through the medium of the book the "illusionist" technique of antique painting, and there can be no doubt that this was one of the most decisive factors in the evolution of art during the Middle Ages. For in thus perpetuating the tradition of classical forms, the illuminated books acted as a sort of reservoir whence the art of succeeding centuries was constantly replenished as the need arose. These returns to the ancient sources lay at the origin of the so-called "renaissances" that took place from time to time in medieval art and recurred, like successive waves, in the centuries preceding the dawn of Romanesque. In Byzantium they followed one another almost continuously during the first millennium of our era, reaching their climax in the 10th century, while in the West they touched England to begin with round about 700, then France in the 9th century, then Germany and England once again towards the year 1000. Particularly striking is the intimate understanding of classical style displayed in the imitations of antique models that were made during the Carolingian renaissance. Indeed, even if none of the illuminations of the final period of classical antiquity had survived, we would be able to get a fairly good idea of them from copies made in the early Middle Ages.

The Roman Calendar for 354 A.D. is a case in point; nothing of it survives today, but we have drawings made in the 16th and 17th centuries and reproducing, Peiresc tells us, a Carolingian copy of the original. In the best of these the Roman prototype is reproduced so faithfully that one is hardly conscious of the intervention of a Carolingian copyist; even in the ornamental elements we find nothing suggestive of the art of the early Middle Ages. The original, a de-luxe version of the official Roman Calendar, was a New Year's gift to a high official named Valentinus. The maker of this illuminated manuscript inscribed his signature on a tablet upheld by *putti*, drawn on the opening page. His name was Furius Dionysius Filocalus and we know he was subsequently employed as an epigrapher by Pope Damasus (366-384), for whom he invented a special type of monumental capital letter for use in marble inscriptions in the Catacombs.

The decorations comprise a set of "official" depictions of the four capitals of the Empire, likenesses of the two consuls of the year (Constantius II and Constantius Gallus), an astrological calendar showing the planetary deities and an almanac with full-page representations of the Months. The spirit of these illustrations is still frankly pagan, though the ecclesiastical computation of the year figures among the texts. Both script and illustrations are framed in richly decorated borders, whose motifs are the same as those in the ornaments on contemporary Roman military uniforms. The fact that these decorative frames enclose texts laid out in the form of *tabellae* is not due to the epigrapher's caprice; we learn from an Egyptian papyrus that in book rolls of the Hellenistic epoch it was already customary to frame tabular texts with ornamental colonnettes. Moreover some of the illustrations in Filocalus' Calendar conform to a standard type whose origin is unknown but which persists in all the calendars of medieval psalters and sacramentaries having representations of the months and signs of the zodiac. Although the forms changed, calendar illustration of this kind remained in vogue without a break from classical antiquity until the Renaissance.

ARATUS. CENTAUR. NINTH-CENTURY CAROLINGIAN COPY OF A FOURTH-CENTURY ORIGINAL. (8⅛ × 8⅝″)
HARLEY MS 647, FOLIO 12, BRITISH MUSEUM, LONDON.

During the decline of the Empire (as can be seen from copies made in the early Middle Ages) there was a vogue for illuminated manuscripts dealing with astronomy. No less than seven such texts, some with and some without illustrations, have survived, and all derive from models dating to the end of classical antiquity. Among the illustrated texts we may mention two manuscripts by Aratus, one at Leyden (University Library,

Voss. lat. 79) and the other in London (British Museum, Harl. 647). The former contains personified representations of celestial bodies standing out on a grey-blue sky and enclosed in fiery-red frames. Each picture has the form of a rectangular tablet and fills an entire page, the verses that explain the subject illustrated being written on the opposite page and containing interpolations from the writings of Avenius. It is possible that the model used for this illuminated manuscript was produced under the personal supervision of that writer, who flourished in the mid-4th century.

Illustration page 91While of much the same type as those in Leyden, the depictions of celestial bodies in the London manuscript have neither frames nor backgrounds. Moreover, on close examination, we find that the bodies are composed of a closely written explanatory text in *capitalis rustica*, only the heads, extremities of limbs and parts of the outlines being actually painted. The origins of this curious technique, known as *technopaignion* ("art game"), may be traced to the Greek poems representing objects (calligrams). This literary device was employed in the 4th century by Constantine the Great's court poet, Publilius Optatianus Porfyrius. Speaking of the ornate editions of his *carmina figurata* made in earlier days, the exiled poet says that these poems had painted contour lines and he wrote them *picto limite dicta notans*, that is to say fitting the written text within outlines indicated with the brush, just as in the London Aratus.

Some of the panegyric poems by Porfyrius are cast in the form of crosswords, and Carolingian copies of these are extant. Copying the methods of this eccentric early poet, a 9th-century writer, Hrabanus Maurus, made a sequence of hymns celebrating the Holy Cross, some richly illuminated versions of which exist, one being written in gold and silver on a purple ground. This, we learn, was the presentation Porfyrius had adopted five centuries before for his own poems. It seems quite possible that the full-page picture on the first pages of Hrabanus' manuscripts and the depiction of Louis the Pious as a Christian hero holding a long staff with a cross at the top also stem from prototypes of the Constantinian age; indeed this portrait may well be a reminiscence of the famous statue of the Emperor which, according to the annalists, was erected by him in Rome to commemorate his victory over Maxentius.

However, for our knowledge of the state of book illustration during the last centuries of the Roman Empire, we do not depend solely on Carolingian copies or imitations, since, by a happy chance, some originals have survived. These are the four sheets of the translation of the Old Testament known as the Itala Manuscript (Berlin, former Staatsbibliothek, Theol. lat. fol. 485), and the two Vergil manuscripts in the Vatican Library: Illustrations pages 94-96the Vergilius Vaticanus (Vat. lat. 3225) and the Vergilius Romanus (Vat. lat. 3867).

The Itala has come down to us in a particularly fragmentary state. It consists of a few sheets that were torn from a manuscript of the four Books of the Kings in the 17th century for binding legal and other documents. (At that time the manuscript was in Quedlinburg, Saxony.) The condition of the painted surfaces in these miniatures varies according to the care with which the sheets were detached by the binders. But, from the art historian's point of view, the injury done these miniatures as works of art has not been without some compensation. Where the paint has been rubbed off we can now read instructions to the painter written in a running hand. "Put here a prophet with a zither, another with a double flute, a third with a cymbal and lastly Saul and his young God-inspired servitor with a psaltery." Such inscriptions seem to prove that the artists concerned were not expected to work from a given model but to provide an original interpretation of each scene.

The format of these miniatures is a large square filling an entire page, this being subdivided with red lines into four small squares or two rectangles. The effect of this division of the picture surface into compartments is not unlike that of looking through a casement window; an effect heightened by the fact that most of the picture consists of atmospherically graduated sky. Sometimes the ground is not indicated at all, sometimes by pale, greenish-yellow stripes which give place in the middle distance to a band of pale blue, before changing first to a luminous pink, then, in recession, to a deeper blue. Placed in this dreamlike ambience of changing colors are a company of figures in ceremoniously stylized attitudes. Sometimes they seem to be advancing in a line like soldiers on parade; sometimes marching past, taking long strides, their swinging arms and legs displayed in profile. This frieze-like presentation of the figures is reminiscent of the style of Roman bas-reliefs; the same attitudes and gestures can be seen on sarcophagi and triumphal pillars—indeed at a first glance it might well be imagined that these are episodes of Roman history rather than biblical incidents.

Judging by the illuminations of this period, no clear distinction was drawn as yet between Christian and pagan methods of expression and the same teams of craftsmen worked both for high government officials and for the ecclesiastical authorities. Thus the resemblance between the miniatures in the Itala and those in the Vatican Vergil need not surprise us; nor the fact that the two manuscripts were almost certainly the work of the same atelier, though the Vergil appears to be a slightly later production. It is generally dated to about the turn of the 4th century, whereas the Itala may well have been made a decade or two before.

Though the layout in window-like compartments is found also in the Vergil, most of the miniatures are presented singly and their dimensions adjusted to the width of the columns of writing. In the Vergil, too, we have the same atmospheric backgrounds and for the most part color schemes resembling those of the Itala, with blues, vivid reds and violet predominating. However the presentation of the figures is less "military," the grouping less schematic. Their location in space and the angle of vision vary from scene to scene, and besides frieze-like arrangements of figures aligned on narrow strips of ground we often find quite different compositional schemes, with the groundline sloping up towards the top edge of the picture. On the whole these Vergil illustrations give a fuller idea of both the technical equipment of the workshop and the artists' remarkable powers of imagination—particularly apparent in the nightpieces and scenes of the netherworld, where brown or dark mauve backgrounds create an appropriate atmosphere of mystery. In two cases we are shown interiors in which the handling of three-dimensional space proves that the geometrical perspective employed by the ancients in their renderings of such scenes was still in use.

VERGILIUS VATICANUS. THE BUILDING OF A CITY (AENEID, BOOK I, 419). EARLY FIFTH CENTURY. (6¼×6½″) VAT. LAT. 3225, FOLIO 13, BIBLIOTECA APOSTOLICA, VATICAN CITY.

In these pictures the world of pagan antiquity comes to life so vividly, so convincingly, that we might be tempted to see in them copies of much older panels or frescos, were it not that their great number renders it unlikely that they were composed for any purpose other than the illustration of a book. For it is estimated that the Vergil originally contained no less than 245 scenes, and a picture cycle of this magnitude could not have been meant to serve elsewhere than in a codex. Here we have a last, belated flowering of that pagan art of Rome which now was *in extremis*. Unlike the Terence illustrations (probably made a little later), these paintings had no sequel, never being copied either during the Carolingian renaissance or in the succeeding centuries. Obviously they were too pagan in spirit to be approved of by the all-powerful Church; indeed pious minds of the early Middle Ages accounted it a sin to relish Vergil, "the sorcerer."

VERGILIUS VATICANUS. THE DEATH OF DIDO (AENEID, BOOK IV, 663). EARLY FIFTH CENTURY. (4⅝×6⅛″)
VAT. LAT. 3225, FOLIO 41, BIBLIOTECA APOSTOLICA, VATICAN CITY.

VERGILIUS ROMANUS. SHEPHERDS TENDING THEIR FLOCKS (GEORGICS, BOOK III). FIRST HALF OF THE FIFTH CENTURY. $(8\,^5/_8 \times 8\,^{13}/_{16}'')$ VAT. LAT. 3867, FOLIO 44 VERSO, BIBLIOTECA APOSTOLICA, VATICAN CITY.

Of the same style as the Itala and the Vatican Vergil, and perhaps a production of the same workshop, was a richly decorated Bible, used as a model by a group of miniature painters at Tours in the 9th century (see p. 148). Though the original is lost, Carolingian copies give us a fairly reliable idea of what it looked like. Four large-size pictures, two for the Old and two for the New Testament, sponsor an interpretation of the doctrine of Redemption intended to act as a counterblast to the Manichean heresy. Wilhelm Koehler, who has studied the question with a rare combination of meticulous thoroughness and constructive imagination, has come to the conclusion that the cycle was a "proclamation" of Pope Leo the Great (440-461). Thus for the first time themes based on Christian doctrine make their appearance in illumination, and the basic difference between symbolical imagery and the narrative depictions familiar in monumental art becomes apparent in book illumination as well. In the Carolingian copies we can see that the classical technique of the Itala and Vergil was still followed in the Bible, in the handling of details such as heads, hands and gestures. Likewise the atmospheric backgrounds and the rendering of an interior in perspective link up its illustrations with those in the earlier manuscripts. Everything goes to show that they derive from the same school. They differ, however, from their predecessors in the new emphasis on monumental composition. Though spatial recession is not yet wholly abolished, the tendency to bring all the figures forward on to the picture surface becomes more pronounced, and we find the diversity of forms and movements in the Itala replaced by the smaller selection of types that was to prevail more and more in the near future. We have here, in fact, the beginnings of a new pictorial language that, after steadily gaining ground in the second half of the 5th century, attained its culmination in the first phase of Byzantine art, during the reign of Justinian.

One of the forces behind this new development, which did much to reduce and dissipate the heritage of classical antiquity, was the "provincialism" that had resulted from the decentralization of the imperial power. Already in the reign of Constantine we find it influencing the official art of the day and thereafter, like an underground river, it permeated the entire course of art throughout the 4th and 5th centuries. Its influence can be clearly seen in one of the key works of Latin illumination, the Roman Vergil (Vergilius Romanus). The illustrations of this manuscript seem to have hardly anything Illustration page 96 in common with those of the Vatican Vergil. In the Vergilius Romanus, instead of a continuous series of pictures illustrating successive episodes of the text, illustration is limited to a single miniature at the beginning of each Book of the Aeneid. The rigid postures of the figures foreshadow the art of the ikon painters. Line plays the leading part and the shadows enveloping figures are thickened into heavy black bands. The folds of garments are deeply grooved, eyes are staring, almost vacuous. The naivety of this artist and the absence of the spatial relations and atmospheric backgrounds found in the other works we have been dealing with have led some to ascribe the Vergilius Romanus to a much later period. But the elegant script in *capitalis rustica*, wholly classical in spirit, and the striking similarity of several motifs to those on 4th-century sarcophagus reliefs seem to tell against this dating. On the whole we are inclined to date this manuscript not later than the first half of the 5th century. Its peculiarities can easily be accounted for on the assumption that it was made in some provincial atelier. Also, there are reasons for believing it to be the work of a Christian scribe; firstly, the fact that two *nomina sacra* (i.e. names of God like *deus* and *dominus*) are written, following Christian usage, in abbreviated forms (*ds* and *dns*), and secondly that scenes of pagan sacrifice, which would have been particularly repugnant to Christian taste, have been scrupulously omitted.

During the 6th century book production passed more and more into the hands of the Church and the copyists were chiefly employed on making Gospel Books. But the time was not yet ripe for a final break with the art tradition of antiquity by amalgamating ornaments and script. Judging by the works that have survived, the only decorative elements of the Gospel Books in four cases out of five (the reverse is true of the Middle Ages) were limited to simple linear ornaments around the colophons. Only the canon tables or "concordances," invented by Eusebius, bishop of Caesarea (who died in 339 or 340), formed a real exception, being given a setting composed of decorative arches. This type of decoration, providing as it were a multiplex portico through which the reader approached the sacred text, soon became standardized throughout the Christian world. In the Western part of the Empire St Jerome employed them in his new translation of the Bible, and there can be little doubt that Gospel Books including ornamented canon tables were being produced in Rome during his lifetime. That no examples earlier than the 6th century are extant can be explained by the pillaging of Italian churches in the intervening period. The finest specimen still existing consists of two sheets in the Vatican Illustration page 99 Library (Vat. lat. 3806), while the completest is in the London Gospels (Brit. Mus., Harl. 1775). There were two distinct types of canon page in use: one with twelve arches, the other with sixteen. In some exceptional cases brief résumés of the contents have been added to the tables of Eusebian canons; for example in the sumptuous purple Gospel Book at Brescia which, like the famous Codex Argenteus in Upsala, was probably made in Ravenna to the order of Theodoric the Great. These two manuscripts have also small "canon arches" at the bottom edge of each page, upholding the text much as the pillars of a Christian basilica support its walls.

So few miniatures datable to the final phase of antiquity have been preserved that each can claim an individual significance. Hence the great interest of the Cambridge Illustration page 100 Gospels (Corpus Christi College, MS. 286), of which two illuminated pages prefixed to the Gospel of St Luke have survived. The value of the manuscript, relatively slight from a purely artistic point of view, lies in its association with an event of great historical significance: the mission of St Augustine (the apostle of England, not to be confused with the earlier St Augustine, bishop of Hippo and author of *The City of God*), who was sent to England by Pope Gregory the Great in 596 and became the first archbishop of Canterbury. The Cambridge Gospels is believed to be one of the books that the pope gave his envoy in connection with his mission oversea. Be this as it may, it proves that about this time workshops of Roman illuminators were engaged in producing books for use in church services. The affinities between the architectural setting of the

GOSPEL FRAGMENT. EUSEBIAN CANON TABLES. ITALY, SIXTH CENTURY. (13⅜ × 10¾″)
VAT. LAT. 3806, FOLIO 2 VERSO, BIBLIOTECA APOSTOLICA, VATICAN CITY.

SO-CALLED GOSPEL BOOK OF ST AUGUSTINE. ST LUKE. ROME, LATE SIXTH CENTURY. $(7\frac{7}{8} \times 6'')$
MS 286, FOLIO 129 VERSO. CORPUS CHRISTI COLLEGE LIBRARY, CAMBRIDGE.

frontispiece, showing St Luke seated on a throne, and that of the Filocalus calendar of the year 354 are astonishing and go to show that the 4th-century Roman art tradition was still alive in the time of Gregory the Great. Similarly the sequence of twelve scenes of the Passion in small square compartments reminds us of the "casement window" layout of the Itala Bible. But the rendering of space and atmosphere has been abandoned and replaced by flat, plain backgrounds, sometimes shaped like spreading leaves. The paint is applied in thin coats, and the white of garments and flesh is rendered by leaving the parchment bare. The artist rings the changes on three dominant colors—grey-blue, crimson and yellow—with an eye to decorative effect, while figures are bound in contour lines which, though firmly drawn, lack vigor. These scenes would lend themselves to reproduction in cloisonné enamelwork such as that on a famous reliquary cross in the treasure of Sancta Sanctorum in Rome.

For propaganda purposes—that is to say, for the conversion of the Anglo-Saxons—this type of art may well have been too subtle and restrained to be effective, and so far as is known it had no immediate influence on local art. All the same it subsequently played a considerable part in shaping the course of British art during the Middle Ages. When in the 8th century an indigenous school of painting arose at Canterbury, it to some extent took these pictures as its starting-off point, and some four centuries later we still find Romanesque book illustrators drawing inspiration from the small biblical scenes figuring in the Cambridge Gospel Book.

The missing Gospels of the other Evangelists must have had the same type of miniatures on the opening pages as those in the Gospel of St Luke; thus the work originally contained no less than a hundred depictions of New Testament episodes. This wealth of illustration reminds us of the often cited dictum of Pope Gregory that pictures are intended for those who cannot read. There can be no doubt that the earliest painters commissioned to make decorations in English churches took these and similar illuminations as their models. This is known to be the case with an Apocalypse manuscript which Benedict Biscop brought back from Italy to England in the 7th century to serve as a pattern book for English fresco painters. And so far as we can form an idea from Carolingian copies of what this Apocalypse looked like, it must have had much in common, stylistically, with the Cambridge Gospels.

During the period before political upheavals and particularly the Arab invasions of the 7th century had almost extinguished the art of the illustrated book in the Latin countries around the Mediterranean basin, an important atelier somewhere in the southwest of Europe—its location has never been precisely identified—produced a manuscript whose full-page pictures, such is their exuberant vitality, excel those in all other cycles of Bible illustrations of this early period. We are referring to the so-called Ashburnham Pentateuch. Shortly after 1842 Count Libri, inspector-general of libraries Illustrations pages 102-105 under Louis-Philippe, purloined the book from the library at Tours and sold it to the Earl of Ashburnham, an eminent bibliophile. Thanks to the efforts of Léopold Delisle, the great French medievalist, this precious manuscript was restored to France forty years later and it is now in the Bibliothèque Nationale, Paris (Nouv. acq. lat. 2334).

ASHBURNHAM PENTATEUCH. THE STORY OF ADAM. NORTH AFRICA OR SPAIN, SEVENTH CENTURY. $(14\,^{9}/_{16} \times 12\,^{9}/_{16}\,'')$
NOUV. ACQ. LAT. 2334, FOLIO 6, BIBLIOTHÈQUE NATIONALE, PARIS.

ASHBURNHAM PENTATEUCH. THE STORY OF JACOB AND ESAU. NORTH AFRICA OR SPAIN, SEVENTH CENTURY.
(14 9/16 × 12 9/16″) NOUV. ACQ. LAT. 2334, FOLIO 25, BIBLIOTHÈQUE NATIONALE, PARIS.

The nineteen full-page pictures which have survived illustrate the Old Testament narrative from the creation of the world until the departure of the Israelites from Egypt under the leadership of Moses. Each picture comprises several associated but distinct scenes, grouped as the painter's fancy took him. The kaleidoscopic effect of this mode of presentation is often intensified by the settings: architectural motifs of a complex and somewhat curious nature. When the incident depicted takes place in an interior the housefront is given the form of an arcade. But since there is no longer any regard for three-dimensional space, the figures are always brought up to the foreground and appear to be standing in front of the openings of the arches rather than behind them. Everywhere the eye is caught by a medley of men and animals disposed on the picture surface with a skill that testifies to the artists' feeling for decorative rhythm. Despite persistent stylization, the forms are strongly charged with life and in each brushstroke we perceive, as in the art of classical antiquity, the painter's instinctive sense of color relations.

Illustration page 103

Biblical cycles of this kind can be seen in certain Byzantine illuminated manuscripts and it is probable that all alike derive from a very ancient Eastern tradition. But more important than any tradition is what the artists themselves made of it thanks to their highly original personalities and gift for pictorial narrative. Particularly notable is their keen interest in rendering incidents of everyday life. Thus when dealing with the tale of Jacob and Esau they seized on the opportunity of depicting a kitchen and a sheep-pen, and in the picture of Joseph entertaining his brothers, they also show us, in the lower portion of the picture, a company of Egyptians likewise eating and drinking. Scenes of house-building and work in the fields, of birth and death, of love and hate—in a word, the rich variety of incidents narrated in the Pentateuch—come vividly to life upon these pages and it is obvious that to a certain extent the artists drew inspiration from direct visual experience of the world around them. We are shown exotic flora and fauna, date-palms, camels, lions and scorpions drawn with remarkable verisimilitude. Negroes figure in some scenes, notably in those concerning the lives of Joseph and Moses, where quite half the Egyptian population represented consists of Negroes. Here we may have a clue to the provenance of this manuscript—somewhere in North Africa or, maybe, southern Spain. This is borne out by the kinship between these pictures and the illustrations in the Apocalypse of Beatus, an affinity first observed by Wilhelm Neuss and particularly

Illustration page 105

noticeable in the depiction of the Flood with its gruesomely realistic renderings of corpses.

The culture mirrored in the illustrations of the Ashburnham Pentateuch has completely disappeared and we have no contemporary works enabling us to situate it in any precise historical context. It is almost as though a flood, as disastrous as that recorded in the Book of Genesis, had caused it to disappear—a lost Atlantis, sole surviving vestige of whose mysterious, highly developed civilization is an illuminated manuscript that has escaped destruction by some happy fluke. However, this is by no means a unique case; one of the many fascinations of illuminated manuscripts is that, better perhaps than any other form of art, they make the remote past live before our eyes. We shall see this time and again when we come to deal with the illuminated books of the Middle Ages, many more of which are extant.

ASHBURNHAM PENTATEUCH. THE FLOOD. NORTH AFRICA OR SPAIN, SEVENTH CENTURY. (14 $^{9}/_{16}$ × 12 $^{9}/_{16}$″)
NOUV. ACQ. LAT. 2334, FOLIO 9, BIBLIOTHÈQUE NATIONALE, PARIS.

# PRE-CAROLINGIAN ILLUMINATION

THE transition from Late Antiquity to the Middle Ages properly so called took place in the 7th century and one of its earliest manifestations was a new emphasis on ornament in all domains of art. In the Near East the Arabs revived the Jewish ban on "imaging," reducing even the forms of plants to an abstract play of lines, the Moslem arabesque. At Byzantium the influence of Sassanian decorative art on book illumination is evidenced by the fragments of a richly decorated Greek Gospel Book on gilded parchment in the British Museum, London (Add. 5111). The Lombards who now were overrunning Italy adopted the interlace as their leitmotiv, while the Germanic races exploited with brilliant success the decorative possibilities of combining it with animal ornament. In England this was the century of Sutton Hoo, and here, as in Ireland, the metal workers drew new inspiration from their pagan past by resuscitating that typically Celtic ornament, the spiral. Such, in brief, was the situation when the books of the Christian Church in the West opened their pages to the ornamental idioms current in other branches of art, and from now on decoration became the chief concern of medieval illumination in this, its earliest phase.

The Greeks and Romans had made only a very limited use of ornaments in their manuscripts. These were usually confined to small calligraphic tailpieces at the ends of chapters. This, in any case, is the lesson gleaned from the many fragments of papyrus rolls discovered in Egypt and at Herculaneum. It would seem that for the man of classical antiquity the word was essentially an uttered sound, and a written text something whose main purpose was to be read aloud. Thus the idea of decorating a roll containing a text would have seemed to him as preposterous as would seem to us that of adding decorations to a sheet of music.

When, during the first centuries of our era, the roll was replaced by the leaved codex, a new element was introduced: the page of a restricted size, suitable not only as a support for framed pictures but also for richly decorated titles. Nevertheless the opinion that ornament was uncalled-for in the text itself held good. True, there were exceptions and the decorated initial letter makes a somewhat premature appearance towards the end of the 4th century. To start with, it was little larger than other capital letters and curiously enough was used to mark the beginning of a page, not that of a new paragraph or chapter. Thus, as we learn from the Vergilius Augusteus (Vatican, lat. 3526 and Berlin, lat. fol. 416), an initial might crop up in the middle of a sentence. But a reaction against this innovation quickly followed, and St Jerome, speaking in a famous passage of so-called "*litterae unciales*," probably referred to the type of de luxe editions represented by the Vergil fragments in Berlin and Rome, "burdens rather than books," as he calls them. Even in the 6th century, when initials were first employed to mark the beginning of a new chapter, they remained rather unusual in Christian manuscripts.

Such was the state of affairs when in the 7th century the center of gravity of European culture shifted north of the Alps. When the new monastic scriptoria set to producing books they started off, naturally enough, by modeling their work on the manuscripts of Late Antiquity. But it soon became apparent that these did not tally with their program. Being still virtually "barbarian" craftsmen, they saw no objection to the use of ornaments in conjunction with a written text. On the contrary, they regarded decoration as a means of impressing readers with the value and importance of the text under their eyes and far from banning ornament they made the utmost use of it. Decorative initial letters, employed more and more frequently, were constantly enlarged until finally they came to occupy an entire page—almost as if they were not so much parts of the text as independent, "non-objective" pictures.

Thus ornamentation became the chief concern of both the monastic ateliers on the Continent and those in the British Isles. But since there were few contacts between them, they followed widely divergent paths and the ornamental repertory in Merovingian manuscripts has little resemblance to that of the Irish scribes and illuminators. Fundamental differences in the manner of the writing contributed to this cleavage. In fact continental and insular methods of expression were never so completely differentiated from each other as in the period preceding Charlemagne. No compromise was possible and inevitably one of these styles ended by supplanting the other. It was the "insular" style that gained the day and provided the basis of all that was to follow. None the less it was not in the British Isles that the next phase originated but on the Continent during the reign of Charlemagne. Not that Merovingian art died out completely and definitively; it survived in Spain and, re-emerging in the South of France at the end of the 10th century, enriched Romanesque art with a wealth of lively animal ornaments.

IRISH GOSPEL BOOK. ST MARK AND THE FOUR EVANGELIST SYMBOLS. IRELAND, EIGHTH CENTURY. (9×6⅞″)
CODEX 51, FOLIO 78, STIFTSBIBLIOTHEK, ST GALL.

# IRELAND AND ENGLAND

THE style of ornament we find in books made in the monasteries of the British Isles may be described as a last flowering of prehistoric art. Thus they belong to a field of research in which the art historian needs assistance from the archeologist. For before being used in Christian manuscripts these motifs had already figured in many kinds of pagan metalwork. The origins of the decorations of the Book of Durrow, the Book of Lindisfarne or the Book of Kells are not to be found in the south of Europe (whence their texts derive), but in the adornments of helmets, shields and harness, or on the escutcheons of the "hanging bowls." Even the characteristic mingling of Celtic and Germanic motifs with interlaces was transmitted to Christian art from this source, as has been confirmed by the finds made in the tumuli at Sutton Hoo in East Anglia in 1939. The metal objects glittering with gold discovered there cast a revealing light on the decorations employed in the famous Gospel Books of this period.

Between the artifacts of Sutton Hoo and the Book of Durrow there intervened a momentous event: the conversion to Christianity of the Anglo-Saxon tribes. This is known to have been for the most part the work of Irish missionaries from Iona; St Aidan (d. 651) and his successors had a larger share than the Roman emissaries at Canterbury in the foundation of a national church in England. The Irish monks were intelligent enough to enlist in the service of the Church the artists employed by the pagan chieftains, without forcing them to replace the indigenous craftsmanly tradition with idioms of foreign provenance. An artificer skilled in decorating shields with spirals, interlaces and animal figures was allowed to adorn in much the same manner a chalice, a reliquary or the cover of a Gospel Book. An 8th-century specimen of this type of binding is extant: the back cover of the Lindau Gospels (Morgan Library, New York).

Once these artists had learnt to transpose the patterns of Celtic metalwork into line and color, the next step was to transfer the decorations of the bindings into the interiors of books. And the craftsmen working in the Northumbrian monasteries gradually acquired much competence in this form of art. By the same token this explains the almost metallic precision distinctive of the Hiberno-Saxon style of illumination.

The indebtedness of the decorations in Christian manuscripts to the art of the heathen goldsmiths is particularly noticeable in the Book of Durrow, earliest of the Illustrations pages 110-111 famous Hiberno-Saxon Books. Each Gospel has as its frontispiece a "carpet page" with an ornamental composition. That at the beginning of St John has a central medallion containing a cross surrounded by closely plaited interlaces, and in the square borders a medley of quadrupeds interlocked in a chain pattern. The medallion reminds us of the boss of a circular shield, and the border decorations look as if they had been copied line for line from those on the scabbards of pagan swords. Only the initials called for a serious effort to adjust the decorative pattern to a given shape, that of the alphabetic form of the letter in question. But even here the relatively great freedom allowed the decorator is plain to see.

BOOK OF DURROW. CARPET PAGE. IONA (?), SEVENTH CENTURY. $(9\frac{1}{8} \times 5\frac{5}{8}'')$
FOLIO 192 VERSO, TRINITY COLLEGE LIBRARY, DUBLIN.

BOOK OF DURROW. SYMBOL OF ST MATTHEW. IONA (?), SEVENTH CENTURY. $(7\,^7/_8 \times 4\,^{15}/_{16}\,'')$
FOLIO 21 VERSO, TRINITY COLLEGE LIBRARY, DUBLIN.

ECHTERNACH GOSPELS. SYMBOL OF ST MARK. IRELAND (?), CA. 690. (10¹/₁₆ × 7 ⁹/₁₆″)
MS LAT. 9389, FOLIO 75 VERSO, BIBLIOTHÈQUE NATIONALE, PARIS.

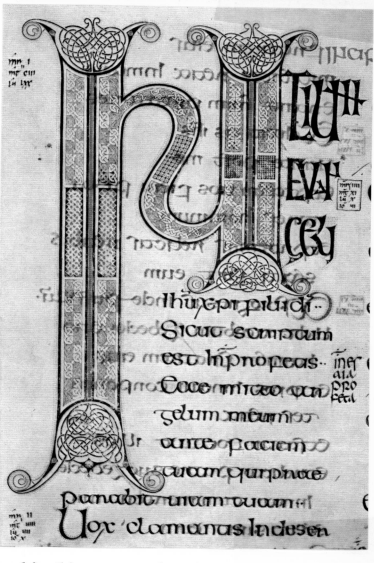

Two basic types of linear ornament figure largely in this art: the spiral and the interlace. Animal forms are included only for the purpose of enlivening the interlaces, the bodies being adapted to them by being woven into twisted, convoluted ribbons. The draftsman's constant aim is to get the maximum of movement into the smallest possible space. Thus a decorated surface like that of the monogram shown on page 115 is charged, down to its tiniest cell, with a dynamism whose tensions make the whole composition seem to be in a state of perpetual motion. The wealth of linear ornament is nothing short of prodigious; one has an impression that were it possible to unravel the fine-meshed skein of tangled lines into a single thread, it would be long enough to span the entire circumference of a small church. Indeed there is nothing to surprise us in the fact that a manuscript like the Book of Kells was thought in the Middle Ages to be the work of angels rather than of men.

This linear structure is characteristic of Hiberno-Saxon art, whatever its nature, goldsmith's work or illumination. But in the latter it is naturally associated with pen drawing and for this reason tends to develop into calligraphy; there is in fact a curious affinity between Anglo-Irish manuscripts and the pattern books of Renaissance and Baroque calligraphers and in both we find the same amazing manual dexterity. Particularly striking is the absolute regularity and precision of the spirals, drawn freehand, it seems, whether the line be thick or gossamer-thin. One feels that to do them justice they should be studied through a watchmaker's lens.

However this trend of insular illumination towards an elegant calligraphy is not yet fully developed in the older manuscripts, such as the Book of Durrow and, notably, in the fragments of the still earlier Durham Gospel Book (Cathedral Library, A. II. 10), where thick interlacing bands are still employed. The first approach to a purely calligraphic style was made by the artist of genius responsible for the Echternach Gospels, now in Paris (Bibl. Nat., lat. 9389). This book was made, seemingly around 690, for the use of the Anglo-Saxon missionary St Willibrord. Here for the first time we find initials

Illustrations pages 112-113

embellished not only with spirals added so to speak from the outside, but also with interlaces prolonging the contours of initials and developed out of the letter itself. This structural innovation was destined to have a decisive influence on the treatment of initials in Carolingian manuscripts.

Though dynamic line is a basic element of insular illumination, it is used to build up compositional schemas which, if enlarged, might very well serve as designs for carpets. The various motifs are carefully balanced and there is a notable predilection for symmetry based on the diagonal. Peter Meyer has made an excellent study of the syntax of the insular esthetic, his conclusion being that it is almost totally opposed to the classical Hellenic norm of beauty. For whereas the latter subordinates parts to the whole in terms of an organic structure, insular art tends always to subdivide figures into details, each of which has a more or less autonomous validity. This process of segmentation is applied to small as well as to large elements of the composition, to ornaments pure and simple as well as to the figurative motifs, with the result that even the latter seem to serve a purely decorative purpose.

Illustration page 111
In their representations of human beings these artists had no qualms about indulging in the most singular distortions, especially in their treatment of the folds of garments. In the symbol of St Matthew in the Book of Durrow the body is represented as a cube with decorations in enamel, like the Celtic idols found in Viking graves. Everywhere organic structure is transmuted into ornament, while in frames not only the motifs used to fill up empty spaces but even the main structural lines are handled in this manner. Though continuous, the frame is subdivided into a number, small or great as the case may be, of self-contained compartments, while its angles and intermediate sections are given independent decorations often taking the form of circular brooches or crosses. The structure of the frames may also be given a form matching the long shafts of the lettrines. In the case of full-page initials the frame is sometimes broken off abruptly and the lettrine itself made to do duty for it. We also find a preference for forms that lend themselves to diverse interpretations; a frame may have at one extremity an animal's head and forefeet and at the other end the hind legs and tail of the animal, its body being absorbed into the geometric pattern of the frame. The constant interplay of geometric and zoomorphic motifs gives rise to astonishing metamorphoses which almost seem like early intimations of Romanesque art.

The outlines of each element are governed by the artist's strictly two-dimensional conception of space yet, despite their stylization *à outrance*, the animal and human forms retain an almost startling vitality. Behind the microscopic precision of the calligraphy we often sense the presence of an observer gifted with the keen eye of a trained huntsman and it is not surprising that in the Book of Kells, which generally speaking eschews naturalism, we find here and there small animals drawn with an amazing naturalness. This applies especially to the cats and mice and to the otter with Illustration page 115 a fish on the illuminated page bearing the sacred monogram XPI. Some of the more grotesque compositions curiously anticipate the "drolleries" of Gothic miniatures and strike the same profane, not to say blasphemous note.

BOOK OF KELLS. THE SACRED MONOGRAM XPI. IRELAND, EIGHTH CENTURY. $(12\,\tfrac{5}{8}\times9\,\tfrac{1}{2}{}'')$
FOLIO 34, TRINITY COLLEGE LIBRARY, DUBLIN.

BOOK OF LINDISFARNE. CARPET PAGE. LINDISFARNE, LATE SEVENTH CENTURY. (10 $^{13}/_{16} \times 9 \frac{1}{4}$ ")
COTTON MS NERO D. IV, FOLIO 2 VERSO, BRITISH MUSEUM, LONDON.

imagohomi uis:... OAGIOS MATHeus

BOOK OF LINDISFARNE. ST MATTHEW. LINDISFARNE, LATE SEVENTH CENTURY. (11 $^{1}/_{16}$ × 8 $^{15}/_{16}$″)
COTTON MS NERO D. IV, FOLIO 25 VERSO, BRITISH MUSEUM, LONDON.

For we cannot disregard the fact that this ornamental vocabulary—with the exception of a few sporadic motifs that include the cross—is barbaric not only in origin but in spirit also. It is an almost inhuman art, so ruthless is its stylization, rooted in the tribal past and traversed with savage accents; utterly opposed, in short, to all that Christianity stood for. Nevertheless, by a strange paradox, this heathen art served the cause of the new religion and in fact went far to body forth the sanctity and transcendence of the Word of God. It was in its magical suggestions that illumination found the common denominator enabling the metamorphosis of pagan art into Christian. For prehistoric ornament had always been charged with otherworldly powers and these the Christians of the West enlisted in their service. Moreover, writing in itself was regarded by the Irish church with almost superstitious reverence, all the more so when its function was to propagate the message of the Scriptures. This conception found its most significant expression in the huge illuminated initial letters, which in fact "held up" the reading of the script; in them the divine word was arrayed in ornaments, just as shrines containing holy relics were bedecked with gold and precious stones.

There has been much controversy as to the racial origins of Hiberno-Saxon illumination. Formerly its Celtic provenance was taken for granted, but in recent times a theory (which has much to commend it) has gained ground: that the leading role in the formation of this art should be assigned to the monasteries located in Northumbria rather than to Ireland. In the same way as Arab art took its rise not so much in Arabia as in Syria and Egypt, so (if this theory be accepted) the true originators of the new style of illumination were less the Irish monasteries than their affiliated foundations in various parts of England.

Actually, however, it is not a question of choosing between two clean-cut alternatives; the facts are of a more complex order. Though it may be granted that the type of illumination we are dealing with would remain inexplicable if we left out of account the ornamental art patronized by the Anglo-Saxon monarchs, and though the Irish would never have attained the exquisite perfection of the Book of Kells had not the artistic achievement of the North of England already existed, it remains true that the Irish contribution cannot be thus lightly brushed aside. For the more we go back towards the sources, the greater is the preponderance of purely Celtic elements in this art. The insular minuscule script is unquestionably an Irish creation, and the same is true of the very special preparation of the parchment, the technique of the actual writing and the general layout of the text. As for the rows of tiny red dots duplicating the outlines of initials and frames, while ultimately of late classical origin, they make their appearance in Irish manuscripts as early as the 6th century. And the interlaces resembling strapwork in the oldest Durham manuscript (Cathedral Library, A. II. 10) and in the Book of Durrow are paralleled by designs on 7th-century Irish stone crosses.

From Ireland, too, so far as can be judged, came the practice of prefixing the Gospels with symbols of the four Evangelists in a presentation differing from, and prior to, that popularized in the West by St Jerome: namely, the man for St Matthew, the eagle for St Mark, the calf for St Luke, and the lion for St John. Thus the normal

CODEX AMIATINUS. THE SCRIBE EZRA REWRITING THE SACRED RECORDS. JARROW-WEARMOUTH, EARLY EIGHTH CENTURY. (13¾×9¹³/₁₆″) AMIATINUS I, FOLIO 5A, BIBLIOTECA LAURENZIANA, FLORENCE.

MAESEYCK GOSPEL BOOK. AN EVANGELIST. YORK (?), SEVENTH-EIGHTH CENTURY. (6¼×4½″)
FOLIO O, ST CATHERINE'S CHURCH, MAESEYCK.

symbols of St Mark and St John are transposed—and this in the Book of Durrow whose text, however, is based on Jerome's Vulgate. That these illustrations derive from very ancient models is proved by the fact that the symbols have neither wings nor aureoles. Similarly, the order in which the symbols are placed corresponds to that set forth in the prologue to a biblical poem written by the Spaniard Juvencus; evidently this text was known in Ireland, since it was copied in the MacRegol Gospels at Oxford (Bodl. Libr., Auct. D. II. 19). Moreover we find the same Evangelist symbols, without aureoles and wings, in Spanish versions of the Apocalypse. Presumably they originated somewhere in the East, and this may explain their presence in the margins of a famous Gospel Book in the library of the Stavronikita monastery on Mount Athos (Cod. 43).

In Hiberno-Saxon illumination we find other motifs of eastern origin, but it is usually hard to say whether the Irish or the English were the first to adopt them. There is, however, no question that, from the second half of the 7th century onward, it was chiefly by way of Northumbria that foreign art forms entered the British Isles. Even in this early age the English had acquired the reputation of being great collectors of books and works of art. Benedict Biscop (628?-690), founder of the monasteries of Wearmouth and Jarrow near Durham, made no less than five trips to Italy for the purpose of buying books and, in conjunction with other collectors, imported to Northumbria a portion of the great library which that erudite 6th-century historian, Cassiodorus, had got together at Vivarium in Calabria. Biscop had these volumes copied by his Northumbrian scribes with such meticulous care that it is sometimes difficult to distinguish copies from originals. Most famous is the big Bible he intended to give to the pope, the Florence Codex Amiatinus, the illustrations on whose opening pages Illustration page 119 exactly reproduce those in Cassiodorus' Codex Grandior. So complete is the fidelity with which the picture of Ezra has been copied that even the cast shadow of the ink bottle is included—a unique phenomenon in early medieval art.

The Cassiodorus Ezra also served as model for the St Matthew in the Book of Lindisfarne. But though the contours of the two figures are almost identical, they differ greatly Illustration page 117 in style. The artist responsible for the Lindisfarne Gospels did not, like the Jarrow artist, set out to make a literal, archeologically faithful reproduction; he brought to his work a style of such compelling power that the model underwent a total change. One might well be tempted to see in this an original creation were it not that a very similar style is found in some 7th-century ivories said to have belonged to St Mark's episcopal throne and known to be of Byzantine or Eastern provenance. The explanation of this resemblance may lie in the fact that not long before the Book of Lindisfarne was made the English Church had been reorganized by a Greek, Theodore of Tarsus, who was sent by Pope Vitalianus to England in the year 668. He did much to promote an understanding of contemporary Byzantine art in England and, following the example of Rome, this most northern of the provinces of the Catholic Church in Europe had no qualms about recognizing the primacy of Byzantium in the field of culture. How proud the English were of their new-won erudition is shown by the fact that the master of the Book of Lindisfarne prefixes the names of the Evangelists with the Greek word *hagios* ("saint").

Illustration page 120

Italo-Byzantine influence makes itself felt also in the Northumbrian stone crosses (dating to the last three decades of the 7th century and subsequently). The earliest was erected at the time when Wilfrid (ca. 634-709) set on foot the reunion of the church of Northumbria with that of Rome. This enlightened prelate, who was abbot of the monastery at Ripon and for a time bishop of York, did much to raise the standard of insular culture to an international level. He played a memorable part in English history and among his many claims to fame is the fact that he commissioned the making of a sumptuous Gospel Book in gold on purple vellum. It is clear that he had at his disposal an atelier of quite exceptional proficiency, and the absence of any manuscript that can be positively assigned to this important art center is a regrettable lacuna in the history of the illuminated book. The only surviving work that can, with some probability, be assigned to this source is the fragment of a Gospel Book inserted in another of a later date, now in the church of Maeseyck. The fragment contains eight canon tables and the portrait of an Evangelist. The decoration consists of foliate motifs, lozenges and interlaces, all exquisitely wrought and very similar to the designs on Northumbrian stone crosses. One of the canon tables has a line of birds used as filling along one of its arches, a motif closely paralleled in the wall paintings of the Omayyad castle at Kusejr Amra in the Syrian desert. We find the same birds in the Book of Lindisfarne, but in a more complicated form, already combined with interlaces (see p. 117). The massive figure of the Evangelist has striking affinities with the reliefs on the cross of Ruthwell, where the rendering of drapery in heavy, little differentiated folds is exactly similar. Everything goes to show that we have here a Northumbrian work datable, at the very latest, to the beginning of the 8th century. Since its source can be neither the school of Lindisfarne nor that of Jarrow, it well may be that this is what we have been looking for: a manuscript of Wilfrid's time deriving from the school of York. This hypothesis is borne out by the fact that it has had its home for many centuries in a region affected by Wilfrid's missionary activities on the Continent.

While Anglo-Irish artists took little interest in the narrative aspects of illustration, the Anglo-Italian schools on the contrary practised an art whose trend was humanistic, and paid no less attention to figurative representation than to ornament. They even went so far as to take over, not single pictures, but whole narrative cycles figuring in the manuscripts imported from Italy. Both the originals produced in late antiquity and the copies made by English artists have disappeared and we have only Carolingian reproductions, but there can be no doubt as to their existence. Thus it is evident that the illustrations to the works of Caelius Sedulius (a 5th-century Christian poet) which included scenes of the life of Christ—now in the Plantin Moretus Museum, Antwerp— and the Apocalypse cycle at Valenciennes (Bibl. Comm. 99) derive from copies made in Northumbria round about the year 700. Though there is no denying that these Anglo-Italian miniatures are on a lower level as works of art than the essentially ornamental compositions, they reveal the interesting fact that insular illumination was already beginning to shed its pagan trappings and place itself at the service of the Catholic doctrine of redemption; a trend that was to become more pronounced in the next period.

CODEX AUREUS OF CANTERBURY. ST MATTHEW, EIGHTH CENTURY. (15 $^{7}/_{16}$ × 12 $^{3}/_{16}$ ″)
A. 135, FOLIO 9 VERSO, KUNGLIGA BIBLIOTEKET, STOCKHOLM.

In fact the simultaneous presence of these two forms of expression, Anglo-Irish and Anglo-Italian, gives the art of the British Isles a Janus-like ambivalence, one face turned towards autochthonous tradition, the other towards Rome and Byzantine culture. But the two tendencies were not mutually exclusive; we often find them operative in one and the same manuscript. Oddly enough, the setback to the Irish church at the Synod of Whitby (664) seemed to foster rather than weaken Hiberno-Saxon art in Northern England, and at Lindisfarne, under English auspices, the traditions of Irish illumination still held their own. But by now the English church was exercising a reciprocal influence on the Irish, and Egbert, an English friend of Wilfrid, seems to have done much to convert the Irish church to the English rule. He even succeeded in enforcing the use of the Roman tonsure at Iona. St Willibrord of York studied under him for ten years before going on his mission to the Continent. It was perhaps from the school of Egbert that this great "apostle of the Frisians" procured the Celtic Gospel Book (Paris, Bibl. Nat., lat. 9389) which he brought to the monastery he founded at Echternach; the text and illustrations are best accounted for if we assume the book to have been made in an Irish scriptorium impregnated with English influences. The frontispiece of the Gospel of St Matthew in which the Man by whom this Evangelist is symbolized, while stylized in the typically Irish manner, has a Roman tonsure, is striking evidence of the shift of attitude. Willibrord's companions, who founded at Echternach a branch of the insular school, worked partly in the Hiberno-Saxon tradition of the Celtic Gospel Book and partly in the Anglo-Italian style of the Maeseyck fragment, as can be seen in the Gospels signed by a scribe named Thomas, now in the Cathedral Treasure (no. 141) at Trier.

Illustrations pages 112-113

In the 8th century Canterbury, in the South of England, became the headquarters of British illumination. The missionaries sent to England by Pope Gregory the Great had brought with them liturgical books made in Italy, one of them the Cambridge Gospels (Corpus Christi College, MS 286) mentioned in the previous chapter (pp. 98-101). But it does not seem that production of manuscripts made on the spot began at once; periods of evangelical activity are not always favorable to a flowering of art, time must be given for the missionaries' labors to take effect. It is not until the 8th century that we find works of a high quality being produced at Canterbury, the first example being a psalter with a frontispiece representing King David among his scribes and musicians (London, Brit. Mus., Vespasian A. I). At this time the influence of Northumbrian art was strongly felt in Canterbury, as we can see from the initials of this manuscript. But the great cathedral city also rallied to its ancient Gregorian traditions, as is evidenced by the

Illustration page 123

Stockholm Codex Aureus, another masterpiece of the Canterbury School. From the iconographical point of view, as Francis Wormald has aptly pointed out, there are striking parallels between the Evangelist symbols in this codex and those in the Cambridge Gospels of St Augustine mentioned in the previous chapter.

After being introduced into England by Archbishop Wilfrid, the practice of writing in gold ink on a purple ground was adopted by the Canterbury School in the Codex Aureus. But, oddly enough, only every other page is purple, the rest having plain white parchment grounds. The general effect is one of a curious polychromy, an effect enhanced by the use of inks of various hues. The text itself is dappled with crosses, lozenges and other forms, rendered in a diversity of colors: gold and silver, red, black and white. This procedure was borrowed from the *carmina figurata* of Porfyrius, who was, as already stated, Constantine's court poet; as it so happens, a passage in a letter mentions that a copy of his poems was at Canterbury round about 750, and we probably should date the Stockholm manuscript not long after that period.

The Codex Aureus has preserved the portraits of two Evangelists, painted in body color and aureoled in gold. They are seated frontally on stools with red cushions, indued with all the pomp and circumstance of Emperors of the East seated on their thrones. Here, however, the hugeness of the pillars and curtains flanking them tends to dwarf the figures. The Hiberno-Saxon illuminators had always been chary of tackling the problem of the third dimension and arrayed forms side by side on the picture surface —this applies to the illustrations no less than to the decorative elements. In the Canterbury Codex Aureus, however, there is some attempt at modeling and suggesting plastic form. Heads are given relief, garments and curtains have shadows along the folds. Also the background is divided into three color zones which, though sharply demarcated, give a vague suggestion of open space behind the figures. This is perhaps the first time we find a Nordic artist attempting to create plastic values. The emphasis on stylization and the heavily marked contour lines may perhaps owe something to contemporary monumental painting—none of which, unfortunately, has survived.

Illustration page 123

This new concern with volumes and plasticity can also be seen in the ornaments; arches are adorned with meanders rendered in perspective and similar motifs—which suggests that these artists were working from a 6th-century model. The animals in the Northumbrian manuscripts are no longer given the form of lacertines woven into interlaces, and their bodies are now surrounded with a slender filigree of loops starting from the tail, the tongue or the tuft of feathers on the heads of birds, as the case may be. New, grotesque animals, usually confronted, also make their appearance. The same themes are found in contemporary Merovingian illumination, but it is hard to decide where they first were used. Oddest of these are the quaint beasts in the Cutbercht Gospels at Vienna, illustrated at Salzburg by an artist hailing from the South of England.

In several other manuscripts we find such close stylistic affinities with the Codex Aureus that it is clear that they too emanate from Canterbury. Instances are a Psalter in the Morgan Library, New York (M. 776), and a Bible originally consisting of several volumes, of which only the Gospels have been preserved (London, Brit. Mus., Royal I. E. VI). The influence of the Canterbury School spread to the Continent (e.g. the Corbie Psalter, Amiens). But the development of this art in the British Isles was soon arrested by the Viking inroads. A 9th-century inscription in the Codex Aureus mentions that Nordic pirates carried this book away amongst their booty and exacted a heavy ransom for its return. The political climate no longer lent itself to the production of works of art of a religious nature. And in these troubled times the decorative arts, deserting for the nonce the illustrated book, flourished once more on the shields and helmets of warriors. The wheel had come full circle.

# MEROVINGIAN ILLUMINATION

CONCURRENTLY with the first flowering of the miniature in the British Isles the art of the illuminated manuscript made a great forward stride in the lands ruled by the Merovingian dynasty. However the aims pursued were very different, as is apparent even in the nature of the texts selected for illumination. In Ireland and England, as we have seen, these were mostly copies of the Gospels and they testified to the apostolic fervor of the northern Church whose missionaries needed them for use in their many newly founded churches and monasteries. The French monasteries, on the other hand, showed relatively little zeal in propagating Christianity among the heathen. Their chief duty, as they saw it, was to tend the sacred flame of faith within the precincts of their own or affiliated establishments. Thus their activities were largely directed to the production of theological and liturgical texts, and the Merovingian counterparts of the Books of Durrow, Lindisfarne and Kells were the Missale Gothicum, the Sacramentarium Gelasianum (both in the Vatican Library, Reg. lat. 317 and 316), and the Gellone Sacramentary (Paris, Bibl. Nat., lat. 12 048). Also we find a predilection for decorated versions of the works of the Fathers of the Church, St Augustine and St Gregory in particular. Indeed the scarcity of Gospel Books in Merovingian illumination seems to hint at a certain awe of the Word of God itself and a preference for interpretations of it sponsored by the Church.

Illustrations pages 130-132

A corresponding difference can be seen in the method of decoration. In Merovingian illuminated manuscripts we do not find big letters covering an entire page and acting as sacred monograms. Capitals are usually incorporated in the text or else used in decorative titles set off by ornamental arches. Also there are frontispieces containing Illustration page 128 no text, often with a large cross in the center. In the Sacramentarium Gelasianum each of the three chief sections of the missal is preceded by an ornamental composition of this kind given the form of an arcaded portico. Is this an early intimation of the richly decorated portals that were to bulk so large in French architecture (but not in English)? Though they have no liturgical significance whatever, even the numbers in the lower margins, marking the beginning or end of each quire of a book, are sometimes ornamented. This same procedure was followed in Coptic and Armenian manuscripts, and is one of several indications of the intimate relations that existed between Merovingian illumination and the East.

Ornament predominates even more in Merovingian illuminated manuscripts than in those of the British Isles. Owing to the paucity of illustrated Gospels, portraits of Evangelists are practically never found in them, the one exception being the Gundohinus Gospels of 754 A.D. (Autun, Bibl. Mun. 3), in which an excellent model of late antiquity with portraits of standing Evangelists has been copied in a rather amateurish way. As a general rule the Merovingian illuminators avoided representations of the human figure, and this presumably was a reflection of the iconoclastic tendencies then prevailing in all the lands around the Mediterranean. The symbol most favored by the Byzantine

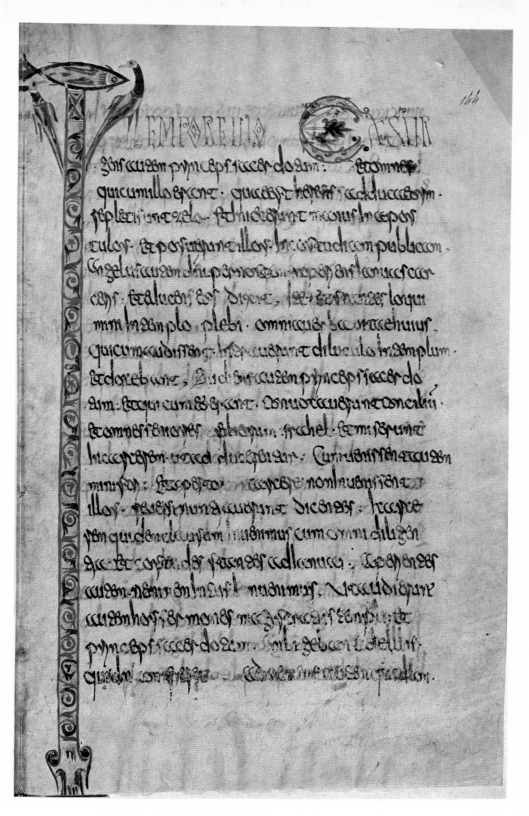

LUXEUIL LECTIONARY. INITIAL T. LUXEUIL, LATE SEVENTH CENTURY. (11 $\frac{1}{16}$×7 ″)
MS LAT. 9427, FOLIO 144, BIBLIOTHÈQUE NATIONALE, PARIS.

iconoclasts was the cross and, significantly enough, this is always given a central place in Merovingian illuminations. The return to favor of the human figure took place only at the end of the 8th century; premonitory signs of it can be seen most clearly in the Gellone Sacramentary. This manuscript, however, belongs rather to the period of transition between the Merovingian and Carolingian styles.

Characteristic of Merovingian, no less than of insular illumination is a love of ornament combined with calligraphy. Instead of drawing lines in freehand, relying solely on his manual dexterity, the Merovingian artist made frequent use of compasses and rulers. Initials consisting of circles gave opportunities for tracing single or double outlines of the letters with the former instrument; thus a plain circle represented the

SACRAMENTARIUM GELASIANUM. FRONTISPIECE AND INCIPIT. FRANCE, MID-EIGHTH CENTURY. (EACH PAGE: 10 $^3/_{16}$×6 $^7/_{16}$″) REG. LAT. 316. FOLIOS 131 VERSO AND 132, BIBLIOTECA APOSTOLICA, VATICAN CITY.

letter "O" or the body of an uncial "D". The uprights in an "R", a "P" or a "T" were sometimes elongated so as to form a decorative border along the whole column of text, and in these cases a ruler was used instead of compasses.

Almond or sickle-shaped letters were constructed by interlocking the arcs of two circles described round different centers. And all that was needed to give a letter thus constructed the appearance of a fish was to insert an eye at one of its extremities. This device, however, could not be employed where bird forms were concerned. The bird —frequent in the tailpieces of manuscripts of late antiquity—had to be more or less violently squeezed into the curves of the initials. Letters adorned with birds and fishes are characteristic of Merovingian technique and enable us to identify it at a glance. When geometric or zoomorphic forms are integrated into the structure of capitals, there results a curious ambivalence; such letters are at one and the same time living animals and non-figurative geometric designs. To start with, however, there was no question of making the forms of birds or fishes merely act as shafts of letters (as is done in "picture alphabets"); in the earlier manuscripts the animal outlines are identified for the most part with those of the entire letters. Thus plant motifs included in the shafts of the letters also serve as fillings for the bellies of the birds and fishes of which the letters are composed and since flat patterning was the order of the day, the animals often look more like anatomical diagrams than living creatures. Hence a crop of "double meanings": the shaft of an initial can be at once an animal and a piece of an ornamental border, and it is hard to tell which is primarily intended. This ambiguity is heightened by the habit of drawing the outlines of animals in very thin strokes, whereas the filling-up passages are done in vivid colors.

In the development of Merovingian illumination we can detect a growing tendency to break away from geometric constraints, birds and fish become more and more like real animals and even quadrupeds appear on the scene, their curved backs following the outlines of the lettrines, and initials end up as letters built up with "living" figures.

Besides animal forms, plant and vegetable ornaments bulk large in Merovingian illumination from the very start. Whether used as filling-up or taking the form of leafage sprouting from the margin of a circle, these vegetable motifs represent as it were an escape from the tyranny of the ruled or compass-drawn line and add a touch of life to the geometric rigor of the letters. On close examination we find that the plant forms used as fillings often consist of chopped vine shoots. Thus Merovingian ornament followed the practice, already noted in the art of the British Isles, of "segmentation." This also applies to the "plaid" and "tuft" designs on which these artists set such store. Leaf forms are often given double outlines as though the artist were imitating three-dimensional effects of an earlier age whose plastic meaning was no longer understood. For the third dimension was totally excluded from this art which dealt exclusively in flat planes, and the frequent inversions of background and decorative elements emphasize the purely abstract nature of its composition.

In Merovingian illumination there is a suppleness in the patterns used for filling up what would otherwise be empty spaces that reminds us of the designs on textiles;

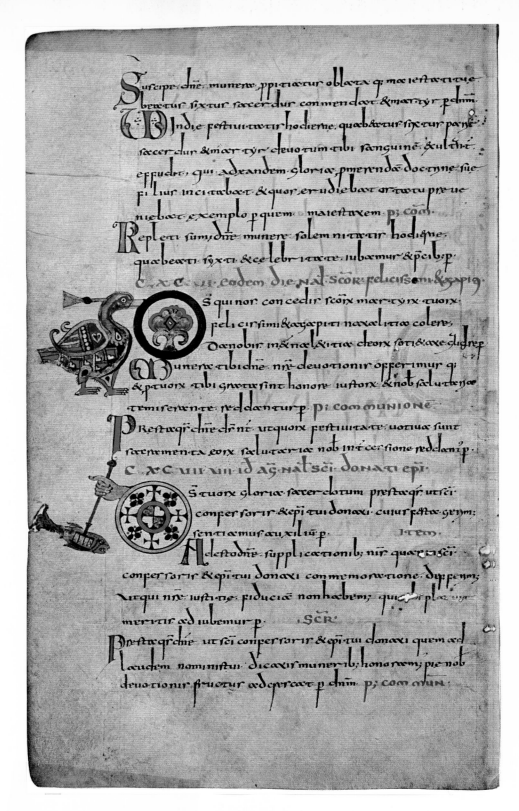

Suscipe dne munera propitiatus oblata quae maiestati tue beatus sixtus sacerdos commendat &martyr per dnm.

Unde festiuitatis hodierne quae beatur sixtus pane sacerdos &martyr deuotum tibi sanguine &ultri effudit, qui ad eandem gloriam promerendam doctrine sue filius incitabat &quos erudiebat orato preue niebat exemplo per quem maiestatem per com.

Repleti sumus dne munere solemnitatis hodierne quae beati sixti celebritate iubemur &pcib; p.

CXCII eadem die nat scorum felicissm &agapiti.

S qui nos concedis scorum martyrum tuorum feli cisimi &agapiti natalicia colere, dnobis infer &letitie eorum sorti &axe diligere p.

Munera tibi dne nre deuotionis offerimur qui & pro tuorum tibi grata sint honore iustorum &nobis salutem te miserente reddantur per com MUNIONE.

Presta qr dne utquorum festiuitate uotiua sunt sacramenta eorum salutarie nobis intercessione reddant p.

CXCIII VIII id ag nat sci donati epi.

S tuorum gloriam sacerdotum presta qr utsci confessoris &epi tui donati cuius festa geym; sentiamus auxilium p. ITEM.

Adesto dne supplicationibus nris quas in sci confessoris &epi tui donati commemoratione dependem; ut qui nre iustitie fiducie non habem; quis prece placatus meritis ad iubemur p. SCR

Presta qr dne utsci confessoris &epi tui donati quem ad laudem nominis tui dicatis muneribus; honorem; pie nob deuotionis struetur ad deprecet p dnm. p; com mun.

GELLONE SACRAMENTARY. DECORATED PAGE. MEAUX (?), LATE EIGHTH CENTURY. ($11\frac{3}{8} \times 6\frac{5}{8}$ ")
MS LAT. 12 048, FOLIO 99 VERSO, BIBLIOTHÈQUE NATIONALE, PARIS.

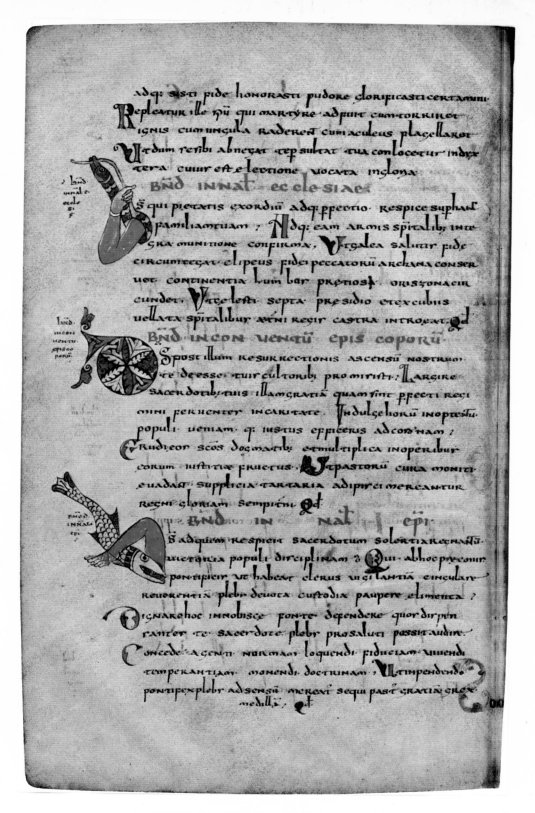

Adq: sisti fide honorasti pudore glorificasti certamini.
Repleatur ille hū qui martyre adfuit cum torriher
ignis cum ungula raderent cum aculeus flagellaror
Uerdum resibi abnegat cep subtat tua conlocetur inder
tera cuiur est e lectione uocata inglona
BŇD INNAT ECCLESIAE
S qui pietatis exordiū adq: ppectio respice suphat
familiam tuam ; Adq: eam armis spiritalib; inte
gra munitione confirma, Urgalea salutir fide
circumtegat clipeus fidei peccatorū archana conser
uot continentia lum bar pretiosa oriszonacir
cundos Urce lesti septa presidio erexcubiis
uellata spiritalibur atni regir castra introeat Qd
BŇD INCON VENTŪ EPIS COPORŪ
S post illum resurrectionis ascensū nostruo
re deesse tuir cultonib; pro mirirti; Largire
sacerdotib; tuis illamgratiā quam sint ppecti regi
mini feruenter incaritate. Indulge horū inoptesitu
populi ueniam q: iustus eppicerus adcoronam ;
Erudieor scos docmatib; et multiplica inoperibur
corum iustitiae fructus, Utpastorū cura moniti
euadad supplicia tartaria adipirci mereantur
regni gloriam sempiterni Qd
BŇD IN NAT EPI
S adquem respicit sacerdotum solertia regnantū
arietatuia populi disciplinam ? Qui abhoc cominr
pontificir ut habeat clerus uigilantia singulari
reuorentia plebs deuota custodia paupere elimenta ?
Dignare hoc innobisce fonte defendere quor dispen
ranter te sacerdote plebs prosaluti passit audir.
Concede agenti normam loquendi fiduciam uiuendi
temperantiam monendi doctrinam, Ut impendendo
pontifex plebr adsensū merear sequi past gratiā grex
meduls; Qd

GELLONE SACRAMENTARY. DECORATED PAGE. MEAUX (?), LATE EIGHTH CENTURY. (11 3/8 × 6 5/8″)
MS LAT. 12 048, FOLIO 164 VERSO, BIBLIOTHÈQUE NATIONALE, PARIS.

GELLONE SACRAMENTARY. INITIALS. MEAUX (?), LATE EIGHTH CENTURY. $(11\frac{3}{8} \times 6\frac{5}{8}'')$
MS LAT. 12 048, FOLIO I VERSO, BIBLIOTHÈQUE NATIONALE, PARIS.

insular art, on the other hand, had more affinities with metalwork. It would seem that Merovingian illuminators borrowed some of their motifs from the oriental fabrics used for wrapping the sacred relics, such as bones of saints, for which there was then a great demand in all parts of the Continent.

Color plays an important part in Merovingian illumination. The dominant hues are the same as those in insular art—green, red and yellow—but we also find other colors, for example dark lilac. The use of similar colors for purely calligraphic initials indicates that usually one and the same person acted as both scribe and painter. The general effect of the color schemes of these manuscripts is one of gaiety and charm. Outlines are drawn in very fine pen strokes and seem curiously pale alongside the patches of color they enclose. This patchwork technique, somewhat reminiscent of enamel and mosaic work, achieves an effect that can almost be described as impressionist in the Codex Ragyntrudis of Fulda (now in the Cathedral).

As regards the origins of Merovingian illumination there has been much heated controversy. Some authorities see in it a Western creation, others a decorative program imported wholesale from the East. One thing is certain: initial letters with the characteristic bird-and-fish theme are found in many oriental books, those produced by the Copts for example, and, more especially, by the Armenians. The Armenian initials, however, are definitely of later date than those in the Merovingian manuscripts and, assuming the latter stem from eastern prototypes, these must be still earlier. But, as it so happens, no such prototypes have survived; it is impossible to say whether they have been lost or if in fact they ever existed. Long and patient research work would be needed to resolve these problems. It would be necessary to begin by collating all late antique manuscripts with fish-pattern initials, particularly those produced in Latin countries from the 6th century on, but without neglecting the Greek manuscripts of the iconoclastic and pre-iconoclastic periods. Only if this is done will it be possible to trace in any satisfactory way the evolution of the initials figuring in Merovingian and Oriental manuscripts.

Anyhow there can be no doubt that on the Continent the art of the illuminated book during this period owed much less to prehistoric "heathen" art forms than did the corresponding art in the British Isles. French monastic scriptoria never lost touch with the art tradition of the ancient world and felt no need to revive the Germanic art of the epoch of the *Völkerwanderung*. But the humanistic tendencies we can detect in Anglo-Italian illumination were no less foreign to the spirit of Merovingian art. They found real favor on the Continent only with the advent of the Carolingians.

The insular style of ornamentation spread from north to south, whereas Merovingian illumination took another direction, spreading from the southeast northwards. The French monastery at Luxeuil in the Vosges, founded in 590 by the Irish missionary Columban, may be taken as its place of origin, though actually the production of illuminated manuscripts did not begin there till some fifty years later. To Luxeuil falls the honor of having created the first minuscule script that can properly be described as calligraphic. The earliest dated work goes back to 669 (New York, Morgan Library,

Illustration page 127

M. 334), and its decoration is still rather hesitant and rudimentary. But, soon after, the Luxeuil school settled into its stride. The key works of the developed style—such as the Missale Gothicum and the Luxeuil Lectionary—belong to the end of the 7th century, while a manuscript of the works of St Augustine, now at Wolfenbüttel (Weissenburg 99), exhibits the baroque tendencies of this school's final manner. There is no reason to date it later than 732, the year when Luxeuil was wrecked and pillaged by the Saracens.

It is usual to identify manuscripts made at Luxeuil by their script, a calligraphy derived from that of the Merovingian charters. But it remains an open question to what extent this book-hand was peculiar to Luxeuil. It seems also to have been employed for a certain time in affiliated monasteries.

This is the case with, for example, the abbey of Corbie, near Amiens, a royal foundation dating to about 660. The decorations of the earliest illuminated manuscript made in this monastery, the Leningrad Gregorius (Public Library, Q.v. I. 14), have all the characteristics of the Luxeuil style. But thereafter the art of Corbie developed a greater independence. That this process was relatively rapid is proved by a manuscript now in the Vallicelliana Library, Rome (B. 62), containing an acrostic poem built round the name of Bishop Basinus of Trier, who died in 704. In the initial letters of the Corbie manuscript drawing plays a larger part than in those of Luxeuil, the bird theme is more rarely employed and a new, characteristic filling-in motif makes its appearance: the circle with a dot at its center known as a "bull's eye." Next, shortly after the middle of the 8th century, the interlace begins to figure among the ornaments favored by this school. While initials become stiffer and heavier, the writing settles down into a sophisticated cursive (the so-called "a-b-script") typical of the conservative spirit obtaining in the monastery. This survived even when the Carolingian minuscule began to be used at Corbie and enjoyed an early vogue under Abbot Maurdramnus (772-781).

Meanwhile other schools are known to have been active in the north and east of France, but it is impossible to give them a more precise location. Recently it has been suggested that the double monastery of Chelles, not far from Paris, was an active center for the production of manuscripts, and Bernhard Bischoff has seen in this the headquarters of the scriptorium in which nine nuns, identified by their signatures, made three manuscripts for Bishop Hildebald of Cologne, Charlemagne's Head Chaplain (Cologne Cathedral Library, nos. 63, 65, 67), towards the close of the Merovingian era. Another large group of manuscripts, akin to these but older, seems also to have been produced in the neighborhood of Paris. Its key work is the famous Sacramentarium

Illustration page 128

Gelasianum (Vat. Reg. lat. 316) mentioned above. Perhaps these works originated from Saint-Denis, a monastery under the direct patronage of Charles Martel and Pippin, which was a leading cultural center in the days of its enlightened abbot Fulrad (751-784).

Mention must also be made of Laon, where there still are two 8th-century codices (Bibliothèque Municipale, 137 and 423), remarkable for the curious intermingling of Merovingian and insular strains in their decorations. Strangely enough, no manuscript hailing from Metz has so far been discovered, though it is known that books were made there in the time of Archbishop Chrodegang (742-766). Initials of a remarkable beauty are to be seen in the more recent portion of the Missale Gallicanum Vetus (Vatican, Pal. lat. 493) and on the first page of text in the Ashburnham Pentateuch; it has been suggested that these books were made at the monastery of Fleury (now Saint-Benoît-sur-Loire). But this is little more than a working hypothesis. The difficulties we so often encounter in trying to determine the provenance of Merovingian manuscripts are strikingly exemplified by the problem of the Gellone Sacramentary. For a long time it was assigned to the South of France or even Spain; in the light of recent paleographical discoveries, however, Meaux now seems more likely to have been its place of origin.

This manuscript has always been popular with connoisseurs owing to the great variety of themes employed in its initials. Besides geometric and vegetable motifs there are animals—birds, fishes, quadrupeds of various kinds—and even human limbs. Thus on the reverse of folio 164 we find a curious intermingling of arms and legs with fishes. Illustration page 131 This type of initial was not a Merovingian invention, it is also found in some Byzantine books; and we may assume that the maker of this manuscript drew inspiration from Greek and Eastern sources.

Sometimes comic touches add to the liveliness of the ensemble, as when the artist in a playful mood represents a fish escaping from the letter whose stem it formed and Illustration page 130 a hand promptly pinning it back in place with a harpoon. For the Gellone Sacramentary is a kind of Merovingian counterpart of the Book of Kells and in it, too, we find anticipations of Romanesque and Gothic "drolleries."

Above the initial formed by the fish is another built up of a circle and a duck, the tassel fixed to the duck's neck being unmistakably a reminiscence of the designs of Sassanian and Byzantine textiles. In the course of its evolution the Merovingian miniature made increasingly frequent borrowings from other art techniques. This led to a certain incoherency and lack of formal discipline, against which the Carolingian "reform" vigorously reacted.

CORBIE PSALTER. INITIAL. CORBIE, EIGHTH-NINTH CENTURY. (4 1/2 × 2 15/16″) MS 18, FOL. 133, BIBLIOTHÈQUE MUNICIPALE, AMIENS.

Pre-Carolingian illumination may be described as anonymous in the sense that next to nothing is known about the persons commissioning it. Neither portraits nor the names of kings or great churchmen figure in the illuminated manuscripts that have come down to us. Things are very different in the Carolingian period when so many famous books have names attached to them: Archbishop Ebbo's Gospel Book, Archbishop Drogo's Sacramentary, the Emperor Lothair's Gospel Book and Charles the Bald's Bibles. Thus the illuminated book now takes its place among great historical documents, often linking up with specific political events.

A case in point is one of the earliest manuscripts of the period, whose dedicatory verses inform us that it was commissioned by Charlemagne to commemorate a notable historical occasion. After taking his son Pippin to Rome at Easter 781 to have him baptized by the pope, the monarch instructed a scribe named Godescalc to make a Gospel Book, presumably for use in the Palace Chapel, with as its frontispiece a picture of the "Fountain of Life." This was an accepted symbol for the Gospels, sources of the water of Eternal Life, but here, as Paul Underwood has aptly observed, it was also an allusion to the baptism of the king's son, which had taken place in the baptistery of the Lateran. It was there, according to an ancient legend, that Pope Sylvester had formally admitted Constantine the Great to the Church, healing

Illustration page 139

him of "the leprosy of unbelief." Iconographically the Fountain frontispiece belongs to the art epoch known as Constantinian and its source of inspiration was the symbolic sanctuary figuring at the conclusion of the Canons of Eusebius in their original Greek version as we know it from copies in Armenian, Ethiopian and other manuscripts. Godescalc evidently used as his model an Early Christian manuscript, perhaps a gift from the pope brought back by Charlemagne from Rome.

This reversion to a very ancient prototype is one of the characteristics of Godescalc's Gospels. But along with it we find an opposite tendency—towards innovations of a singularly bold order. The capitularia at the end of the volume are written not, like the main text, in uncials but in a new alphabet, the Carolingian minuscule. This reform of the degenerate Merovingian script (which had become almost unreadable) was sponsored by Charlemagne's advisers, who decided to replace it by a clearer mode of writing, standard throughout the Empire. This was one of the outstanding cultural achievements of Charlemagne's reign and its results were lasting; the printing type you now are reading derives with hardly any change from the Carolingian minuscule. When Charlemagne set out to standardize the weights within his Empire he took as his basis the Monte Cassino *libra* (pound). This was a relatively simple task; whereas that of generalizing the new script involved considerable difficulty, since it meant breaking with age-old practices almost overnight. Nevertheless the new Carolingian script was so successful that after the year 800 there were only a few scriptoria in France that kept to the old modes of writing.

The Godescalc Gospels is one of the earliest manuscripts using the new minuscule. It was made in the "Capella Palatina," the king's chancellery and headquarters of the movement for a reformed script. The name "Capella" (chapel) derived from a holy relic kept there, the *cappa* (cloak) of St Martin. A royal chancellery was already in existence under the Merovingian kings, the officiating priests being influential members of the court. When miniature-painters joined forces with the scribes of the Royal Chapel the first of the aulic schools of illumination known to the early Middle Ages came into being, and thereafter it produced a number of richly decorated Gospel Books under the auspices of Charlemagne. One of these is at Trier (Stadtbibliothek, Cod. 22), another in London (Brit. Mus., Harl. 2788), another in Paris (originally at Soissons, Illustration page 138 Bibl. Nat., lat. 8850), and a fourth divided between Gyula-Fehérvár (in Transylvania) and the Vatican (Pal. lat. 50). The Trier manuscript was commissioned by Ada, supposed half-sister of Charlemagne, and the school in question is sometimes given her name.

A break with the Merovingian past is evident not only in the script used in the Godescalc Codex but also in the ornament. We no longer find letters built up with bird and fish forms; instead, there figure on the first page two big interlace initials forming Illustration page 139 the monogram IN, whose Northumbrian origin can be seen at a glance, though the Celtic spirals are omitted. Also the decorative elements of the frames are, partly, of the insular type. In fact the school of the Royal Chapel was obviously dominated by English influences, and the reason is not far to seek. When Charlemagne visited Italy in 781 to have his son baptized at Rome, he made the acquaintance, at Parma, of the famous Anglo-Saxon scholar Alcuin who from 766 on had presided over the school of York. The king invited him to head the cultural reform then getting under way in France, and the firstfruits of that reform was the Godescalc Gospels. Charlemagne also brought to France an Italian scholar, Paul the Deacon, previously attached to the court of Lombardy. The style of the Christ in Majesty at the beginning of the Godescalc Gospels is quite Italianate—which suggests that Paul was accompanied by a local painter. For, as Hjalmar Torp has pointed out, there is a marked stylistic kinship between this miniature and the Lombard frescos at Cividale.

Thus England and Italy supplied the basic elements of the school of illumination that flourished at the court of Charlemagne. Nevertheless, as with the writing, much

GOSPELS OF ST MEDARD OF SOISSONS. ST JOHN THE EVANGELIST. PALACE SCHOOL OF CHARLEMAGNE, EARLY NINTH CENTURY. (14 $^3/_{16}$ × 10 $^3/_{16}$″) MS LAT. 8850, FOLIO 180 VERSO, BIBLIOTHÈQUE NATIONALE, PARIS.

of its success was due to the native genius and inventiveness of local Carolingian artists. True, the Evangelist portraits in the Ada manuscripts were certainly inspired by earlier models both as regards their general conception and many of the motifs. All the same they give the impression, by and large, of purely Carolingian creations. We need only compare these Evangelists with those in the Canterbury Codex Aureus (whose general Illustration page 123 layout they follow more or less) to see how great is the advance in medieval art to which they testify. Particularly noteworthy is the intense animation of the figures within the arcaded frames, the impression they give of real living presences. One of the iconographic conventions of the Middle Ages was that of representing the dead as naked and the living fully clad. In this respect the Evangelists in Ada manuscripts are very

GODESCALC GOSPELS. FOUNTAIN OF LIFE AND INITIAL. PALACE SCHOOL OF CHARLEMAGNE. 781-783.
(EACH PAGE: 12×8¼″) NOUV. ACQ. LAT. 1203, FOLIOS 3 VERSO AND 4, BIBLIOTHÈQUE NATIONALE, PARIS.

much alive; they wear rich garments and these garments, too, are charged with restless movement. Even the thrones on which they sit are spread with sumptuous drapery, falling in ample zigzag folds. No less ornate are the architectural elements. In the background we see walls rendered in perspective and interspersed with small, niche-like windows giving the illusion that we are looking into real interiors. But it must be admitted that in these attempts at perspective the artists' skill is less conspicuous than their good intentions. The scrolls and books held by the Evangelists are, like their symbols, broadly treated; in fact the general effect these artists aimed at was that of representing visual experience in its utmost plenitude and of creating an impression of truly regal splendor, stressed by the simulated precious stones studding the arcaded frames. It is as though these miniaturists had been allowed to visit Charlemagne's treasure-house and had feasted their eyes on what they saw there.

On some pages of the Soissons Gospel Book, tiny Gospel scenes, lightly brushed in, fill up the spandrels of arched frames and the interiors of initials; evidently these artists had at their disposal one of the early anecdotal Gospel cycles. But the very smallness of the vignettes proves once again the compunction still felt as to depicting scenes from Holy Writ. This may have been a consequence of the lingering iconoclastic tradition against which Charlemagne showed a certain circumspection in letting his theologians make a stand.

In any case, however, these small Gospel scenes are symptomatic, since they prove that Carolingian art prepared the way for a new florescence of descriptive imagery. For conceptions of this kind had been as foreign to the makers of Merovingian manuscripts as to the Anglo-Irish schools. Only Anglo-Italian workshops had practised this form of illumination (from the year 700 on) and England was in fact the place of origin of one of the two Apocalypse cycles which came into vogue on the Continent during the reign of Charlemagne. The other cycle, exemplified in the Apocalypses of Trier and Cambrai, seems to have stemmed directly from Italy.

We can follow step by step the evolution of the Ada School by noting the gradual compositional changes. These artists were clearly seeking to replace the flat imaging of the pre-Carolingian period by a style capable of rendering the plastic values and organic forms distinctive of the art of classical antiquity. It is in the canon tables of the London Gospels (see page 137) that we have the most striking proof of a drastic change. The earlier tables are treated in a two-dimensional technique; then abruptly the artist takes to three-dimensional representation and modeled forms. This change occurred in the last decade of the 8th century and was introduced presumably by the generation immediately following Godescalc's. Alcuin (ca. 730-804) took little or no part in the movement; when in 796 he went to Tours to complete his revision of the Vulgate text of the Bible, he allowed the artists working under his supervision to continue using the two-dimensional technique that had prevailed in the pre-Carolingian era. The leading figure of the new generation was Einhard (ca. 770-840), Charlemagne's biographer-to-be, who in his early twenties succeeded Alcuin in the management of the Court scriptorium. He is known to have been a gifted artist and his works were highly thought of in his day.

EVANGELIST PORTRAIT ON PURPLE VELLUM. NEW PALACE SCHOOL, EARLY NINTH CENTURY. (10 ¼ × 7 ⁷/₁₆ ″)
MS 18 723, FOLIO 17 VERSO, BIBLIOTHÈQUE ROYALE, BRUSSELS.

The "renaissance" begun by the Ada School spread chiefly towards the east. An affiliated school at Fulda (where St Boniface had prepared the ground half a century before) reached the height of its activity round about 820. In southern Germany missionaries from England did much to propagate Carolingian as well as insular art and the "Charlemagne" Psalter, now at Montpellier, was executed in the Bavarian duchy formerly ruled by Tassilo. A special style of initial letter was in use in the provinces near the Alps; we find it in the early manuscripts of Reichenau and St Gall. In these initials Merovingian elements are still intermingled with others of the Carolingian period. In the north of France, on the other hand, the new minuscule and initials with interlaces characteristic of the insular style came quickly into favor and to this period may be assigned the beginnings of the Franco-Saxon school (cf. page 154).

Illustration page 136

Among the earliest manuscripts written in the new Carolingian minuscule were those made at Corbie under the auspices of Abbot Maurdramnus (772-781). Not long after them comes a psalter (Amiens, Bibl. Mun. 18) whose initials rank among the outstanding achievements of medieval art. Most of them contain figures either relating to the text or merely decorative, and there are also animals deriving partly from Oriental, partly from Merovingian and partly from insular sources. One of the artists clearly had an eye for quaint effects and in his initials there are some quite startling metamorphoses; as when we see sprouting from a man's cap the prow of a boat whose stern is metamorphosed into a horse. This might easily be taken for the work of a Romanesque artist in one of his lighter moments. Indeed there are indications that already in the days of Charlemagne European art was moving towards the Romanesque style in which it would have culminated, had nothing deflected it from its path.

What deflected it was the discovery of impressionist painting as practised by the Ancients—a discovery that promptly made the Ada School seem sadly "primitive." From now on artists all over France tended to take authentic classical prototypes for models. Early intimations of the emergence of this classicizing style may be seen in the manuscripts made at Fleury under the supervision of Theodulf, bishop of Orléans. Mention may also be made of a Gospel Book at Bern (Stadtbibl. MS 348) in which, at the end of the canon tables, we find a miniature almost Early Christian in aspect and the symbols of the Evangelists provided with three pairs of wings as in Early Christian Roman mosaics. But the key work of this new renaissance is undoubtedly the famous Coronation Book of the old Imperial Treasury in Vienna. A venerable tradition has it that Otto III found it on the knees of the dead Charlemagne when in the year 1000 he had the imperial sepulchre at Aachen opened, and in fact we are justified in assuming it was made in the last years of the emperor's life.

Illustration page 141

The Coronation Book is not the only extant work of the "new school"; there is another Gospel Book in Brussels containing a portrait of an Evangelist on purple vellum by the same artist. This curious miniature has neither frame nor background. Finally, a third manuscript survives, in the Treasure of Aachen Cathedral, in which after the canon tables the four Evangelists with their symbols are grouped in front of a landscape quite in the late classical manner, divided by deep gorges into four separate zones.

This may be an allusion to the four parts of the world whither, according to an old tradition, the Evangelists were sent forth to preach the Gospel. As can be seen from traces of a linear design that now shows through the color, the artist's original intention was to represent a city wall behind the Evangelists. The overall bluish hue of the landscape (except for a faint pink glow of dawn in the upper portion of the sky) is reminiscent of Late Antique miniatures produced around 400. Was it the artist's plan to hint at the darkness in which the world was plunged before the Incarnation?

There is a fundamental difference between the treatment of Evangelist portraits in these manuscripts and the practice of the Ada School. Bodies and garments are rendered in patches of color whose tonal relationships and values serve both to integrate the composition and to produce an effect of visual reality. Thus the style based solely on linear and plastic elements that characterized the Ada manuscripts is now replaced by an essentially painterly technique, color and light being intimately associated as in the pictorial art of Hellenistic and Roman antiquity.

We can have little hope of ever discovering all the reasons behind this vital change in Carolingian esthetic. The most that can be said is that the stimulus came in some way from Byzantine painting, which had never quite lost touch with the painterly tradition of antiquity. As late as the 7th and 8th centuries works were being produced in Constantinople and, under Greek influence, in Rome proving that there still were artists conversant with the techniques of classical painting. The abrupt emergence of this style north of the Alps may probably be accounted for by the fact that, after the conquest of Italy, the frontiers of the Carolingian and Eastern empires marched side by side. Moreover, though diplomatic relations had been severed after the coronation of the Emperor in Rome in the year 800, they now were steadily improving; in 812, two years before his death, Charlemagne concluded a treaty with the Basileus of Byzantium in which the latter deigned to style the emperor his "brother." We also hear of a Greek embassy to the court of Charlemagne and it may well have been that Greek artists found their way to France about this time. The fact that the name "Demetrius" figures in the margin of the first page of St Luke's Gospel in the Coronation Book is suggestive; though nothing is known about this man, the name implies he was a Greek.

Illustration page 146

Unfortunately we cannot form an idea of the school's place of origin; for example, the complex of curves building up the initial letters does not quite resemble that employed by any other known school. Its classicizing style was further developed in a Gospel Book made to the order of Archbishop Ebbo of Reims in the nearby abbey of Hautvillers; it is now at Epernay (Bibl. Mun., 1). The artist employed on this manuscript was undoubtedly a pupil of the illuminator of the Coronation Book. Like the latter he clothes the Evangelists in robes of shining white, their sheen intensified with passages of gold, telling out on a bluish background. But here a new element has entered into the style: the vibrant, dynamic movement pervading the whole composition, which makes us feel that the figures are in the grip of a divine afflatus. Garments form an avalanche of folds, criss-crossing, twisted into spirals—to such effect that each Evangelist seems enveloped in an aura of swirling white. But the rush of power suggested is of a psychic rather than a physical order—and herein lies the novelty. This painter was seeking to convey not so much the outward aspects as the psychic essence of the persons he portrayed and in so doing he initiated a new mode of expression that was to prevail in all subsequent medieval art.

Illustration page 143

In the Utrecht Psalter (Univ. Libr., Script. Eccl. 484) we find the same tendencies as those of the Ebbo Gospels, but in a still more pronounced form. Were we limited to but a single example of the Carolingian renaissance, no other manuscript could be more revealing and this is why, though it has no paintings, it figures in this volume. The drawings in the Utrecht Psalter show the early medieval draftsman at his best. At the beginning of each psalm is a landscape peopled with a number of figures in active movement, drawn sketchwise with the pen and charged with nervous energy. The setting is a hilly countryside divided into several zones whose arrangement is adapted to the positioning of the figures. Sometimes the ground consists of hummocks that look like the knuckles of a huge clenched fist. At the top of the scene we sometimes see the Savior attended by angels, sometimes the hand of God issuing from a cloud. In the lower portion of the scene are yawning chasms whence the dark powers of the underworld are pouring forth. Midway, on open ground, the Blessed do battle with the unbelievers, and God intervenes with His angelic host to aid the former and wreak vengeance on their enemies. The violence of these battle scenes and the frantic agitation of the tiny figures bear the distinctive imprint of Nordic medieval art; we find just the same dynamic movement in the decorations of insular manuscripts, the only difference being that here the artist imparts it not to ornamental but to human elements. For the rest, everything has an aerial lightness. Moving with elfin buoyancy or poised on tiptoe, figures have the elegance of ballet dancers, while touches of poetic fantasy in the renderings of nature remind us of the idylls of Theocritus or Vergil's Eclogues. For like the many architectural elements, these themes are borrowed from antiquity and there can be no possible doubt that the artist made use of the best models of the Early Christian period.

The Psalms of David do not lend themselves easily to illustration, since (except in their titles, which sometimes relate to David's life) the narrative element is lacking; there is no sequence of colorful events as in an epic poem like the Aeneid. What the artist of the Utrecht Psalter (or the artist of the model he copies) has done is to make the most of the psalmist's verbal imagery; that is to say, he seizes on such words or phrases as allow of concrete illustration. For example in the group of scenes prefixed to Psalm LXXIII, which we reproduce, he illustrates verse 23: "Nevertheless I am continually Illustration page 143 with thee: thou hast holden me by my right hand," by showing God grasping the hand the psalmist stretches out to Him. For verse 20: "As in a dream," we have a picture of two men sleeping in two beds, and the charming scene of the mare and her foal is a picturesque comment on verse 22: "I was as a beast before thee." The illustrations, in fact, are rather like charades and only to be understood by a careful word-by-word study of the text. As Dora Panofsky has aptly pointed out, the pictures, curiously enough, do not always apply to the version they illustrate, the Gallican translation of the Psalms. Some illustrations can only be understood by reference to another version, known as the *Hebraicum*. From which it follows that this picture cycle was originally made for a so-called *Psalterium duplex* (or *triplex*) in which the different versions were written in parallel columns; and in fact the general layout of the text bears this out. It also confirms the view that the Utrecht Psalter illustrations were copied from an Early Christian model. There is in the Stuttgart Library (Bibl. fol. 23) a Psalter dating to the beginning of the Carolingian epoch with illustrations which, if rather crude, do not lack vigor and are obviously copies of some work of Late Antiquity probably made in the 6th century, perhaps in the Vivarium monastery under the auspices of Cassiodorus. In Psalm LXXIII, at verse 22, we again find the mare and foal and there are other parallels with the Utrecht Psalter. But the model of the Stuttgart Psalter must in its turn have derived from a still earlier archetype and it was doubtless from this archetype that the illustrator of the Utrecht Psalter got not only most of his themes and motifs but the peculiarities of his style. It would be interesting to know if in this very early manuscript datable to ca. 400 all the scenes were similarly located in a mountainous landscape. In any case there are good grounds for holding that the miniatures of the Utrecht Psalter are no slavish copies of an ancient model and that these artists introduced many modifications and drew freely on their imagination. But in the process they so successfully recaptured the syntax and idioms of Christian antiquity that it is hard to say which parts are copied and which original.

GOSPEL BOOK OF EBBO. ST LUKE. REIMS, BEFORE 823 (?). (6⅞×5 9/16″)
MS I, FOLIO 90 VERSO, BIBLIOTHÈQUE MUNICIPALE, EPERNAY. (ENLARGED IN REPRODUCTION)

Ebbo, who did much to launch the new style, was an important political figure of his day. Son of a freedman and foster-brother of Louis the Pious, he was appointed by the emperor to the archbishopric of Reims. While the remarkable dynamism of the illustrations in the Utrecht Psalter is due in large part to the missionary ardor prevailing in the pre-Carolingian period, it certainly owes much to the great archbishop's personal zeal, manifested in his campaign for the conversion of the Danes, brought to a successful issue in 823. However, since no mention of this is made in the dedicatory verses of the Epernay Gospels, though his other great deeds are extolled at length, we may assume that this manuscript was made before that date. After breaking with Louis the Pious, formerly his patron, Ebbo joined the party of Lothair and was finally expelled from Reims by Charles the Bald in 845. That we find the Reims style employed in the part of the empire ruled by Lothair is probably due to Ebbo's close relations with that king, whose Psalter, now in London (Brit. Mus., Add. 37768), testifies to his taste as a bibliophile. Subsequently Ebbo quarreled with Lothair also and took refuge with Louis the German. Henceforth the manuscripts produced in Bavarian and Saxon territory bore (in differing degrees) the imprint of the style of Reims, though it is difficult to say if this was due solely to Ebbo's influence.

Once contact with the art of Christian antiquity had been established, there was a marked increase in the repertory of themes employed. The numerous cycles of scientific and literary illustrations made at the close of classical antiquity were collated and copied in Carolingian scriptoria. The *carmina figurata* of Porfyrius which we last heard of at Canterbury (in 750) found their way to the Continent and Hrabanus Maurus, abbot of Fulda, modeled his poem *Liber de Laudibus Sancti Crucis* on them. Carolingian copies were made of illustrated versions of Terence, Prudentius and Aratus; also of the moralized bestiary known as the Physiologus. Pagan or Christian, all these works alike were treated in the same spirit and betokened the intense desire to vie with classical culture that characterized this period.

Besides Reims other ecclesiastical centers in eastern France played a part in this vast cultural renaissance. The finest Prudentius manuscripts were made at Saint-Amand, while Saint-Denis and Korvei (in Westphalia) have been suggested as the places of origin of the illustrated Terence manuscripts. The group of liturgical books produced at Metz center on a splendid Sacramentary (Paris, Bibl. Nat., lat. 9428) which Archbishop Drogo, Illustration page 149 an illegitimate son of Charlemagne, commissioned, perhaps with a view to enhancing his prestige as papal legate. Drogo was also Lothair's chaplain; thus there are reasons for seeing in the Metz atelier a school affiliated to the royal court.

The initials of the Drogo Sacramentary contain scenes of the life of Christ, the deaths of martyrs and rites of the Church. All are quite small, like the Gospel illustrations of the Ada School and the drawings in the Utrecht Psalter. Distinctive of Metz illumination is the use of gold acanthus tendrils twining like ivy around the capital letters and sometimes filling the surrounding space. Before this, in the time of Charlemagne, acanthus leaves, leitmotif of classical antiquity, had been used as fillings in frames and canon tables, but then were treated in a rather heavy manner. Now that Carolingian artists were deliberately harking back to the art of the 4th and 5th centuries the handling of the acanthus theme became more delicate, more classical. And after being transferred from borders to initials, it ended up by proliferating over entire pages.

St Martin's Abbey at Tours ranks high as a center of Carolingian illumination; we are indebted to the greatest expert on Carolingian art, Wilhelm Koehler, for a masterly résumé of its output. This school owes its renown to the large one-volume Bibles thanks to which Alcuin's version spread to all parts of the Carolingian Empire. It seems that the Turonian workshop had at its disposal a very fine Early Christian Bible (commissioned by Leo the Great in Rome) with paintings intended to serve as a papal manifesto against the Manicheans. This Bible may have been brought to Tours by Alcuin, who used this source, however, only for his revision of the Vulgate. A generation had yet to pass before the School of Tours felt capable of integrating the Roman picture cycle into its own

Illustration page 152

productions. We see this happening for the first time in the Grandval Bible (London, Brit. Mus., Add. 10 546) and next in the Vivian Bible of 846 (Paris, Bibl. Nat., lat. 1). Here the number of scenes is doubled and among the new ones is a votive picture showing the members of the Chapter of St Martin, headed by their lay abbot, Count Vivian, ceremoniously presenting the book to the Emperor Charles the Bald. The illustrations in the two Tours Bibles are among the most monumental productions of Carolingian illumination, their special merit being the skill with which a masterpiece of Late Antiquity has been incorporated into medieval art, thus providing a basis for all subsequent works of the kind, up to the Romanesque Bibles of the 12th century.

Between the Grandval and the Vivian Bibles a bare ten years elapsed, but that decade was of capital importance in the evolution of Turonian art. The makers of the Grandval Bible took over some of the methods used by the artists of Late Antiquity for the rendering of space but without greatly troubling about the structural anomalies in which this landed them. Typical are the foreshortenings used in the perspective representation of the coffered ceiling in the scene of Moses, accompanied by young Joshua, giving instructions to Aaron and the Israelites. The same scene figures in the Vivian Bible, but there we find the classical conception of space superseded by a purely medieval schema; henceforth the illusion of real depth gives place to a system of separate planes echeloned tier on tier, within which figures, movements and objects are disposed in strictly defined registers.

Some years after the appearance of the Vivian Bible Charles the Bald, who had temporarily made peace with his half-brother Lothair, his former enemy, authorized the

Illustration page 150

latter to commission a decorated Gospel Book (Paris, Bibl. Nat., lat. 266) from the Tours atelier, as a memorial of their reconciliation. Both in its figure drawing and its ornament this book represents the apogee of Turonian illumination. But the flowering of this admirable school was of brief duration, and it came to an end abruptly in 853, after an inroad of the Northmen. The havoc caused by the Vikings was not, however, the only reason for the rapid decline of Carolingian illumination. And if it is often difficult to localize the centers of this art in the latter half of the 9th century, this is certainly due to a great extent to the Europe-wide political unrest of the age.

SACRAMENTARY OF DROGO. TE IGITUR. METZ, CA. 842. (8¼×7″)
MS LAT. 9428, FOLIO 15 VERSO, BIBLIOTHÈQUE NATIONALE, PARIS.

GOSPEL BOOK OF LOTHAIR. THE EMPEROR LOTHAIR. TOURS, 849-851. (7 13/16 × 4 7/8″)
MS LAT. 266, FOLIO I VERSO, BIBLIOTHÈQUE NATIONALE, PARIS.

One fact, however, is fairly certain: that under the patronage of Archbishop Hincmar (845-882), Ebbo's successor, the Reims atelier remained an important art center. To Reims we may attribute two very fine manuscripts, the Gospels formerly in the Crawford Collection and now in the Morgan Library (M. 728) and the famous Bible of San Paolo fuori le Mura in Rome. The latter derives from a Tours Bible containing miniatures similar to those of the Vivian, but to the Turonian repertory it adds several new scenes, bringing their number to twenty-four. This magnificent book was made to the order of a king named Charles; some say Charles the Bald (in which case it must be dated to before 875), others think Charles the Fat is meant (in which case it was made after 880). But everything tells in favor of the former view and recently an eminent American scholar, Mr E. H. Kantorowicz, has advanced good reasons for dating it to 870, the year of Charles the Bald's marriage with his second wife, Richildis.

Illustration page 153

For a long while the San Paolo Bible was assigned to a group of lavishly illuminated books whose place of origin was thought to be Corbie. But apart from the fact that manuscripts definitely known to emanate from that abbey, e.g. the Paris Sacramentary (Bibl. Nat., lat 12050), display a markedly different style, it is now admitted that there are not sufficient grounds for assuming that the Bible in Rome and its relatives were really executed at one and the same place. The latter form a group apart. Most noteworthy among them are a group of books made for Charles the Bald, for example the king's own Book of Hours, now in Munich, his Psalter (Lat. 1152) and Coronation Sacramentary (Lat. 1141) in Paris, and, last but not least, his Gospel Book, the Codex Aureus of Munich (Clm. 14000). Made for the king in 870, this superb "golden codex" has still its original cover, a masterpiece of Carolingian goldsmiths' work. From the dedication we learn that it was made by two brothers, Beringar and Liuthard. The latter also signed, as scribe, the Psalter of Charles the Bald and, as painter, a Gospel Book at Darmstadt (Landesbibl., Cod. 746), as is recorded in a marginal note at the end of the canon tables, written with gold in the ancient Roman shorthand known as "Tironian notes," which Bernhard Bischoff has been kind enough to decipher for us.

Illustration page 155

It was a mistake to believe (as I myself once thought) that the Codex Aureus and affiliated manuscripts had their origin in Reims. The minuscule employed is definitely different from that in the San Paolo Bible and other products of the Reims scriptorium. Though initials, frames and figures have much in common with the art of Reims, we find discrepancies proving that these works must stem from an independent school and had another place of origin. One of the characteristics of this atelier was an almost excessive use of acanthus-leaf borders and marblings with patches of gold and colors. The general effect of these manuscripts is one of almost reckless lavishness, an eye-filling splendor unsurpassed in all Carolingian illumination.

One thing is clear: the scriptorium in question was under the direct patronage of Charles the Bald. It was in fact his court atelier, just as the Ada group had been his grandfather's. (It may be noted in passing that the Munich Codex Aureus copies a manuscript made in the palace school of Charlemagne.) Hence we are justified in regarding this atelier as a dependency of the imperial chancellery, which would also account for the

THE GRANDVAL BIBLE. MOSES RECEIVING THE TABLES OF THE LAW; JOSHUA, MOSES, AARON AND THE ISRAELITES.
TOURS, CA. 840. (16 × 11 ⅜") ADD. MS. 10 546, FOLIO 25 VERSO, BRITISH MUSEUM, LONDON.

BIBLE OF CHARLES THE BALD. THE ARK IN THE DESERT AND SCENES FROM THE HISTORY OF THE ISRAELITES.
REIMS, CA. 870. (15 9/16 × 12″) FOLIO 30 VERSO, SAN PAOLO FUORI LE MURA, ROME.

frequent use of "Tironian notes." For to this group can be assigned several lexicons and psalters entirely written in this classical shorthand, and it is an interesting point that in these books even the tachygraphical signs at the beginnings of chapters are shaped to look like real initial letters.

Every medieval chancellery, even one that, like Charles the Bald's, was constantly on the move, must have felt the need of having behind it some monastic center with a scriptorium whose artistic style and standard could be relied on. Saint-Denis has been proposed in the present case and the American art historian A. M. Friend, who was the first to put forth this view, has thought to see the influence of the writings of a Greek philosopher, Denis (Dionysius) the Areopagite, in certain iconographic peculiarities of the illuminations and goldsmiths' work produced by this school. A Latin translation of these writings was made at Saint-Denis in the 9th century, and their original author, identified with the disciple of St Paul mentioned in Acts XVII, 34, was held in high esteem there. Moreover he was apt to be confused with the patron saint of the monastery. Friend advances liturgical arguments in support of the view set forth above. But the special interest shown in the saintly martyr and his companions is also explicable by the fact that Charles the Bald was lay abbot of Saint-Denis. If Friend's view is not accepted, an alternative would be the court monastery at Compiègne which Charles the Bald patronized with the same enthusiasm that half a century before his grandfather Charlemagne had shown towards the Palace Chapel at Aachen.

Illustration page 156

Some authorities, however, have seen in Saint-Denis the place of origin of quite another school of Carolingian illumination, the one usually known as Franco-Saxon. Most of the works deriving from this source are Gospel Books and Sacramentaries, and it turned them out in such large numbers that a great many public libraries have one or more. The activities of the Franco-Saxon school extended over more than half a century and everything goes to show that not one but several ateliers practised this form of art. Though these were undoubtedly located in the North of France, their influence made itself felt as far afield as the eastern marches of the kingdom. Of all Carolingian styles this is perhaps the one that lasted longest, since we find its forms being imitated as late as the 12th century.

The Franco-Saxon school showed a certain diffidence in its attitude towards the contemporary renaissance movement. True, we find miniatures containing figures somewhat in the style of Reims and showing the artists' complete mastery of classical illusionism; in, for instance, the so-called Gospels of Francis II (Paris, Bibl. Nat., lat. 257). But representations of human beings are on the whole rare in this school. Usually the manuscripts contain only illuminated initials, framed frontispieces or canon tables treated in a strictly two-dimensional style, the most frequent motifs being interlaces and ornamental animal forms copied from insular models. Yet so finely balanced is the composition that the effect is almost classical, as is splendidly exemplified in the Second Bible of Charles the Bald (Paris, Bibl. Nat., lat. 2), the beauty of whose initials was appreciated even by decorators of the time of Henry II. Perhaps it was the typically French clarity of their formal structure that appealed to them.

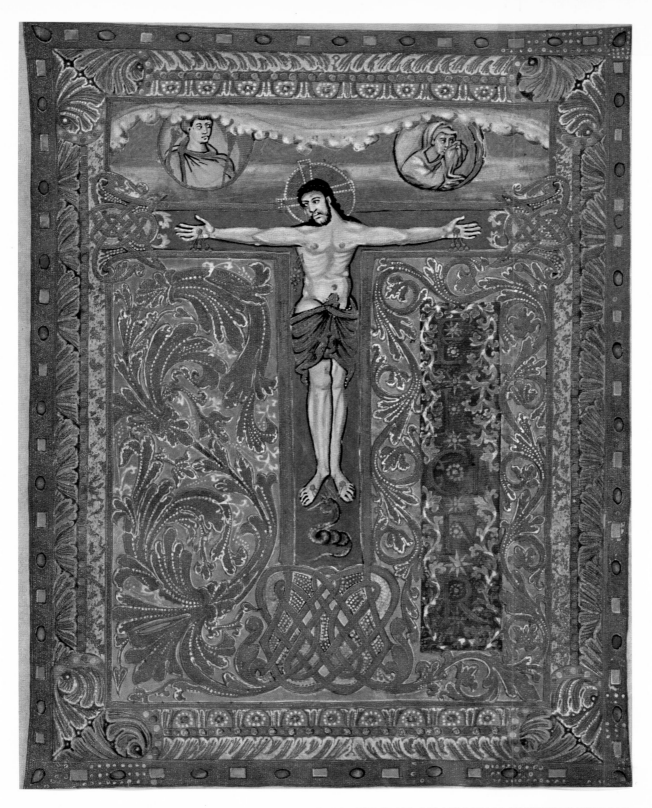

THE CORONATION SACRAMENTARY. TE IGITUR AND CHRIST ON THE CROSS. PALACE SCHOOL OF CHARLES THE BALD. SECOND HALF OF NINTH CENTURY. (9⅜×7″) MS LAT. 1141, FOL. 6 VERSO, BIBLIOTHÈQUE NATIONALE, PARIS.

GOSPEL BOOK. INITIAL PAGE WITH FIGURED FRAME. FRANCO-SAXON SCHOOL, SECOND HALF OF
NINTH CENTURY. (7 ¹⁵/₁₆×7 ⅛″) MS 233 (1045), FOLIO 8, BIBLIOTHÈQUE MUNICIPALE, ARRAS.

Two eminent authorities, Charles Niver and André Boutemy, while following independent lines of research, concur in the opinion that the Franco-Saxon school had its center at Saint-Amand (near Tournai). It was for this monastery, presided over by Milo, poet and friend of Charles the Bald, that the Stockholm Sacramentary (Kung. Bibl. A. 136) was made. Milo acted as tutor to the king's two little sons and they must certainly have learnt the alphabet to perfection thanks to the clean-cut precision of the Franco-Saxon script. The dedicatory verse in the Second Bible of Charles the Bald has been attributed to Milo's successor Hucbald. Clearly the abbey of Saint-Amand was a cultural center favored by the royal bibliophile.

Thinking that its usual name might be misleading, some have described this school as "Anglo-Frankish" or "Franco-insular." But these names have not gained currency. The old term "Franco-Saxon" persists and it is too late in the day to reserve it for the sub-group to which it applies more correctly since the manuscripts of this group are Frankish in style but derive from Saxony. The starting-off point of this school was a Gospel Book now in the Treasure of Prague Cathedral (Cim. 2), remarkable both for its exceptionally rich decoration and the fact that the Evangelists are represented not only in the act of writing (as was customary) but also facing the companion miniature at the moment of receiving the divine afflatus.

After the dethronement of Charles the Fat in 887, the political center of the Empire tended to shift more and more to the East. By a deed of gift the Codex Aureus of Charles the Bald and other *ornamenta palatii* passed into the possession of Arnulf, king of the Germans, who bequeathed them in 899, just before his death, to St Emmeram's monastery at Regensburg, where he was buried. The upper portion of a binding made at the court atelier of Charles the Bald found its way to St Gall, where it was used to cover a new manuscript, the Lindau Gospels now in the Morgan Library, New York (M. 1). This manuscript (which may thus be later than its binding) is itself a noteworthy example of the art of illumination practised at St Gall, seat of the last great Carolingian school and most important center as regards the origins of Ottonian art.

Before and during the Carolingian period the illuminated books produced in monasteries near the Alps had a style peculiar to themselves. The forms of the initials retained more of the Merovingian tradition than did those of the French scriptoria in the West, and there was also some use of motifs stemming from the British Isles —a legacy of the missionary era. Towards the middle of the 9th century French influence became paramount, leading to initials composed of interlaced gold bands. And when finally to these were added vegetable elements (probably of Byzantine provenance) there arose a style distinguished by its frequent use of rinceaux done in gold with buds along the stems, twisted into spirals or twining around each other in elegant interlaces. Their forms are emphasized by boldly marked contour lines in minium red. Silver as well as gold was used. The general effect is one of heavy splendor, more pronounced than that of the initials made in the French schools.

In St Gall, in the Franco-Saxon ateliers, the decoration of the initials and title pages was the craftsmen's chief concern. To enhance the beauty of the initials when these occupy an entire page, they are given a purple ground and richly decorated frames, whereas the rinceaux in the openings of the letters have either green or light blue grounds. There are for the most part few full-page pictures, the chief exception being a David cycle in the Psalterium Aureum of St Gall (Stiftsbibl., Cod. 22), one of the best works of the school.

The majority of St Gall manuscripts have remained at their place of origin—an advantage for the researcher, who thus can follow the evolution of this school under the best conditions (as has been done by Adolf Merton and with even finer understanding by Franz Landsberger). After an initial period of strictly ordered rhythms there developed early in the 10th century an almost baroque luxuriance of forms. The Psalter of Illustration on the title-page Folchard (Cod. 23) was one of this school's first capital works. In it the litanies are surrounded by arcades festooned with leafage and in the spandrels between the arches we find the sprouting acanthus leaves which henceforth were to figure also in the fillings of initial letters. This school reached its apogee under Abbot Salomon (890-920), chancellor of the Frank kingdom of the East and an enthusiastic patron of the arts. It was he who commissioned the Psalterium Aureum (Cod. 22). The names of several St Gall monks of this period, famed for their musical, artistic and literary compositions, have come down to us, among them Notker Balbulus, Waltram and Tuotilo. The last-named was the maker of some famous ivories. Sintram, another member of the group, was held in great esteem as an illuminator; the so-called Evangelium Longum (St Gall, Stiftsbibl., Cod. 53) is by his hand.

In addition to St Gall, the island monastery of Reichenau in the Lake of Constance seems to have been an active center around 900, but so far it is still a moot question what manuscripts can be positively assigned to it. This problem arises notably in connection with the striking pictures of the months in the Martyrologium of Wandalbert in the Vatican Library (Reg. lat. 438) and the Book of Maccabees at Leyden (Univ. Bibl., Periz. 17).

On a general survey of the evolution of Carolingian illumination we get an impression of an immense luxuriance, outcome of a new and lively interest in art. Einhard, Charlemagne's private secretary and biographer, was not mistaken when he said of the Emperor's cultural policy that "it enabled him to bring about a glorious revival of the learning which had well-nigh disappeared in a world given over to barbarism, and thus to transform the vast realm which, when God bestowed it on him, was shrouded in darkness and like a kingdom of the blind, into a land of light where men's eyes were flooded with celestial radiance." For a century the archaism of the early Middle Ages was replaced by an eminently humanistic culture. That this should have happened is all the more surprising when we remember that, after the death of Charlemagne in 814, the political situation steadily deteriorated and that the lands which had enjoyed this great period of cultural enlightenment ended in a state of almost complete exhaustion, from which France made a slow and painful recovery only in the 11th century. It would seem that the soil which nourishes the arts needed to lie fallow for a while before it could once again bring forth a golden harvest.

# FROM CAROLINGIAN TO ROMANESQUE

BY a judicious fusion of classical and Nordic formal elements the Carolingian renaissance achieved a style that was essentially European, and its chief center was located in the very heart of Europe, in the ancient Frankish kingdom of Neustria, between the Loire and the Meuse. Throughout its development it remained a purely continental style, tending to lose its driving force as it neared the sea coast. We look in vain for any traces of it in the larger islands and peninsulas of Europe; whether in still heathen Scandinavia or in the British Isles, hard put to it to safeguard their Christian heritage, in Spain and Sicily, then overrun by the Moslems, or in Italy, still culturally isolated from her neighbors. None of these lands was ready to abandon out of hand its age-old traditions and to fall in line with the new Carolingian culture. Nevertheless the entire period was dominated by this continental art, since none of the countries named above had an art of its own strong enough to be set up against it. Hence our justification for regarding the Carolingian renaissance as the determinant of 9th-century art. The great exception is Byzantium, which after the end of the Iconoclastic Controversy had embarked on a renaissance of its own whose influence was to make itself felt in the art of the West and steadily gain ground from the 10th century on.

As we have seen, the flowering of Carolingian art spanned three or four generations only. When it came to an end, at the close of the 9th century, European illumination had to start out again from the beginning. A tendency towards a somewhat "barbarian" primitivism made considerable headway in many scriptoria during the first half of the 10th century and it is sometimes very difficult at first sight to distinguish between manuscripts of this period and those made in provincial workshops in the early 9th century. Soon, however, in several countries that had been relatively unproductive in the Carolingian period, there came a sudden burst of creative energy and from now on we find the Romanesque style gradually taking form, though not until the 12th century did it come triumphantly into its own. Almost all nations took part in its development, and it ended up by dominating Europe, from Sweden in the north to Sicily in the south. In other words, we have in Romanesque the first art language of the Middle Ages that can properly be described as international; compared with it, all previous styles have the air, more or less, of local dialects. Indeed one might be justified in defining the early Middle Ages as the epoch *par excellence* of diverse regional styles.

In the new efflorescence of art that marked the beginning of the Romanesque period three countries played a leading part: England, Germany and Spain. Lying as they did on the outskirts, north, east and south, of what had been the Frankish empire, each had taken over the heritage of Carolingian art and rightly felt that it offered scope for new developments on lines congenial to the national temperament. Thus, when revitalizing as it were the Carolingian renaissance, the English, German and Spanish schools of illumination joined up with the regional styles of the early Middle Ages. For this reason Anglo-Saxon, Ottonian and Mozarabic illuminations can suitably be dealt with in the present volume. This is all the more justified by the fact that we have to do with movements of limited duration. For a very marked cleavage took place in the development of art in England, Germany and Spain after the middle of the 11th century, a cleavage due to events of far-reaching historical importance: the Norman invasion of England in 1066; in Germany, the struggle between Pope and Emperor over the question of investiture; in Spain, the Cluniac reform of the Church linked up with the Reconquista. All these events tended to diminish the regional isolation of the various forms of art obtaining in these countries and to prepare the way for the internationalization of Romanesque art.

It was inevitable that France and Italy should be affected by the great historical events of the second half of the 11th century. But in these two countries the situation was from the outset rather different. In neither do we find a revival of the art of book illumination in the 10th century comparable to that in England, Germany and Spain. Not until the beginning of the 11th did the French and Italian schools take to producing illuminated manuscripts of an interest and value ranking them beside those of the three countries named above. Furthermore, French and Italian illumination of the 11th century betrays to a large extent the influence of the corresponding art in neighboring lands—so much so that instead of exerting an influence on the English, German and Spanish schools, it tended to borrow and adapt their forms. Similarly Italian illumination owed much to the Ottonian influences prevailing in the peninsula. At the same time, however, Italian artists were finding a new source of inspiration in Byzantine art, and it was owing to this circumstance that Italy was to take the lead in disseminating that fundamental element of the new Romanesque style.

While the beginnings of the French and Italian schools, round about the year 1000, still show a certain lack of confidence and enterprise, they none the less were factors of extreme importance in the subsequent development of art. This is why we have thought best not to deal with them in the present book but to reserve our study of them for the following volume, where they will fall naturally into place as preliminaries of the Romanesque movement in book illumination.

# MOZARABIC ILLUMINATION

THAT appellation "the Dark Ages" so often applied to the first centuries of the medieval era is particularly appropriate to conditions in Spain during this period. The Islamic conquest had isolated the country and largely cut off Spanish culture from contacts with the European community, thus retarding the development of a medieval art on Western lines. When with the 10th century there came a revival of the art of illumination in Spain, it became evident how great had been the setback due to the Moslem occupation. The common idea that Spain profited from the high cultural standards of the Arabs certainly does not apply to illumination. Of all the schools of painting that flourished in Europe during the 10th and 11th centuries the Spanish strikes us as the most primitive and backward. One of the characteristics of the early Middle Ages is a persistent tendency to hark back to a decorative art racy of the soil—a tendency countered by the "renaissances" that took place from time to time. Spain was an exception, the only European country where there were no such "renaissances"—with the result that even the most cultured artists of medieval Spain tended to adopt the idioms of folk-art and their style bears traces of primitivism.

We name this style "Mozarabic" as being the style employed by Christian artists in Spain when they were under Moslem domination or in constant danger of being overrun by their Moorish neighbors. However we must be careful not to overestimate the Moslem strain in Spanish art, for the fact is that, anyhow in its early phase, Mozarabic illumination was little influenced by Islam.

To start with, the Arab invaders adopted a remarkably tolerant attitude towards the Christian culture they found in Spain. This explains why even in the second half of the 8th century a Christian élite was able to keep the art of painting at the same level as that obtaining before the Moslem conquest. Though no Spanish miniatures have survived to prove the point directly, there is much indirect evidence in confirmation of it. In 786 at the latest a monk of a monastery in northern Spain, Beatus of Liebana, wrote commentaries on the Book of Revelation and the Book of Daniel, deriving for the most part from earlier sources, and had them decorated with a wealth of illustrations. Though the original has disappeared, we can get some idea of the style of these illustrations from the copy made in the mid-11th century at Saint-Sever (Paris, Bibl. Nat., lat. 8878), to which we shall revert in our following volume. A careful study of this manuscript makes it clear that the artists working for Beatus must have had a real understanding—remarkable for the age—of the stylistic traditions of Late Antiquity. This explains why the illuminations of the Saint-Sever Apocalypse so strikingly recall those of the Ashburnham Pentateuch, both in their range of colors and in their handling of forms—sometimes so much so that we can hardly believe that four centuries intervened between the two works.

A native of Spain, Bishop Theodulf of Orléans (ca. 755/60-821), had been inured in his youth to the late classical tradition as handed down by the original Beatus miniatures, and for this reason was well qualified to play a part in promoting the Carolingian renaissance. In the mosaics he commissioned for the church of Germigny we find, as André Grabar has pointed out, a variety of influences, Roman, Spanish and Byzantine. The same is true of the canon tables and ornamented titles in the famous Paris Bible (Bibl. Nat., lat. 9380) and in the Le Puy Bible (Le Puy Cathedral Treasure), both of which were executed at Fleury under Theodulf's instructions. Should the Gospel of Livinus at Ghent (Treasure of St Bavo's), dating from the beginning of the 9th century, also be associated with this Franco-Spanish art current? The two surviving illuminations show St Matthew and St John in the presence of a standing witness, and the nearest parallel to this unusual iconographic formula is to be found in the Evangelist portraits of Beatus manuscripts. Even the presentation of the Evangelist symbols in a medallion over the pillar separating the two figures in each miniature is exactly paralleled in a Spanish Beatus Apocalypse now in New York (Morgan Library, M. 429).

Besides the art of the Beatus manuscripts, in which we have belated but short-lived reminiscences of Late Antiquity, there existed in Spain a more primitive style dating to before the 8th century. Works of sculpture surviving from the period of Visigothic rule show how thoroughly the formal language of antiquity had already been superseded, in many cases, by "barbarian" methods of expression. Attention has rightly been drawn to the resemblances between the style of certain Visigothic stone slabs and that of Mozarabic 10th-century illumination (Helmut Schlunk). In both alike we find completely flat and stylized renderings of figures, while the folds of drapery are often marked by double lines. Like the political traditions of the country, this indigenous art seems to have kept to its natural course notwithstanding the Moslem occupation.

In the manuscripts the persistence of this national tradition can be seen most clearly in the minuscule script, known as the Visigothic hand, employed in them. Like the national scripts of the Merovingian period, it is an offshoot of the Roman cursive of Late Antiquity and, so far as is known, took its rise in the 7th century—though the earliest exactly datable manuscripts written in the Visigothic minuscule belong to the middle of the next century. In the oldest Spanish manuscript containing ornamentation (Albi, Bibl. Mun., MS 29), this is limited to decorative frames and initials drawn in pen-and-ink. Their affinities not only with Merovingian but also with Byzantine illuminations are unmistakable. These two influences are fundamental to all the illuminated books produced in Spain throughout the 9th century. The key work of this period is the Danila Bible at La Cava (near Salerno) which, though devoid of illustrations, is remarkable for the extreme elegance of its Mozarabic calligraphy. The title lines of each book of the Old and New Testaments are embellished with a square or circular ornamental frame drawn with the pen, at the bottom lefthand corner of which is suspended (as in some Greek manuscripts) the initial letter. Circular elements in the bodies of letters are traced with the aid of compasses, but even when the scribe has not made use of this mechanical device, the line is always marvelously crisp and clear. As in Merovingian initials, the chief colors are red, green and yellow, but to these is often added a delicate purplish-blue. The rendering of the canon tables, with their marbled columns and plain, broad arches, testifies to the proficiency of this atelier in handling body-color. And, given the high excellence of this manuscript, it seems no less surprising than regrettable that no other productions of this school have been brought to light.

The style persisted, though losing much of its finesse, until the first quarter of the 10th century. Beginning in the year 900, there was a steady increase in the number of ateliers and the output of manuscripts. In one respect the Spanish scriptoria showed themselves in advance of those in other lands: nowhere else do we find so many signed and precisely dated codices. For the Spanish scribe made a point of recording in a colophon his name, the date, and sometimes also the place where the manuscript was produced. These dates follow the Spanish system of chronology, 38 years ahead of ours. Thus in a famous manuscript preserved in the Escorial (d. 1. 2), the Codex Vigilanus, a record of the proceedings of Spanish Councils, we find a colophon stating that it was completed by the scribes Vigila, Sarracino and Garcia in the year 1014, that is to say 976 of our era. Similarly in a copy of this manuscript, also in the Escorial (d. 1. 1), known as the Codex Aemilianense, it is recorded that the writing of it was begun in the same year by Velasco and two scribes bearing the name of Sisebut, one a bishop, the other a scrivener. This excellent practice of recording names and dates may well have been inspired by that prevailing in royal chancelleries.

We have, however, no evidence that there then existed in Spain that close connection between ateliers and the royal courts which played so large a part in the history of Carolingian illumination. No manuscript was made to the order of a monarch before the reign of King Ferdinand the Great of Castile (d. 1065); nor were gold and silver used by the illuminators prior to this period. The production of manuscripts was a monopoly of the monastic scriptoria. We know the names of some of the chief centers, since whole groups of manuscripts stem from their libraries; among others, those of San Millan de la Cogolla, San Pedro de Cardeña and Santo Domingo de Silos. But most prolific were the monasteries in and around León, in northwestern Spain. From the reign of Alfonso III (866-914) onward, León was the headquarters of the Spanish resistance and the campaign that led to the gradual reconquest of the country from the Moors.

Stylistically speaking, Mozarabic illumination falls into two successive periods. The key piece of the earlier period (which covered the second quarter of the 10th century) is the Bible, originally in two volumes, in León cathedral. According to an inscription Illustration page 164 it was commissioned by Abbot Maurus and written and illuminated in the year 958 (i.e. 920 of our era) by the monks Vimara and Johannes at San Martin de Albelda (or Albeares). As in many Mozarabic manuscripts the so-called Cross of Oviedo—emblem of the Christian resistance movement—figures on the front page. Then comes a picture of a "rose of the winds" taken from an illustration in the famous encyclopedia *Originum sive etymologiarum libri XX* of Isidore of Seville (ca. 560-636). In the tympana of the arches in the sixteen canon tables at the beginning of the New Testament are half-length representations of the Evangelist symbols grouped two by two as if conversing—presumably an Early Christian formula, which spread from Spain to Ireland (Book of Kells), France (the Ada School) and Germany (Fulda and various Ottonian ateliers). Finally,

BIBLE OF THE YEAR 920. SYMBOL OF ST LUKE. (9 ³/₁₆ × 8 ⁵/₈ ")
COD. 6, FOLIO 211, LEÓN CATHEDRAL.

each Gospel begins with a full-page illumination in which we see an angel enclosed in a circle bearing on his shoulder the symbol of the Evangelist concerned; in the case of St Matthew the motifs of symbol-carrier and symbol (the winged man) are unified.

Such is the emphasis on decorative values that it is often hard to decipher the iconographical meaning of each illustration. Everything is depicted wholly on the surface—without depth—as in pre-Carolingian miniatures, and not only are plastic volumes omitted but even their superficies is only summarily indicated. Forms have a wispy thinness or, when they possess any breadth, give a curious impression of having been inflated from within. Modeling is altogether absent in the case of angels and symbolic creatures, and replaced by decorative streaks of color. To a certain extent we are reminded of the vibrant, almost impressionist brushstrokes used by the artists of Late Antiquity in their renderings of bodies; here, however, the basic elements are not light and color but ornament and color. Here lies the difference between Mozarabic illumination and the essentially linear style of the Irish miniature, the former tending to exalt color at the expense of drawing and design. We have already seen something of the kind in the illuminated initials of Merovingian manuscripts, but in these Mozarabic works we sense the presence of a distinctively oriental feeling for color. For all their primitivism, the illuminations in the León Bible testify to a highly refined sensibility on the artist's part. One might almost say that the Mozarabic miniature hovers constantly between a childlike incapacity for rendering three-dimensional form and that instinctive feeling for painterly effect which is the gift of great artists who see and realize purely in terms of color.

To implement the representational qualities of this art, a greater mastery of plastic form was called for and the style of its second phase is marked by various attempts in this direction. Round about 930-940 a new influence made itself felt when the Mozarabic illuminators came in touch with Carolingian art. We now find larger initials built up with interlaces, obviously inspired by the school of Tours or Franco-Saxon models. But there are also elements deriving from Islamic influences, for to these are certainly due the small, fleuron-like, serrated leaves on slender stems that now begin to sprout from frames and initial letters. The plaitwork designs, which are now more frequently employed, also have Islamic parallels. Thus the Merovingian-Byzantine phase was followed by an Islamic-Carolingian style.

As in the first period, so in the second the key piece is a dated Bible made at León. Preserved in the collegiate church of San Isidoro (Cod. 2), this manuscript, which is signed Illustration page 167 and dated 960 (of our era), was the joint work of a scribe named Sanctio and his teacher Florentius. On the last page below the big Omega we see them congratulating each other, each with a goblet in his hand, and praising God for the happy issue of their protracted labors. The canon tables of this Bible are of the same type as those in the Bible of 920, but instead of the split palmettes forming the upper and lower extremities of the pillars in the earlier work we now have capitals and bases of the normal kind. Generally speaking, architectural elements are more clearly articulated. The big arches are given the horseshoe form characteristic of Mohammedan architecture. The Evangelist symbols in the tympana are no longer cluttered up with colored strips of ornament, but have coherent, if rather sketchy outlines, and we can speak of a real attempt to render the folds of drapery, although these still are essentially linear and schematic. True, no great attention is paid as yet to the volumes of figures; nevertheless, summarily as these are indicated, we can see that definite progress has been achieved towards making them look more like living beings. In one of the canon tables the artist, in a playful mood, has represented the symbols of St Matthew and St Luke (the man and the bull) confronting each other, the man attacking the animal with a spear—an obvious allusion to that typically Spanish sport, the bullfight.

A series of Old Testament scenes treated in the same style as the Evangelist symbols in the canon tables is included in this second Bible. For the most part they are inter-calated in the columns of writing—enough in itself to show the artist had had recourse to an Early Christian model. But it is evident that the Mozarabic illuminator almost completely failed to understand his predecessor's style. With their beady eyes protruding from expressionless faces and their flat, stiff bodies, his figures look less like real people than like cardboard puppets. All the scenes are a shade too big and overflow into the text, quaintly reminding us of cakes that have "risen" and overspread their molds.

Meanwhile, however, frankly representational elements had found their way into Mozarabic illuminations, and from now on painters began to employ a very large cycle of illustrations: that of the Beatus Apocalypse. Copy after copy was made right up to the 13th century; over twenty are extant and it may safely be said that they are only a tithe of those that once existed. Like the second León Bible the earlier Beatus manuscripts translate the naturalistic style of the original into the decorative idioms of Mozarabic art, abridging or modifying the composition of the models, so that no two of these manuscripts are quite alike. However, on comparing them, we find that they fall into groups or iconographic "families." Wilhelm Neuss, whose research work in this field is authoritative, has carefully examined all the known Beatus manuscripts. On his showing, both philological data and artistic considerations point to the conclusion that by and large the different groups constitute two main families, though the distribution of individual copies within these families is sometimes a moot point.

Illustration page 173

The most active center, to begin with, was the monastery of San Salvador de Távara, north of Zamora, near the southern border of the kingdom of León. It was there that the *archipictor* Magius, maker of several Apocalypses, died in 968; at the time of his death he had just begun his last work—the Beatus manuscript now in the National Archives in Madrid. A certain Emetrius, one of the master's disciples, was called on to finish the task. The atelier of Távara was located in a lofty watchtower, which figures in a famous miniature in this Apocalypse. Work on this manuscript was brought to a conclusion in 970. Five years later Emetrius, now promoted to the rank of master, executed in collaboration with a *pintrix*, a nun named Ende, a second Beatus manuscript

Illustrations pages 170-171

containing over a hundred miniatures; it is now in Gerona cathedral. Since there was a nunnery annexed to the monastery at Távara and this manuscript, though far from being a slavish copy, has many iconographical affinities with the one in Madrid, it seems probable that the Gerona manuscript, too, was made in the atelier of Távara.

BIBLE OF THE YEAR 960. OMEGA. COLOPHON: SCRIBE AND ARTIST CONGRATULATING EACH OTHER. (14⅜ × 11⅜″)
COD. 2, FOLIO 515 VERSO, COLLEGIATE CHURCH OF SAN ISIDORO, LEÓN.

Illustration page 169

The name of Magius reappears in the Beatus Apocalypse in the Morgan Library (M. 644), executed for a monastery dedicated to St Michael, perhaps San Miguel de Escalada. In the colophon the master records his joy at having brought his task to its much-desired conclusion and dates the manuscript as follows: "in the year thrice three hundred and thrice ten times two," which works out at the year 960 of the Spanish era, or 922 of ours. Thus it would seem that this was a work of Magius' youth—he died in 968. However, since some words preceding the date have been struck out and they may have indicated other figures, it is possible that the year 922 represents the *terminus a quo*, not the date the manuscript was finished. Indeed both the style and paleography so closely resemble those of the 970 Apocalypse that it seems more probable that this work should be dated to around the middle of the 10th century. A copy made at Valcavado and now in the Biblioteca Santa Cruz at Valladolid is dated, like the Távara Beatus, 970. The maker of the illuminations—he gives his name as Oveco—belonged, however, to another atelier whose location has not yet been determined.

The production of Beatus manuscripts continued in the 11th century. In 1047 a scribe named Facundus made an exceptionally fine copy for Ferdinand the Great and his wife Sancha (Madrid, Bibl. Nac., B. 31). Then in 1086 a scribe signing himself "Petrus clericus" wrote the manuscript now in the cathedral of Burgo de Osma; the painter gives his name as Martinus. The last manuscript executed in the Mozarabic style (London, Brit. Mus., Add. 11 695) was made at the abbey of Santo Domingo de Silos, near Burgos; work on it began in 1091 but there was a long break and it was not completed until 1109. In some of the miniatures figuring in the latter portion of the manuscript there are intimations of the Romanesque style which, stemming from France, was everywhere beginning to take effect in Spain. A certain Prior Petrus who took part in both the writing and the illuminating of this book concludes the manuscript with a veritable *cri du cœur*. "A man who knows not how to write may think this no great feat. But only try to do it yourself and you shall learn how arduous is the writer's task. It dims your eyes, makes your back ache, and knits your chest and belly together —it is a terrible ordeal for the whole body. So, gentle reader, turn these pages carefully and keep your finger far from the text. For just as hail plays havoc with the fruits of spring, so a careless reader is a bane to books and writing." Excellent advice, which all true bibliophiles will heartily endorse!

The Beatus manuscripts are Spain's outstanding contribution to the art of medieval illumination. They prove conclusively, if proof were needed, that independence of mind, patience and persistence are essential to the flowering of an art that can lay claim to greatness. Spanish art has always displayed the first-named virtue, but the period we now are dealing with shows it at its very best. Among the great illuminated books of the Middle Ages the Beatus manuscripts hold a very special place. It is no exaggeration to say that they have the glamour of exotic flowers—the dark orchids of those libraries fortunate enough to own them. Like flowers, they can often be recognized even with the eyes shut, for the pages have been treated with a special wax giving off a faintly astringent odor.

BEATUS APOCALYPSE. ANGELS HOLDING THE FOUR WINDS AND THE ANGEL WITH THE SEAL (REVELATION VII, 1-2).
SPAIN, 922 OR CA. 950. (15 × 11 ¼ ") M. 644, FOL. 115 V, COURTESY THE PIERPONT MORGAN LIBRARY, NEW YORK.

BEATUS APOCALYPSE. HELL. DATED 975. (14 ³/₁₆ × 10 ³/₁₆″)
FOLIO 17, GERONA CATHEDRAL.

BEATUS APOCALYPSE. THE TWO WITNESSES. DATED 975. (12 15/16 × 9″)
FOLIO 164, GERONA CATHEDRAL.

We need only compare them with other Apocalypse cycles produced in the Middle Ages to appreciate their uniqueness. Not only is the range of scriptural themes chosen for illustration greater than that in any Carolingian or Gothic cycle, but we also find pictures having only an indirect bearing on the Revelation of St John. Portraits of all four Evangelists figure, surprisingly enough, in the forefront of the book, each seated on a throne beside a standing witness; and on the page facing him are once again two angels holding forth the sacred text. Then come the genealogical tables of the four pre-Christian ages: from Adam to Noah, Noah to Abraham, Abraham to David, and from David to Mary, Mother of Jesus. Also, in some manuscripts, the incarnation of the divine Logos is symbolized by a mythical bird at grips with a snake. The bird (signifying Christ) has soiled its gorgeous plumage even as the Savior put on human flesh so as to fight and overcome the Devil incarnated in the Serpent.

Among the Apocalypse illustrations are some relating to the Commentary provided by Beatus. Thus the prologue *De ecclesia et synagoga* contains a big map of the world showing the three continents divided by a T-shaped stream of water—Asia above, Europe on the left and Africa on the right—with the River Oceanus flowing around them. And since the commentator draws a parallel between the Church and Noah's ark, the latter appears in another miniature along with a view of the Flood. Facing the commentary on Revelation VII, 4-12, describing "a great multitude with palms in their hands," is a picture of a palm-tree from which two natives are drawing off palm-wine. So abundant indeed are the illuminations of Spanish Apocalypses that, for contemporaries, they played the part of pictorial encyclopedias. Most manuscripts include St Jerome's commentary on the Book of Daniel and this, too, is illustrated with miniatures, a dozen in all. The text begins and ends with decorative, full-page renderings of the letters Alpha and Omega.

Though the miniatures form a sequence spaced at equal intervals through the book, such is their size and so compelling their power that each produces the effect of an independent, self-sufficient work of art. Some of them spread over two pages, regardless of the fact that this involves a fold in the middle of the picture—a type of miniature seldom or never found elsewhere. The cycle as a whole constitutes a very rich pictorial ensemble and it is no easy matter deciding whether we should speak of a text with illustrations or a picture book with an explanatory text. For text and pictures are on an equal footing; they body forth with like convincingness a tremendous vision of the end of all things, "the great day of His wrath."

This is due to the pictorial language, at once formalized and pictographic, by which events are evoked rather than narrated. "What counts is not the image seen, but the image in our mind" (Neuss)—and the visions of St John in the Book of Revelation have the same transcendental quality. No other illustrators of the Book of Revelation turned their backs so resolutely on the facts of visual experience as did the Mozarabic illuminators; in fact they went even further in this direction than Beatus himself.

Space itself takes on an abstract, visionary aspect. In the 8th-century prototype of the cycle the atmospheric backgrounds of Late Antique painting had already stiffened

SO-CALLED TÁVARA APOCALYPSE. THE TOWER OF TÁVARA. DATED 970. (14×8¾″)
COD. 1240, FOLIO 139, ARCHIVO HISTORICO NACIONAL, MADRID.

into clean-cut bands of color, but now the colors, richly diversified and chosen purely for their decorative values, build up as it were heraldic "fields." When, for example, the sea is represented, it fills space as an expanse of blue, like the ocean in an atlas. Again, in some pictures the composition is built around a hub-like central point whence the figures radiate out in all directions like spokes of a wheel—a geometrical layout reminiscent of the schematic graphs which Isidore of Seville made a habit of inserting in his encyclopedic works. Saints and the Blessed are aligned in orderly ranks, reminding us of soldiers on parade. "Like the letters in a text" (as Meyer Schapiro remarks in his penetrating study of the Apocalypse of Silos), they occupy the exact places assigned them in the God-ordained scheme of things. Only sinners and the dead are dispersed (to some extent) at random on the picture surface.

Buildings, too, are rendered in a stylized, symbolic manner. For example, churches are represented merely by a row of arcades with a T-shaped altar in the open space under an arch. Other buildings are sometimes shown in cross-section, as in architects' designs. In the miniature reproduced on page 173 we have an outside view of the walls of the tower of Távara faced with colored tiles *(azulejos)*, yet they do not prevent our seeing the interior as well; it is as if the walls were made of glass. Noah's ark looks like a child's toy cupboard with a pediment above and shelves packed with animals. Other hollow objects, such as lamps, casks and headdresses, are often depicted in cross-section. Though this curious technique is paralleled by the art of ancient Egypt, it is also to be found in much child art. So we need hardly assume that there was a direct connection, spanning the gap of several millennia, between it and the art of the Egyptian tombs, tempting as it would be to link up Mozarabic art with the immutable esthetic of the East.

For the rest, we cannot fail to be struck by the keen interest of the Mozarabic artists, primitive though they are in some ways, in technical details. In the Távara Illustration page 173 Apocalypse the painter, when depicting the watchtower, is careful to indicate such structural elements as the ladders joining up the successive stories. And, in representing the palm-tree, he shows just how the natives use a pulley for climbing up the trunk. Illustration page 170 Finally, in his visions of hell, the artist has solved the vital problem of ventilation by inserting two chimney shafts permitting the smoke and stench of the hellfires to escape to the upper air.

But sometimes, too, the illustrations of the Beatus manuscripts reveal a desire to represent that which, strictly speaking, cannot be represented. Thus "the silence in heaven about the space of half an hour" (after the opening of the seventh seal) is suggested by a circular colored field sprinkled with stars, and nothing else. Only in an age of intense mystical faith could a purely symbolic image of this kind carry conviction.

While there is no question that the Mozarabic illuminators possessed this faith, it cannot be denied that their style was sometimes inadequate for expressing the grandiose visions of the author of the Apocalypse. The emotions of rage, despair and thirst for vengeance on which he rings the changes so dramatically could hardly be conveyed by these insect-like little beings, with bulging eyes and stereotyped gestures. The expressive power of these strange scenes lies in their color orchestration of sulfur-yellows, reddish browns, dark blue and lilac, charged with mysterious, emotive overtones. Still, despite the artists' skillful handling of color, one is often conscious of a gulf between the tremendous import of the text and the puppet-like antics of the figures; it is almost as if some callous demiurge were making sport of the human predicament, treating his creatures as pawns in some celestial game. Indeed when looking at these miniatures we can hardly help being reminded of a checkerboard divided into many-colored squares on which the "men" are placed or moved according to set rules. Yet, perhaps for this very reason, the artists may be said to have struck instinctively the exact note that was needed for catching the rather inhuman attitude of the author of the Apocalypse. In any case such fatalism was in keeping with the spirit of the age in which most of these Mozarabic manuscripts saw the day; the never-ending struggle against the Moslem occupants, the horrors of a war waged on their native soil, may well have encouraged the belief then prevalent in Spain that the end of the world was near at hand.

But the popularity of the Apocalypse theme in Spanish ecclesiastical circles must have been also due to other causes of which we now know little. It seems that on certain feast days passages from Revelations or the Book of Daniel took the place of the customary readings from the prophets at church services, and presumably Beatus manuscripts were the liturgical books used on these occasions. In this connection attention may be drawn to the striking fact that Gospel Books, which played so large a part in early medieval illumination in other lands, were practically unknown in Spain. The only parallel—though not a complete one—is to be found in Merovingian illumination, to which the corresponding Spanish art was affiliated in its early phase. It would seem that the Apocalypse, rather than the Gospels, was regarded in Spain as the most sacred book of Holy Scripture. Have we here a reason for the curious fact that representations of all four Evangelists figure at the beginning of Beatus manuscripts? No certain answer can be given to this question. Like the Sibylline books, of which in some ways they are a Christian sequel, these Spanish Apocalypses still keep their mystery intact and seem likely, as regards the circumstances that gave rise to them, always to remain a baffling problem to researchers.

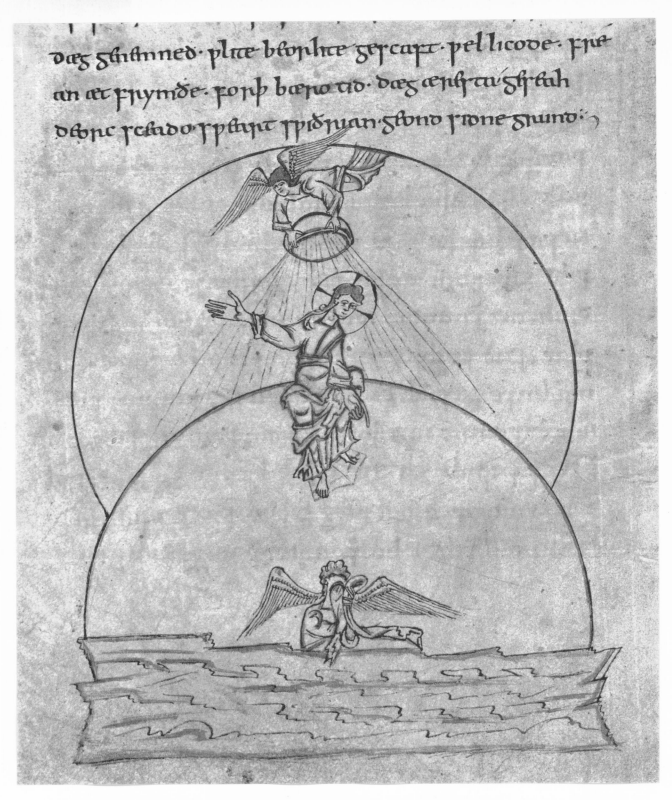

CAEDMON'S POEMS. THE FIRST DAY OF CREATION. ENGLAND, SECOND HALF OF TENTH CENTURY.
(5⅞×4⅞″) MS JUNIUS II, FOLIO 6, BODLEIAN LIBRARY, OXFORD. (ENLARGED IN REPRODUCTION)

# ANGLO-SAXON ILLUMINATION IN THE TENTH AND ELEVENTH CENTURIES

THE cultural situation in England at the close of the 9th century had a good deal in common with that of Spain, for at this time the Carolingian renaissance had not yet crossed either the Channel or the Pyrenees. In so far as any art activity persisted in these countries, it still kept in line with the ancient pre-Carolingian traditions, and such monasteries as still had scriptoria employed the old national forms of writing: in Spain the Visigothic minuscule, in England the so-called Irish or insular script. Similarly manuscript decoration, limited as it was to sparely ornamented initial letters, conformed to the practice of an earlier era. So far as England is concerned, two manuscripts in the Bodleian Library at Oxford may be taken as representative of this phase. One of them (Hatton 60), containing King Alfred's translation of St Gregory's *Cura Pastoralis*, is dated to 890-897; the other, an Ovid (Auct. F. IV. 32), was made at about the same time.

Though these manuscripts may have little artistic merit, they are important as marking a half-way stage between the pre-Carolingian period and the new style of initial that was to make its first appearance in Anglo-Saxon manuscripts at the beginning of the 10th century. Our knowledge of this intermediate style is chiefly due to research work by Francis Wormald and T. D. Kendrick. As a rule these initials have animals' heads with snapping jaws, capriciously combined with interlaces and acanthus leaves. Sometimes the heads are fitted on to winged, two-footed reptiles, direct ancestors of the Romanesque "dragon" initials which appeared in the 11th and 12th centuries. Thus their importance in the history of medieval illumination is considerable.

It is a noteworthy fact that most of the manuscripts adorned with these initials were written, wholly or in part, in the insular minuscule script and that many of them contain Old English texts. Examples are the Codex Vercellensis, which includes a delightful florilegium of Anglo-Saxon poems; the Caedmon manuscript presented by Illustration page 176 Francis Junius to the Bodleian; the English translation of the Venerable Bede's *Ecclesiastical History* (Bodl. Libr., Tanner 10), and the Helmingham Orosius. Obviously we have here a national art current that makes itself felt not only in the decoration but in the choice of texts. Thus there are justifications for comparing it to the similar trend in Spain that found expression in the Mozarabic Beatus manuscripts.

But remarkable though these manuscripts are for the originality and fine execution of the initials, they played only a minor part in the general development of Anglo-Saxon illumination in the 10th century. Most of the illuminated books produced in this period followed another path both in the writing and in the style of ornament. In them the Carolingian minuscule is used in preference to the Irish, while heads of animals and interlaces give place to patterns of acanthus leaves in a great variety of colors.

The whole outlook of the makers of these manuscripts was opposed to that of their 7th- and 8th-century predecessors. When we move on from the plates on pp. 108-123 to those on pp. 176-189, we feel we are entering a different world, more cheerful, more accessible, and more civilized; the world which 9th-century Carolingian culture had brought into being and which the English illuminators now took over with the zest of converts to a new religion. For these neophytes the intricacies of insular ornament —its spirals, interlacing animals, stopped knots and mazy convolutions—had lost their appeal and one of the reasons for this doubtless was that such "barbaric" motifs were closely related to the art of the Vikings who for almost a century had been the scourge of the British Isles. Hence the welcome given to the more naturalistic, classicizing art trend which, though stemming from the Continent, soon acquired a national significance. Indeed some art historians would have us regard the 10th-century miniatures as more truly "English" than the productions of the Hiberno-Saxon illuminators of the 7th and 8th centuries. This much is clear: that here for the first time we find certain basic elements whose specifically English character was to persist well into the Gothic age and even later. Among these characteristics are a predilection for elongated figures with small, aristocratic heads and dainty hands and feet, and a habit of caricaturing the "villains of the piece" on almost Hogarthian lines.

There can be no question that the foundations of this new development were laid by Alfred the Great (d. 899), the English monarch who after checking the inroads of the Danes in Wessex set on foot the unification of the country. Like Charlemagne he invited foreign men of learning to his court. His "Alcuin" was a continental scholar named Grimbald, monk of the monastery of St Bertin at Saint-Omer, who after the king's death became first abbot of New Minster Abbey at Winchester. But the new links with the Continent did not make themselves felt in the field of illumination at once, and it was not until the reign of Alfred's grandson, Aethelstan (925-939), that the first finely illuminated manuscripts saw the day. With this king are associated several outstanding books, amongst them Bede's *Life of St Cuthbert* (Cambridge, Corpus Christi College, MS 183), whose frontispiece represents King Aethelstan offering the manuscript to the saint. It was also at his behest that the Winchester scriptorium enriched a small Psalter (Brit. Mus., Galba A. XVIII) imported from the Continent with a calendar and a set of full-page miniatures, one of which was subsequently removed from the book and is now at Oxford (Bodl. Libr., Rawlinson B. 484). These miniatures have exceptional interest as being the first depictions of biblical scenes in 10th-century Anglo-Saxon illumination. Though stylistically they have a good deal in common with Carolingian art, they are not copies of Carolingian originals but derive, it seems, from still older models: Italian and Byzantine 7th- and 8th-century works. And since insular art is known to have come under Mediterranean influence as far back as the pre-Carolingian period, we are justified in assuming that these English artists drew inspiration once again from prototypes that had been in the country since a much earlier period. In which case the Carolingian look of these Anglo-Saxon miniatures is due mainly to the fact that they stem from sources which had served the turn of the French artists of a century before. Moreover, curiously enough, we sometimes find English miniaturists of the 9th and 10th centuries harking back to themes directly connected with the religious controversies of a much earlier age; as when we see the heresiarch Arius lying prostrate at the feet of Christ, or St Pachomius receiving from an angel tables for the computation of the calendar, showing how to fix the correct date of Easter (Brit. Mus., Arundel 155 and Caligula A. xv).

Aethelstan's reign, however, was only the beginning of the revival of English art. From the mid-10th century on, the movement rapidly gained strength as a result of the thoroughgoing reform of monastic life initiated by St Dunstan and his colleagues, Sts Aethelwold and Oswald. The headquarters of the movement was Glastonbury where Dunstan held the post of abbot from 943 to 957. It is probably to this period that we should date the drawing (often reproduced) of Christ adored by St Dunstan, a tiny figure humbly kneeling at His feet (Oxford, Bodl. Libr., Auct. F. IV. 32). An old tradition, which may well be reliable, has it that this drawing was made by the saint himself. After his appointment to the Archbishopric of Canterbury in 958, Dunstan vigorously promoted a revival of the religious life of the entire country. The zeal of the reformers strengthened the links between the Anglo-Saxon church and the Continent. In his years of exile (957-958) Dunstan had taken refuge in St Peter's monastery at Ghent, and at the same time Oswald was studying at Fleury. Aethelwold, who subsequently became Bishop of Winchester, had close connections with this center and later, between 987 and 989, that fine scholar Abbon, abbot of Fleury, held a teaching post at Ramsey. As a result of this intimate association between the monastery of Fleury and various English religious centers, the library of the former came into possession of several handsome Anglo-Saxon books; some miniatures in a Boethius manuscript now in Paris (Bibl. Nat., lat. 6401) may be the work of an English artist active at Fleury in the third quarter of the 10th century.

Edgar, King of "All England" (959-975), gave his full support to the English reformers. In the royal charter granted to the New Minster of Winchester in 966, written in gold and presented in book form, the miniature on the first page shows him standing between the patrons of the abbey (the Virgin and St Peter) holding up his charter to Christ, enthroned in a mandorla upheld by angels. The scene is surrounded by an ornamental border of acanthus leaves in several colors. This lively composition, which justly ranks among the early masterworks of the new style, was undoubtedly executed by a miniaturist attached to the monastery of Winchester, then under royal patronage. While the Archbishop of Canterbury had the whip hand in ecclesiastical affairs, the course of art in England was determined mainly by Winchester, where the kings had their chief residence and Aethelwold, a great lover of richly illuminated manuscripts, held the bishopric from 963 to 984. The same intimate alliance between the royal and the ecclesiastical power which, in an earlier day, had led to the flowering of Carolingian book illumination sponsored the remarkable development of this form of art in 10th-century England. For this reason it is not entirely wrong to name the whole English school of illumination of this period after Winchester, even if in point of fact the production of illuminated manuscripts was far from being confined to that city. On the contrary, thanks to recent research work, it is becoming more and more evident that very active scriptoria flourished in several of the "reformed" monasteries in the south

BENEDICTIONAL OF ST AETHELWOLD. THE BAPTISM OF CHRIST. WINCHESTER, 975-980. (9 $^{7}/_{16}$ × 7 $^{7}/_{16}$ ″)
FOLIO 25, DEVONSHIRE COLLECTION, CHATSWORTH.

THE GRIMBALD GOSPELS. ST JOHN THE EVANGELIST. WINCHESTER SCHOOL, EARLY ELEVENTH CENTURY.
(9¾×8¼″) ADD. MS 34890, FOLIO 114 VERSO, BRITISH MUSEUM, LONDON.

of England. But the movement unquestionably took its rise at Winchester and throughout the first half of the 11th century this school, alongside that of Canterbury, held the lead in the development of insular illumination.

Illustration page 180

Most magnificent of Anglo-Saxon illuminated books is the Benedictional made at Winchester for Bishop Aethelwold between 975 and 980, probably under his direct supervision. Now in the Duke of Devonshire's collection at Chatsworth, this is doubtless the most valuable book of its class to be still in private ownership. The effect of dazzling splendor produced by its miniatures is due not least to the frames and border decorations, at once elaborate and beautifully executed. The dedicatory verses at the beginning of the book explain the program the illuminator was required to follow. They tell us that Bishop Aethelwold instructed the "humble monk" in question to include a great number of *circi* and to paint within them figures rendered *multigenis miniis pulchris*—i.e. in all kinds of beautiful colors. (In this context it is interesting to note that the word *minium* had already lost its literal meaning of "red" and come to include all the colors used in book illumination, a usage which survives in the term "miniature.") By *circi* were evidently meant the rectangular or arcaded frames enclosing the illustrations and the big initial letters at the beginnings of the more important passages of the text. These consist of parallel gold bands broken off at the corners, sometimes at the center as well, so as to make room for ornamental squares or circles. We have already seen this type of frame figuring in the full-page designs of 9th-century Franco-Saxon sacramentaries. Also, the fillings of brightly colored acanthus leaves between the gold bands are of Carolingian origin. In some of the oldest English *circi* these acanthus leaves proliferate beyond the gold bands only at the corners, where they take the form of rosette-like bursts of leafage; but soon they begin to overlap the frames from end to end. This is what we find in King Edgar's Charter of 966 (which, however, has no corner motifs) and on the more richly decorated pages of the Aethelwold Benedictional. In fact from now on the frame seems to play the part of an espalier from which flowers and many-colored foliage sprout in all directions. This type of structure (which may be described as the "espalier-frame") became a distinctive feature of English illumination and remained in use until the 12th century. On closer examination we can detect another important characteristic of the English style; the acanthus leaves have gracefully curled tips, resembling ostrich plumes. Thus their forms, no longer flat, exist in three dimensions, while the leaves cling to and wind themselves around the espaliers, as though endowed with animal life.

Such are the dimensions of the frames and such is the wealth of floral ornament that they tend to overpower the scenes depicted. For they do not merely enclose the miniature, but also form part of the setting in which the action is taking place. Indeed it often happens that a scene overlaps the frame, sometimes encroaching deeply on it. The *circi* act as grounds for scenes and figures, and in some cases it seems as though the latter were projecting from the picture surface forward, into real space. On the other hand there is hardly any suggestion of spatial recession behind the figures and the plane formed by the frame. The gaps between them and the frame are left empty, except when occupied by clouds in the form of wavy bands of color. So as not to lose all homogeneity with the frame, figures are made to touch each other at certain points, thus creating a plastic continuum like that of trelliswork or the structure of the early medieval goldsmiths' work known as *opus interrasile*.

The illustrations in the Benedictional concern chiefly Christ's incarnation and His triumph after death, but there are also representations of the Virgin and the most venerated saints: the Apostles, Sts Benedict and Etheldreda (Aethelthryth). Towards the end of the book a miniature, only partly colored, depicts the consecration of an Anglo-Saxon cathedral—a scene of unique documentary interest for the historian of architecture. The pictures of biblical incidents derive from various models, for the most part lost. However a fortunate discovery made by Otto Homburger has enabled us to trace the prototype of the scenes of Christ's nativity and baptism; this is the relief-work on an Illustration page 180 ivory casket, executed in France at the end of the Carolingian period and now in Brunswick Museum. As in the reliefs, the baptism scene in the miniature shows us the Dove of the Holy Spirit carrying in its beak a double phial of the sacred oils, signifying Christ's dual function as *rex et sacerdos*, King and Priest.

The artists employed on the Aethelwold Benedictional were sometimes hard put to it to adapt the scenes provided by their models, in which the composition was horizontal, to the vertical layout imposed on them by the format of the manuscript. For this reason we are often conscious of an incongruity between the frieze-like extension of the scenes depicted and the height of the frames surrounding them. In a second Benedictional (or Pontifical) produced by the same atelier as that responsible for the Aethelwold manuscript but a few years later in date, which is now in Rouen (Bibl. Publ., MS 369), figures are already better adjusted to the picture space provided by the frame. This manuscript, which may have been made to the order of Aethelgar, abbot of New Minster (Winchester), who became Archbishop of Canterbury in 988, was later presented to Rouen Cathedral by the Norman prelate Robert of Jumièges, who after becoming Archbishop of Canterbury was expelled from his see in 1052 and returned to his birthplace. To the monastery of Jumièges, where he had once been abbot and where he ended his days, he made the gift of another outstanding English manuscript, a sacramentary, mistakenly termed the "Missal of Robert of Jumièges" (Rouen, Bibl. Publ., MS 274), which illustrates a later stage in the evolution of English book illumination. The discrepancy between the format of the frames and that of the scenes enclosed by them has practically disappeared, and by the same token the trelliswork composition with all the figures brought forward to the surface has given place to landscape settings in which the figures act as staffage, with their size necessarily reduced. It is likely that this structural change was motivated by the Utrecht Psalter.

Next after the manuscripts mentioned above come the Gospel Books. Their decorations consist of full-page, framed initials at the beginning of each Gospel; sometimes of portraits of Evangelists and, finally, of canon tables, the finest specimens of which are surmounted by representations of the Virgin and the Trinity under various aspects, attended by saints and angels. Nothing is known as to who commissioned these Gospel

COTTON PSALTER. THE HARROWING OF HELL. WINCHESTER, CA. 1050. $(9\frac{3}{4} \times 6\frac{9}{16}'')$
COTTON MS TIBERIUS C. VI, FOLIO 14, BRITISH MUSEUM, LONDON.

Books, the earliest of which, datable to the close of the 10th century, seems to have been made in Malmesbury and Canterbury. Two particularly handsome examples call for mention: the Duke of Aremberg's Gospel Book recently acquired by the Pierpont Morgan Library and the Gospel Book (B. 10. 4) in the library of Trinity College, Cambridge. Whereas no use is made as yet of *circi* of acanthus leaves in the Aremberg manuscript, they make their appearance in the Cambridge Gospels—perhaps as a result of the transfer of Aethelgar from Winchester to Canterbury in 988. The first Gospel Book produced by the school of Winchester is the so-called Grimbald Gospels (Brit. Mus., Add. 34890), dated to around the year 1000. The composition of the two illuminated pages prefixed to the Gospels of St John is exceptionally sumptuous; the frame consists no longer of acanthus leaves but contains instead a host of tiny figures: apostles, saints,

Illustration page 181

Old Testament kings and angels, and the whole Court of Heaven grouped around the Evangelist. On the eve of the Norman Conquest the Anglo-Saxon schools produced several Gospel Books in the pure "Winchester" style. In the case of two manuscripts (Morgan Library, New York) we know their entire "life history." They were made for Judith of Flanders, wife of Count Tostig who fell in the battle of 1066 against the Normans. When after her husband's death she fled to the Continent, she took the two books with her. Later, after her marriage to her second husband Henry IV of Guelph, Duke of Bavaria, she donated them to the Benedictine monastery of Weingarten (in Württemberg, near Lake Constance). After the Napoleonic Wars the books found their way back to England, where they figured in the library, at Holkham Hall, of the first Earl of Leicester. Finally, in 1926, they reached their present home on the other side of the Atlantic. *Habent sua fata libelli.*

A third group of liturgical manuscripts consists of Psalters. Mention may first be made of the Bosworth Psalter (Brit. Mus., Add. 37517) which according to tradition

PSALTER FROM BURY ST EDMUNDS. ILLUSTRATION OF PSALM LXXXIII, 13. ENGLAND, FIRST HALF OF ELEVENTH CENTURY. (4⅛×2″) REG. LAT. 12, FOLIO 90 VERSO, BIBLIOTECA APOSTOLICA, VATICAN CITY.

was owned by St Dunstan. With its interwoven bands and animal heads this manuscript may be taken to typify the style prevailing at Canterbury during the early years of Dunstan's tenure of the see. This Psalter has no illustrations and it is not known whether the Utrecht Psalter, which did so much to shape the evolution of the Canterbury school, had already crossed the Channel at this time. From the end of the 10th century on, however, its presence in England is vouched for by the unmistakable influence it exercised on English illuminators in general and in particular on those of the Canterbury school. A complete copy of the Utrecht Psalter, in a rather larger format than the original, was begun about the year 1000 (Brit. Mus., Harl. 603); one man was not enough to cope with this grueling task, which called for three or four successive spells of labor.

Illustration page 185

Two manuscripts testify to the existence of a cycle of English illustrations of the Psalms, independent of the Carolingian tradition. These are a manuscript in Paris (Bibl. Nat., lat. 8824), that once belonged to the library of the Duc de Berry, and another in the Vatican (Reg. lat. 12) made at Bury St Edmunds. Both are handled in a manner resembling that of the Utrecht Psalter in so far as the similes in the text are represented so to speak *verbatim*. Thus the imprecation of the enemies of God in Psalm LXXXIII, 13, "O my God, make them like a wheel; as the stubble before the wind," is illustrated by a man standing on a wheel, trying in vain to keep his balance.

Illustration page 184

The English artists working on the Psalters devised a system of illustration of their own which was widely adopted in other countries during the following centuries: the addition to the psalter of a set of full-page frontispiece pictures. An example is a manuscript in the British Museum (Tiberius C. VI), considerably damaged in 1731 by the fire at the Cottonian Library, then housed in the Strand, London. It contains a cycle of scenes from the lives of David and Christ. The idea behind the introduction of New Testament episodes into a Psalter was to reveal the prophetic import of the Psalms and perhaps also to provide a starting point for pious meditations on religious themes. Much stress is laid on Christ's victory over the Devil, particularly in the scene of the "Harrowing of Hell," interpreted with startling dramatic power.

Illustration page 189

Illustration page 176

In addition to the liturgical manuscripts we have illustrated texts of other kinds, those written in the vernacular Old English being the most interesting. There are two famous books of this type: Aelfric's metrical paraphrase of the Pentateuch and Joshua (Brit. Mus., Claudius B. IV) and Caedmon's poems on the Creation and early history of mankind (Oxford, Bodl. Libr., Junius 11). Quite unrhetorical in their approach, the illustrations have the naivety of folk-songs. The first picture of the Creation shows God seated on the vault of the firmament; with a sweeping gesture He is creating Light, an angel pouring it forth on Him from a huge goblet, while on the earth below, still without form and void and covered with "the waters under the firmament," is another angel with his eyes blindfolded, signifying the darkness of the world's beginning.

A product of the artist's free fancy, this scene is at a far remove from the sophisticated artistry of the professional illuminators who were obliged to follow more or less closely a pre-existing model furnished by some older manuscript. Even the not infrequent lapses in the drawing are charmingly atoned for by its naïve verisimilitude. We shall find this happening time and time again in the illustrated medieval manuscripts written in the vernacular, from the chivalric romances of the Gothic age up to the 15th-century German *Volkshandschriften*.

The Scandinavian influences apparent in certain decorations of the Caedmon manuscript have led some to date it to the reign of Knut, King of Denmark, who ruled England from 1016 to 1035—a view which seemed to be confirmed by the fact that it contains a portrait in a medallion inscribed "Aelfwinus" and a man of this name was abbot of New Minster at Winchester from 1035 onward. But the name was far from rare and the Aelfwin in question might equally well be the Aelfwin employed as a scribe by King Aethelred II in 993. Moreover, if we confine ourselves to stylistic considerations —the internal evidence of the manuscript itself—everything points to the fact that the Caedmon manuscript should be dated no later than the 10th century. The artist who made the first illustrations stopped work at an early stage, before finishing the pictures of the Deluge. At page 73 a second artist, with a quite different style, stepped in. After representing the scene of Noah and his family landing from the Ark, he too ceased work (at page 88). At once more cultured and more formal, his style is clearly affiliated to that of an illustrated Prudentius in Corpus Christi College Library (MS 23) and his active period evidently dates to around the year 1000, since influences of the Utrecht Psalter are already visible in his work.

The illustrators of Anglo-Saxon manuscripts made use of two different techniques; sometimes they painted in gouache, using an opaque, often somewhat milky medium, and sometimes they drew with the pen. In some drawings the same brown-black ink is used as for the writing of the text, but the most frequent technique is polychrome drawing with different colored inks: red, green, blue and black. This colored-outline procedure may strike us as something of an anomaly since the natural function of color is that of covering surfaces, not that of drawing outlines. The effect is rather one of hinting at polychromy than of actually realizing it. The number of colors varies from two to five, and as a rule the artists use them to differentiate between parts of bodies that are left bare and the garments, between tunics and cloaks and so forth. Hence that curious phenomenon of "segmentation," a stylistic peculiarity we have already noted in pre-Carolingian art and one which was subsequently to play a far from negligible part in Romanesque. Though the bare parts of bodies are mostly done in a reddish tone, the fact remains that the choice of colors by and large is purely arbitrary. Garments and solid objects such as furniture and buildings are given blue, red or green contours according to the artist's whim, and this multiplicity of colors contributes greatly to the decorative effect of the illustrations. What is more, it links them up with the titles and initials of the text which, likewise, are often drawn in inks of various colors. This all-over harmony of blue-red-green directly pointed the way to the color schemes we find in Romanesque manuscripts.

The practice of drawing in inks of different colors and in tinted outlines seems to have been an Anglo-Saxon invention dating to the 10th century; in any case no earlier example of it is known. Quite possibly it derived from the sister art of embroidery which enjoyed so great a vogue in England during the Middle Ages. Anyhow there is no question that England was the country of origin of this technique which came to be widely employed on the Continent from the Romanesque period on. Dürer himself resorted to it when in 1500 he made the Book of Hours of the Emperor Maximilian, and quite recently Picasso has employed it in some of his lithographs.

It would seem that the practice of drawing with different-colored inks became generalized as a result of copying early manuscripts—or else simply for reasons of economy. As compared with illustrations which are merely drawn, those which are fully painted in gold and color unquestionably produce a more sumptuous effect, such as we find in the Benedictional of Aethelwold. It is, however, clear that such considerations were not always a decisive factor when it came to choosing the technique to be employed; the Ramsey Psalter (Brit. Mus., Harl. 2904) is a case in point. True, the large initials in this handsome book are painted in gold and colors; which goes to show that the atelier concerned was familiar with the technique of painting in full color. But the page-size miniature of the Crucifixion, obviously the work of an exceptionally gifted artist, is nevertheless drawn in reddish-brown ink, with some accents of dark blue and black. As is sometimes the case in English drawings, the outline is shaded off so as to create a suggestion of modeled form, without however detracting from the essentially linear structure of the ensemble. When as here the artist elected to use a draftsmanly technique, the outline style, he may have felt that this method allowed him more freedom of execution than would have been possible had he painted in body colors. The result is that this miniature has a dignity combined with grace that could hardly have been achieved by other means.

Whether drawn or painted, drapery arranged in elaborate folds plays a large part in English miniatures of this period. Not only figures but, whenever an opportunity presents itself, even articles of furniture are covered with draperies. In their representations of Evangelists these artists always made a point of decking the reading-desks on which are placed the sacred books with materials falling in ample folds; even the footstools are frequently draped. There can be no doubt that this profusion of the rich surface patterns made by folded drapery derived from the Ada School. But it was a gradual process; in manuscripts made for King Aethelstan during the first half of the 10th century the folds of garments are still hardly distinguishable, whereas in the second half of the century they become more numerous and more pronounced. This development seems to run parallel to the ever richer fillings of acanthus leaves within the panels of the frames. At the same time as leaves begin to flicker forth, like tongues of flame, beyond the framework, folds and swirls of garments become increasingly intricate and exuberant, tending almost to usurp the place of the bodies clad in them. This is particularly noticeable in the Aethelwold Benedictional, where what chiefly holds the eye is the complex pattern of short wavy lines formed by the folds and bottom edges of the draperies. The general effect might be compared to a melody enriched by trills, and the comparison with music is all the apter since in both arts the trills serve less as functional elements than as the embellishments styled in Italian *fioriture*.

AELFRIC'S PARAPHRASE OF THE PENTATEUCH AND JOSHUA. THE BUILDING OF THE TOWER OF BABEL.
ENGLAND, ELEVENTH CENTURY. (11 3/8 × 7 7/8″) COTTON MS CLAUDIUS B. IV, FOLIO 19, BRITISH MUSEUM, LONDON.

Later on, when the Reims style superseded that of the Ada School, the "trills" became more and more agitated, set to an ever quicker tempo, with which the miniatures painted in full color had difficulty in keeping pace. Thus, thanks to its greater freedom of movement, the technique of pen drawing stole a march on that of painting. So rapid now are the pen strokes that they strike flashes along the folds, as if the drapery were charged with electricity. The dynamic movement of the garments is sometimes carried over to the figures. As Wilhelm Worringer observes, movement reaches its maximum intensity in arms and legs, which are wildly agitated even when the body itself is at rest in a chair. The knees of frontally seated figures are widely extended, while the small head with its over-long neck "almost gives the impression of a fifth limb." Often the vibrancy of clothes and figures has no real appropriateness to the theme of the picture; it seems, rather, to be due to a nervous tension of a subjective order.

Such methods involved a straining after effect that ran the risk of degenerating into stereotyped and empty formalism. Inherent from the start in the dynamic style of Anglo-Saxon illumination, this danger becomes yet more insistent as we reach the middle of the 11th century. Folds of drapery grow stiffer and the movements of the figures tend to lose their vivacity in proportion to the ever increasing emphasis on the architectonic Illustration page 184 qualities of the design. The "Harrowing of Hell" in the Cotton Psalter (Brit. Mus., Tiberius C. VI) is a case in point. Though the Norman Conquest made a break in the evolution of English art, it did not suppress the indigenous tendencies described above; on the contrary, the style imported by the artists from abroad was such as to reinforce them. Since Norman art itself derived to so large an extent from England, the fundamental conceptions of English illumination were at first hardly affected at all by the transfer of political power and, as we shall see in our next volume, the Romanesque style did not really dominate English illumination until the third decade of the 12th century.

At its climax Anglo-Saxon illumination achieved a splendor and a happy freedom entitling it to a place among the noblest manifestations of English art. For despite the strict austerity imposed by the reform movement then in progress, the English monasteries produced an art instinct with life, frolicsome and free. We have here the first Midsummer Night's Dream of British culture—how often do the dainty little figures in the miniatures remind us, with their graceful movements, of Titanias or Ariels! Drawn in rapid, glancing pen strokes, they seem exempt from the law of gravity. Even the canon tables, so solidly and massively constructed in Carolingian manuscripts, acquire the aerial fragility of espaliers. The half-circles forming the contours of the arches are played off against each other and produce almost the effect of sails bellying in the wind. Similarly a gentle summer breeze seems to be toying with the foliage in frames and the draperies around figures, calling them to quivering life. All is lightness, grace and *joie de vivre*.

Though saints and angels play a leading part in the world conjured up by these English artists, the powers of evil are not excluded. Well aware of the dramatic value of contrasts, light and shade, Shakespeare offset Ariel with Caliban in *The Tempest*, and the Anglo-Saxon miniaturists did the same. Their "Caliban" is the Devil, and they give him that grotesque, caricatural aspect which was to be his type-form throughout the Middle Ages. With his preposterous nose, huge mouth and beast-like body he cuts the figure of an alarming adversary of the heavenly hosts. In a drawing often reproduced we see St Peter launching his big key at his head—an aggression amply justified by the "victim's" obvious malevolence. Moreover the English artists were the first to represent Hell by the gaping jaws of an enormous monster, a practice destined to obtain in Christian iconography for many centuries to come.

But striking representations of the infernal powers were not the only iconographic innovation which the Middle Ages owed to Anglo-Saxon art. Another motif that originated in England and later was widely adopted on the Continent was a new rendering of the scene of the Ascension, in which we are shown, in the top of the picture, only Christ's feet and the lower part of His body, the rest being hidden by the clouds through which He is rising heavenwards. The fact that two of the earliest examples of this presentation of the scene figure on the edges of a page where the whole of the central portion is taken up with text suggests that it perhaps was lack of space at the top of the page that first gave an artist the notion of this ingenious device. If this surmise be correct, it follows that the new type of Ascension was first created by an illuminator resourcefully turning to account the restrictions imposed on him by the layout of the page. At the same time, however, Meyer Schapiro is certainly right in regarding the new formula as an example of early medieval realism. It illustrates the scene of the Ascension from the viewpoint of the disciples standing on the ground and watching their ascending Lord. The exact way the Ascension took place—its "mechanism" so to speak—was a constant subject of debate in theological literature. A remarkably audacious theory regarding it, written in the Anglo-Saxon tongue, was enounced in the "Blickling Homilies" (ca. 970), which may well have had some bearing on the new iconographical formula now adopted by illuminators in depictions of the Ascension.

Again and again we are struck by the originality and inventiveness of these Anglo-Saxon artists. In most medieval calendars the months are represented by single figures, busy with some seasonal task and enclosed within the narrow confines of a medallion. But in two English manuscripts (Brit. Mus., Tiberius B. V and Julius A. VI) the action is carried boldly right across the page, forming a small landscape frieze of a kind that does not reappear in art until the 14th century.

Like Carolingian illumination, from which it stemmed, the corresponding Anglo-Saxon art had an early flowering; but, if it was to survive, it needed a climate of a very special kind and exceptionally favorable conditions. Hence the relative brevity of its heyday. Nevertheless, before succumbing, it played an outstanding part in the general development of medieval art. It imposed its imprint on the Romanesque which supplanted it and by the same token did much to mold the Gothic style of book illumination.

MASTER OF THE REGISTRUM GREGORII. THE EMPEROR OTTO II OR III WITH THE SYMBOLS OF THE FOUR PARTS
OF HIS EMPIRE. TRIER, CA. 985. (10⅝×7⅞″) MUSÉE CONDÉ, CHANTILLY.

# OTTONIAN ILLUMINATION

IN the 10th century, under the rule of the emperors of the Saxon royal house, Germany not only became the greatest European power but also outstripped all neighboring countries in the field of art. The revival started under the three emperors bearing the name of Otto and continued under the first monarchs of the Salian Line. During the hundred years which may be described as the great age of German art (ca. 960-1060), its evolution was relatively little affected by dynastic changes and, until the death of Henry III (1056), it kept to the path mapped out for it during the preceding century —for which reason the art of the whole period is rightly termed "Ottonian."

Like the German empire established by Otto the Great, Ottonian illumination took over the legacy of Charlemagne. Carolingian art had established itself on German soil in the first half of the 9th century and the schools of the Alpine regions were still keeping it alive well after 900. Yet it may be questioned if we are justified in speaking of a continuous stylistic evolution extending through the 10th century. For by and large what the Ottonian renaissance stood for was the invention of a new art style—despite the fact that Carolingian models played a considerable part in its formation and artists of the Ottonian schools began by copying Carolingian originals.

However the background of Ottonian illumination was narrower than that of Carolingian; it was less open to the lessons of pagan classical antiquity and thus its sources were less varied. Illuminated copies of the works of Late Antiquity, such as the Aratus, Physiologus, Terence and Prudentius manuscripts, are wholly absent and in this respect it also differs from Anglo-Saxon illumination, in which we find, if not firsthand reproductions, anyhow copies of Carolingian copies of such works.

Similarly the Ottonian artists were narrower in their choice of the liturgical books to be adorned with illuminations. None of the German monasteries specialized in the production of decorated one-volume Bibles as did St Martin's monastery at Tours, and were it not for a Bible with an illuminated frontispiece commissioned by St Bernward of Hildesheim (Hildesheim Cathedral Treasure, 61), this type of manuscript would be entirely lacking. Moreover we have practically no illustrated Psalters made by Ottonian artists. In a general way Old Testament subjects were far less in favor with them than with the Carolingians. If we wish to know how Germans of the period pictured to themselves such biblical personages as Adam and Eve, Joseph, Moses or Samson, we glean little or no information from the illuminated manuscripts. But this neglect of the Old Testament was counterbalanced by an ever increasing interest in the New. Sparsely illustrated and usually reduced to the smallest possible dimensions in Carolingian art, Gospel scenes bulk large in the richly ornate Ottonian sacramentaries, Gospels and books of pericopes (extracts from the Gospels) produced during this period. In fact the books required for use in public worship acted like a lodestone, drawing to them all that was most dynamic and creative in Ottonian illumination. No less care was lavished on the bindings, which were sumptuously decorated with gold, ivory and precious stones.

Looking at these manuscripts we realize that the chief concern of the monastic ateliers was not to gratify the cultured bibliophile but to create objects worthy of the House of God in which they served a sacred purpose.

The historical origins of Ottonian art have not been fully cleared up, but this much we know: that its flowering was preceded, as in England, by a widespread reformation of monastic life. The movement took its rise in the monastery of Gorze, near Metz, founded in the year 933, and it was from Gorze that it spread to Lorraine. The monastery of St Maximin at Trier, reformed in 934, was one of its most active centers and it was thence that the reformation of the monasteries at Reichenau (972) and Regensburg (974) was promoted. Next, following the lead of Regensburg, other monasteries in Bavaria, Franconia, Austria and elsewhere adopted the new rule. Thus the movement spread by a sort of chain-reaction throughout Germany, and wherever it took effect it created more favorable conditions for the activities of local illuminators.

The reformed monasteries were not merely linked to each other by a more or less intimate community of religious outlook; several and in fact some of the greatest were, as *Reichsabteien*, under the direct control and patronage of the emperor. One of the chief political aims of Otto the Great (936-973) was the creation, by means of these monasteries, of a close alliance between Crown and Church against the power of the feudal lords. Thus he viewed with satisfaction the efforts of the reformers to raise the cultural and religious standards of the monasteries, and did his utmost to aid them. The "State Abbeys" became the most favored places for recruiting the personnel of the chancellery or "palace chapel" which accompanied the monarch on all his journeys. This was nothing new—for no less characteristic of the Carolingian era had been this close association between the royal court and monasteries capable of producing de luxe books, in particular those whose ateliers the king employed to fill his own commissions.

An illustration of this co-operation is to be found in two magnificent state documents produced under Otto I, the Great, executed in gold ink on purple vellum in a monastic atelier—so far unidentified—under state control. One of these documents, the *Ottonianum* (dated 962), is preserved in the archives of the Vatican; in it the emperor confirms the pope's dominion over the Papal States. The other, an illuminated roll of parchment, now in the Records Office of Wolfenbüttel (Brunswick), is a document recording the marriage gifts made in 972 by Otto II, then a boy of sixteen, to Theophano, daughter of the Eastern emperor Romanus II, who had come from Byzantium to wed him.

It was in the ten years' interval between these documents that Ottonian illumination came into its own. For whereas the *Ottonianum* is ornamented only along its narrow borders (with palmettes and disks), the dowry roll is richly decorated. The upper edge, done in gold, is adorned with medallions containing figures of saints between confronted peacocks and lions, while the purple ground beneath the text, which is written in a golden minuscule, is patterned (in the manner of Byzantine textiles) with rampant griffins and lions *en camaieu*. This singularly gorgeous roll must have created something of a sensation when it was ceremoniously unfurled for the first time at the marriage service, celebrated at St Peter's in Rome.

Stylistically, the decorative borders of the *Ottonianum* have affinities with the fragment of a Sacramentary from Lorsch, now at Erlangen (Universitätsbibl., Cod. 2000), while the narrow strip of acanthus leaves running vertically along the edges of the Wolfenbüttel dowry roll is almost exactly paralleled by a similar border decoration in a Lectionary, now at Aschaffenburg (Schlossbibl., Cod. 2), which has been attributed to the School of Fulda, though it might equally well have been made at Mainz, whence the manuscript originally came. Lorsch, Fulda and Mainz all formed part of the same diocese —that of Mainz—and it is perhaps significant in this connection that Willegis, chancellor of Otto I, was given the archbishopric of Mainz in 975.

Like Mainz, the famous abbey of St Boniface at Fulda had already made its name as a center for the production of illuminated books. One of these was the richly illustrated Sacramentary at Göttingen (Universitätsbibl., theol. fol. 231); another, stylistically akin and even more sumptuous, the so-called Codex Wittechindeus, now in Berlin (Staatsbibl., theol. lat. fol. 1). Masterwork of the School of Fulda, the latter derives, so far as its canon tables and Evangelist portraits are concerned, from a now lost Gospel Book stemming from the Ada School which had been used in Fulda in the 9th century as a model for other works. However, the style and colors of the Codex Wittechindeus are quite different from those of Ada manuscripts; the dominant hues are cool blue-greens and lilac-blues, while modeling is done in the thick, rich white characteristic of manuscripts produced by the palace atelier of Charles the Bald. In view of the striking resemblance of the color schemes and "trill-like" folds of garments with those of Anglo-Saxon miniatures produced in the time of King Aethelstan and King Edgar, it has recently been suggested that the School of Fulda came under English influence as well. Since Aethelstan was Otto the Great's brother-in-law, it is quite likely that he presented his German kinsman with illuminated books made in Winchester.

In any case it is evident that the Ottonian illuminators and the Anglo-Saxons followed essentially the same program: that of assimilating the heritage of Carolingian art. But the German artists were heavier-handed than their English contemporaries. *Saxonica rusticitas* kept breaking through, and the fact that the Fulda artists had at their disposal illuminated manuscripts of Late Antiquity (as is proved by certain iconographical peculiarities in the New Testament scenes of the Göttingen Sacramentary) made little difference. Only at the beginning of the 11th century can classical influences be discerned—notably in a Sacramentary at the Vatican (Vat. lat. 3548).

To the same early phase of Ottonian illumination belong some handsome liturgical manuscripts hailing from Saxony, whence the Ottonian dynasty originated. For the most part their decoration is purely ornamental, characteristic being the use of purple grounds embellished with patterns borrowed from Eastern textiles, like those in the Wolfenbüttel roll. One of the best is the Wernigerode Gospels in the Morgan Library (M. 755); so Illustration page 196 sumptuous is its presentation that it may well have been commissioned by the emperor himself. It is generally, and probably correctly, ascribed to the monastery of Korvei. But other ateliers were also in existence. Recent research work into the history of the royal court of the Ottos has proved that Hildesheim was one of the chief places where

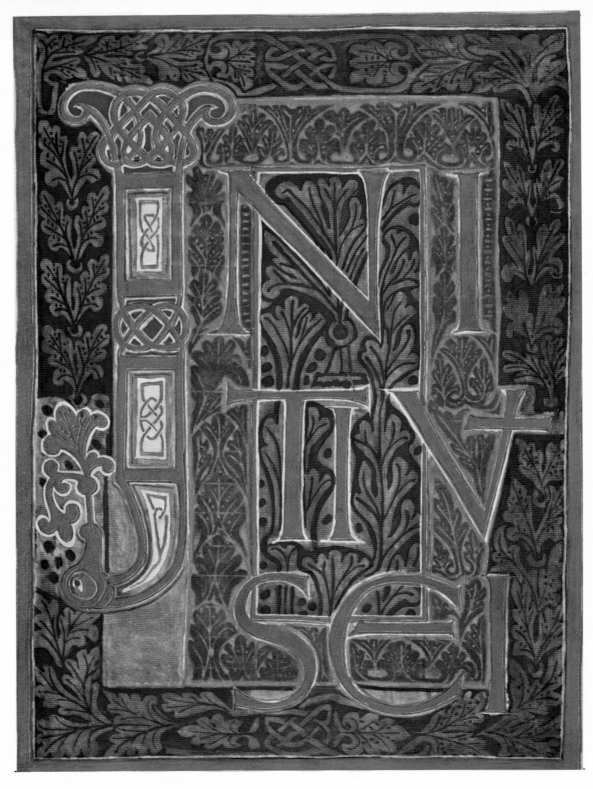

THE WERNIGERODE GOSPELS. INITIUM. KORVEI, THIRD QUARTER OF THE TENTH CENTURY. (11¾ × 8⅝″)
M. 755, FOLIO 16 VERSO, COURTESY THE PIERPONT MORGAN LIBRARY, NEW YORK.

THE GERO CODEX. INITIAL S. REICHENAU, BEFORE 976. (7 $^9/_{16}$×5½ ")
MS 1948, FOLIO 103, LANDESBIBLIOTHEK, DARMSTADT. (ENLARGED IN REPRODUCTION)

GOSPEL BOOK OF OTTO III. ST LUKE. REICHENAU, CA. 1000. (9$^{13}/_{16}$×7$^{7}/_{16}$″)
CLM. 4453, FOLIO 139 VERSO, BAYERISCHE STAATSBIBLIOTHEK, MUNICH.

the kings' ecclesiastical personnel was recruited. And by the same token this city may well have been the chief center of Saxon illumination in the reigns of Otto I and Otto II, since well into the 11th century, during the episcopate of St Bernward (992-1022), the use of backgrounds imitating textile patterns was characteristic of the Ottonian miniature and this was a speciality of the school of Hildesheim. A typical example is the Gospel Book commissioned by Bernward for use in his cathedral.

A third atelier whose origins go back to the reign of Otto I is that of Reichenau. Under the enlightened rule of Abbot Roudmann (972-984), this state-sponsored abbey situated on a picturesque island in the Lake of Constance developed into one of the leading art centers of the Empire. Here, as elsewhere, the illuminators used the Carolingian heritage as their starting-off point, as can be seen in the book of pericopes (Darmstadt, Illustration page 197 Landesbibl., MS 1948) made for one "Custos Gero"—presumably this means Gero, Archbishop of Cologne from 969 to 976, whom Otto I sent as his ambassador to Constantinople. The miniatures in this book derive from the sumptuous Gospel Book executed by the royal ateliers of Charlemagne which is now divided up between the Vatican and Gyula-Fehérvár in Transylvania. We may assume that since this Carolingian Gospel Book was owned by the abbey of Lorsch, it was lent to Reichenau for copying.

To the same category as the Gero Codex belong some other liturgical books produced by the Reichenau School at the beginning of Abbot Roudmann's rule; for example two Sacramentaries, one of them in the University Library of Heidelberg (Sal. IX b) and the other in Switzerland, in the church of Solothurn. The calligrapher, who in the dedicatory miniature at the beginning of the Solothurn manuscript is shown presenting the book to Abbot Adalbert, gives his name as Eburnant, and for this reason the manuscripts affiliated to the Gero Codex are generally described as the "Eburnant Group." Characteristic of their ornamentation are elegant gold initials which, in the later manuscripts, fill an entire page; as to their style they obviously stem from the Carolingian school of St Gall. On the exceptionally white and skillfully prepared parchment these initials proliferate in graceful spiral rinceaux and interlaces set off by blue, green and purple grounds. We find the influence of the Eburnant style making good in all contemporary German schools, and even in France and Italy. And from now on the ornamental initials produced in all other Ottonian schools, from the Rhine to the Danube, were little more than variations on the admirable prototypes created in the Reichenau atelier under the abbacy of Roudmann.

Paradoxically enough, the one exception to this rule was the School of Reichenau itself. Its predilection for the harmonious beauty of the Eburnant initials was comparatively short-lived. Perhaps this elegant style seemed to lack the expressive power needed to convey to full effect the message of the sacred texts. In any case we find the tendrils worked into the initials growing shorter and thicker, the flowing spiral rhythms becoming syncopated and the leafage, driven outward by a centrifugal force, proliferating in all directions. Similarly the interlaces binding the big initials to their frames are so tightly drawn that they remind us of the thongs used to secure medieval madmen. Soon the trefoil flowers at the extremities are replaced by spiky, dagger-like leafage. Stems, too, are contorted into zigzag lines like shafts of lightning. All this goes to show a striving after violently expressionistic effects calculated to strike awe into the beholder and to inspire veneration of the Word of God. This second style of Reichenau, a wholly new creation, ranks among the most original achievements of medieval decorative art.

As an example of its first phase we may take the Psalter made for Archbishop Egbert of Trier (now in the Biblioteca Comunale, Cividale), whose publication by Arthur Haseloff has greatly contributed to our knowledge of Ottonian art. It would seem that this art-loving prelate was presented with the manuscript when he crossed the Alps in 983 to attend the Diet of Verona. A man named Roudpertus, otherwise unknown, is represented as the donor in the illustration on the first dedication page; hence the attribution of this Psalter and its next-of-kin, a Gospel Book stemming from Poussay (Paris, Bibl. Nat., lat. 10514), to the so-called Roudprecht Group, successor of the Eburnant Group described above.

Besides the illustrations on the dedication page the Psalter contains a series of portraits of Egbert's predecessors, the ten sainted bishops who had occupied the see of Trier since its foundation. Each of them is shown standing frontally against a background adorned with geometric and zoomorphic figures drawn in gold. Caught up in the same movement as the foliage of the initials, the birds and other background animals are lashing out in all directions, writhing and biting their own bodies. While the ultimate origins of this decorative scheme may be oriental, the spirit behind it is typically Nordic. But the essentially linear structure of the human figures and their treatment as surface patterns are in the tradition of the monumental art of the frescos of North Italy and those at Reichenau-Oberzell, and it is easy to see how effective these portraits would be if monumentalized into large-scale works, as murals.

Illustration page 192 Though the Egbert Psalter is on every count one of the masterworks of Ottonian illumination, it cannot have been altogether to Egbert's taste. For the artist whom the art-loving archbishop summoned to Trier, seat of his archepiscopate, practised a style very different from that of the Cividale Psalter. This man is known as the "Master of the Registrum Gregorii" on the strength of two isolated miniatures, one of them at Chantilly and the other at Trier, which once formed part of a manuscript containing the Epistles of Pope Gregory the Great. It is a pity we do not know his real name for he is one of the few artists of the early Middle Ages whose work bears the stamp of a forceful personality. Nothing is known as to where he came from, but there can be no doubt that the style of decoration he employs in his initial letters, as revealed in a Sacramentary now at Chantilly (Musée Condé, Cod. 1447), was developed under the influence of the Eburnant Group. Possibly he worked for a time in the imperial chancellery over which Egbert presided for a year before being appointed in 977 to the archbishopric. This much is certain: that shortly after Egbert settled in Trier the Master of the Registrum was commissioned by him to illuminate a number of manuscripts and that his works throw all other Ottonian paintings of the period into the shade. The importance of this artist lies, furthermore, in the fact that he acted as a pioneer of the renaissance movement which was to influence Ottonian illumination from the last decade of the 10th century on.

CODEX EGBERTI. THE MASSACRE OF THE INNOCENTS. REICHENAU, TENTH CENTURY.
(4×5³/₁₆″) COD. 24, FOLIO 15 VERSO, STADTBIBLIOTHEK, TRIER.

It is thanks to the Master of the Registrum that the esthetic of Christian antiquity, as revealed in the Quedlinburg Itala (see page 92) and affiliated works, reappears on the horizon of early medieval art.

The two surviving miniatures of the Registrum Gregorii were meant to go together and their separation is to be regretted. On one we see Pope Gregory, inspired by the Holy Spirit, dictating a text that his secretary is taking down in shorthand on a wax tablet. This text does not form part of the pope's letters but is an except from Proverbs, III, 13: "Happy is the man that findeth wisdom, and the man that getteth understanding." On the other page is a portrait of the emperor (Otto II or Otto III) whose memory Egbert evokes in the dedicatory poem. He is shown seated on his throne under a canopy and Illustration page 192 receiving homage from four persons representing the four parts of his empire. When we lay the two miniatures side by side we find that they correspond to each other, not only as regards their subjects but in their layout; the pope is turning to the right, that is to say towards the emperor, and it is to the emperor that the quotation from the Bible is addressed. Since Egbert was hoping at this time to make of Trier a *Roma secunda*, it is more than likely that he had himself in mind when he had the great pope represented in the act of counseling the German emperor and that what we have here is an allegorical depiction of the imperial chancellery suggesting how well the empire is being administered under the joint rule of the monarch and the highest ecclesiastical power.

Particularly striking in these two miniatures is the happy ease with which the artist has solved compositional problems that baffled his contemporaries. Space is represented by an intricate system of echeloned planes combined with skillfully adjusted gradations of tones. The weak point of Ottonian art in its early phase was that its innovations were confined to decorative patterning and expressionistic effects; as regards the rendering of plastic values and the disposal of figures in space the Ottonian artists showed little or no advance on their Carolingian precursors. All this was changed when the Master of the Registrum came on the scene. With his quite exceptional gift for spatial representation he built up, so to speak, a fund of plastic forms on which his successors could henceforth draw and which they turned to good account. His exemplary success in this field was due undoubtedly to a careful and comprehending study of outstanding late classical works dating probably from the 4th century. One at least of his sources is known to us, since five of the miniatures in a book of pericopes presented to Egbert Illustration page 201 by two Reichenau monks, Kerald and Heribert—the famous Codex Egberti in Trier (Stadtbibl., Cod. 24)—were the Master's work and these clearly derive from the Quedlinburg Itala or some other manuscript made at about the same date in the same atelier. In both we find the same aerial backgrounds and frames adorned with squares of gold, while in the Codex Egberti the weeping mothers of the children massacred by Herod are Illustration page 95 remarkably like the women in tears surrounding Dido's pyre in the Vergilius Vaticanus.

To this Master and his atelier at Trier is attributed another Gospel Book written in gold which had found its way to the Sainte-Chapelle in Paris by the 14th century if not earlier; it is now in the Bibliothèque Nationale (lat. 8851). Though not all the miniatures in this gorgeous manuscript are by the Master's hand, it has very close affinities with the Registrum Gregorii and must have been made at about the same time. Its date can be approximately fixed by the reproductions of coins on one of the initial pages; they bear the effigies of Henry I, Otto I, Otto II and another Henry—which suggests that it should be assigned to the period of uncertainty following the death of Otto II (in 983) when Egbert saw in Henry the Quarrelsome, father of Henry II, the natural successor to the throne. The artist had recourse to various models; for his representation of St John the Evangelist he used an Ada manuscript, for the page depicting Christ in Majesty an illuminated Turonian Bible (both manuscripts were then available at Trier). But for the architectural backgrounds in the miniatures of St Mark and St Luke with their characteristic shadows indicating spatial recession, he evidently depended on an Early Christian model, probably of the 4th century. For the Christ in Majesty he has used a gold ground and this is the first time we find this technique in Western early medieval painting. It indicates that the Master of the Registrum was influenced by Byzantine art, which was now beginning to cast its spell on Ottonian artists of other schools as well.

A Gospel Book made after the coronation of Otto III (i.e. after 996) and now in the John Rylands Library, Manchester, belongs to a later phase of the Master's stylistic evolution. It found its way to Cologne soon after it was made and was used there as a model. From 11th-century copies made in Cologne we can get a fairly good idea of the Evangelist portraits, now lost, in the original. Their iconography follows that of the Coronation Book of Charlemagne and this (or some similar work of the School of Reims) was presumably its model. The decorative motifs, however, seem to have been taken from a manuscript made in the court atelier of Charles the Bald—probably the Gospel Book now in Darmstadt (Landesbibl., 746). The two imperial Gospel Books in Paris and Manchester make it clear that the Master of the Registrum had no scruples about borrowing freely from foreign sources; however, he never lapses into eclecticism but integrates his borrowings into a style that is thoroughly personal.

The date of the Manchester Gospel Book (after 996) proves that the Master of the Registrum outlived his first patron, Archbishop Egbert (d. 993). It is not known whether he continued working at Trier under Egbert's successor, but the fact that coins with the emperor's effigy figure in the Manchester Gospels shows that he must have kept in contact with the court. If he is to be identified with the sculptor who made the ivory relief on the Notker Gospel Book at Liége, as I have sought to demonstrate elsewhere, it well may be that he ended his days in that city—like another famous painter, Johannes Italus, who was asked by Otto III to paint the *Kaiserloge* in Aachen cathedral. Like the Master of the Registrum, this artist must have been one of the foremost painters of his time and helped to shape the course of Ottonian art. Is this pure coincidence, or have we here in point of fact one and the same man? The latter alternative cannot be proved, but it certainly has much to commend it.

With the Master of the Registrum the art of representing spatial recession, as practised in the early Middle Ages, reached its culminating point. Echeloned in successive, well-defined planes, the picture space seems to be unfurling itself towards the spectator, in an arrangement at once intricate and completely logical. All forms are clearly demarcated and related to each other in a counterpoint of finely balanced curves. That restless expressionism we find in so many German miniatures is here ruled out. Also, the Master shows an exceptionally fine feeling for color, particularly attractive being a soft, saturated blue whose only equivalent is to be found in illuminations made in northern Italy during the 10th and 11th centuries.

As was only to be expected, an artist gifted with such technical proficiency had many followers in other schools within the Empire. One of the first to recognize his importance was that of Reichenau, which seems to have come into direct contact with him towards the end of Egbert's life, since five miniatures by the hand of the Master of the Registrum figure in the Codex Egberti made in the famous abbey on the Lake of Constance, which Egbert's favorite artist presumably visited with a view to assisting in its production.

Witigowo (985-997) had by then succeeded Roudmann as abbot of the monastery, and records of the time testify to his artistic interests. Under him and his successors there was so notable a flowering of art at Reichenau that round about the year 1000 it came to rank as one of the leading schools of Germany, and indeed of all Europe. This eminence was sponsored by a series of exceptionally handsome manuscripts made for various emperors: the Gospel Book of Otto III (not Otto II as is sometimes thought)

BOOK OF PERICOPES OF HENRY II. ST PETER RECEIVING THE KEYS. REICHENAU, EARLY ELEVENTH CENTURY.
(10⅜×7½″) CLM. 4452, FOLIO 152 VERSO, BAYERISCHE STAATSBIBLIOTHEK, MUNICH.

at Aachen, another Gospel Book of the same emperor at Munich (Staatsbibl., Clm. 4453), Illustration page 198
the Book of Pericopes of Henry II at Munich (Clm. 4452) and the Bamberg Apocalypse Illustration page 204
(Staatsbibl., A. II. 42). To these may be added a number of liturgical books made for
exportation. The workshop seems to have remained active until the middle of the
11th century, but the quality of its productions declined with the years. In order to
distinguish them from the earlier output of the school, these later manuscripts, about
twenty in number, have been assembled under the name of "the Liuthar Group" (Liuthar
being the otherwise unknown donor or maker of the Aachen manuscript). The Aachen
Gospel Book stands, with the Codex Egberti, at the beginning of this stylistic development. In its New Testament scenes, as in those of the Aethelwold Benedictional, we
are conscious that the artists did not feel quite at ease in combining them with the
ornamental arcaded frames, and the compositions do not always fit into the space
allotted them within the rather tall, narrow arches.

For the initial letters the Liuthar Group kept to the expressionist style of the
Roudprecht manuscripts. In the pictures, on the other hand, they mostly followed the
style of the best miniatures in the Codex Egberti; that is to say the style of the Master
of the Registrum. But already in the Codex Egberti we can see that the program the
Reichenau artists set themselves differed from his; their adherence to Early Christian
models was only superficial and they indulged from the beginning in quite unclassical
forms and proportions. The truth is that the Reichenau artists never really understood
the Master's aims. Nothing was further from their intentions than a revival of the art
of classical antiquity. They tended to regard the study of such late antique prototypes
as came to their notice merely as a means of learning how to make their figures even
more expressive and inevitably this led them to depart from the style of their teacher,
the Master of the Registrum. The effects of this cleavage, which became definitive in the
early 11th century, can be clearly seen in the Bamberg Apocalypse. In this development,
which involved at once a retrogression and an increasing emphasis on the idiosyncrasies
of the school, a contemporary Byzantine manuscript played a certain part.

In the new Reichenau style the tendency towards violent movement which we find
in the "lightning-flash" rinceaux of the Egbert Psalter is extended to figures as well.
Losing much of their plastic volume and harmonious structure, and sublimated by intense
emotion, bodies seem to be transfigured into ideograms charged with the utmost possible
expressive power. Jantzen has described the type of man depicted by the Reichenau
artists as a being reduced as nearly as possible to one dimension. Be this as it may,
there is no question that by its "disembodiment" of human forms the art of Reichenau
opened vistas on a world of pure transcendence.

In Reichenau miniatures like those illustrated on pages 198 and 204 each gesture
is given an ample sweep and the emotive impact of the figures is heightened by the great
empty spaces behind them, against which they tell out. To start with, the Reichenau
artists used the atmospheric backgrounds, bathed in light in the late antique manner,
favored by the Master of the Registrum. But little by little they enlivened these with
bands of pure, unbroken color. Also the use of gold backgrounds soon became more

GOSPEL BOOK. INCARNATION AND TRANSFIGURATION OF CHRIST. COLOGNE, SECOND QUARTER OF ELEVENTH CENTURY. ($6^{11}/_{16} \times 4^{5}/_{8}$″) BIBL. 94 (A. II. 18), FOLIO 155, STAATL. BIBLIOTHEK, BAMBERG.

frequent; in the Book of Pericopes of Henry II no other backgrounds are employed.

Set off by this all-pervading golden sheen, such eminently cool, bright hues as lilac, sea-green, sand-yellow, pink and bluish-white (characteristic of Reichenau miniatures) seem to shine with their own light, as Wolfgang Schœne has pointed out in his magisterial work *Über das Licht in der Malerei* (On Light in Painting). True, luminosity of color is one of the distinctive characteristics of medieval illumination in general, but nowhere else do we find it so pronounced as in the great manuscripts produced by the Reichenau school round about the year 1000.

The miniatures in the manuscripts of the Liuthar Group—for the most part illustrations of the life of Christ—are sometimes free copies of archetypes available in the workshop, with occasional variants; sometimes, though rarely, original creations. No one miniature is exactly like another. Wilhelm Vöge, the first to make a full-length, detailed study of this school, has pointed out that the manuscripts can be grouped according to their iconographic variants. The artists constantly endeavored to think up new ways of depicting each incident of the gospel story. In this connection it is worth while comparing the pictures in the Munich Gospel Book of Otto III with the corresponding scenes in the Codex Egberti and the Aachen Codex; the increase of expressive power is very marked. But it is above all when the scenes of two momentous episodes in the life of Christ are painted on pages facing each other, side by side, that this expressive power reaches its maximum intensity—and this is due in large part to the way each picture complements the other.

In the wholly original creations (more limited in number) where the artist has given free rein to his constructive imagination, the Reichenau school is seen at its admirable best. Striking examples of this inventiveness can be found in two manuscripts at Bamberg (Staatl. Bibl., MSS 22 and 76). Most famous, however, is the rendering of the Evangelists "in ecstasy" in the Gospel Book of Otto III at Munich. In the majority Illustration page 198

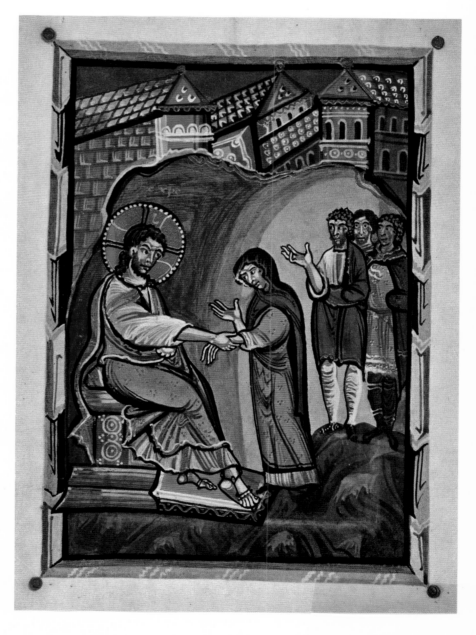

of medieval Evangelist portraits they are shown writing down the gospel tidings, bent over their task. But here they are depicted frontally, facing us, like the trance-bound ministrants of the ancient Hellenic oracles. St Luke is shown with his arms stretched up to the medallion containing the apocalyptic symbol assigned to him, like an Atlas upholding the heavens. In the Evangelist's lap repose the five Books of the Old Testament whose authors, the prophets, are gathered around the symbol hovering in mid-air. The idea behind these elaborate arrangements of prophets, Evangelists and symbols is that the coming of Christ, the divine Logos, was heralded in the Old Testament and that the Evangelists were the prophets of the New Dispensation. The speaking gaze of the Evangelists' widely opened eyes and the dramatic movement of their arms lifted heavenwards in an ecstasy of adoration create an atmosphere of numinous enchantment; never had their sacred mission been more tellingly conveyed.

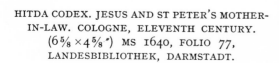

HITDA CODEX. JESUS AND ST PETER'S MOTHER-IN-LAW. COLOGNE, ELEVENTH CENTURY. (6⅝×4⅝″) MS 1640, FOLIO 77, LANDESBIBLIOTHEK, DARMSTADT.

The other German art centers were hard put to it to hold their own beside the school of Reichenau. St Gall, which Otto the Great had vainly tried to subject to the strict discipline of the reformers, failed to regain its former eminence and Einsiedeln, though it played an active part in the reform movement, was artistically never more than a dependency of Reichenau.

Further north, however, in other German schools, the art of illumination developed on independent lines; most notably in Cologne. Whereas the school of Reichenau sponsored a mainly linear expressionism as against the new plastic style of the Master of the Registrum, the artists of the capital of the Lower Rhine exploited the possibilities of color *per se* with remarkable success. In a series of medium-sized Gospel Books —Cologne (Stadtarchiv., 312), Milan (Bibl. Ambros., c. 53 sup.), Giessen (Univ. Bibl., 660) and Illustration page 207 Darmstadt (Landesbibl., 1640)—we find striking illustrations of this tendency.

The decorative program of these manuscripts clearly derives from that of the Manchester Gospel Book described above, a work of the Master of the Registrum dating at the earliest estimate to 996. Hence we are justified in assuming that the school of Cologne took its rise at the turn of the century, when Heribert became archbishop of the see (999-1021). This is borne out by the fact that the execution of a Lectionary made for his predecessor Archbishop Everger (Cologne, Domschatz, Cod. 143) is markedly inferior. Before his appointment to the archbishopric, Heribert, a personal friend of Otto III, was *logotheta* or chancellor of Germany in Italy where he frequented the Greek ascetics who are reputed to have had some influence on Otto III towards the close of his life. This may account for the inscriptions in a curiously highflown style, with Greek turns of phrase, facing the illustrations in several Cologne manuscripts. Also, what we know of Heribert's character explains why it was that Cologne, unlike all the other great Ottonian schools, never worked for the German kings or emperors. After taking up his post too late to be of service to Otto III, who died early in 1002, the archbishop was constantly at odds with Henry II. Under these circumstances the school of Cologne could hardly expect to enjoy such marks of royal favor as orders for sumptuously decorated manuscripts.

As was the case at Reichenau, the artists of the Cologne school had access to a 10th-century Greek manuscript and this obviously exercised a considerable influence on the evolution of their style. Whereas the essentially painterly qualities distinctive of the middle period of Byzantine art met with little response at Reichenau, they played a large part in the formation of the Cologne school. Taking their lead from a manuscript resembling the Bible of Queen Christina of Sweden in the Vatican (Reg. gr. 1), most painterly of all 10th-century Greek manuscripts, the Cologne illuminators not only made the most of color but utilized the fluid properties of their medium with an eye to pictorial effect. They seem to have painted directly with the brush, without preliminary drawing, and in some miniatures we get an impression that they deliberately allowed the paint to "run." One effect of this technique is that the outlines of forms are often blurred and tremulous, while garments worn by the sacred figures have a strangely ragged look, as if the material had not been cut but torn—a look in keeping with the gaunt, ascetic aspect of their wearers. Such is the dynamic flow of color that even buildings appear

PRAYER BOOK OF OTTO III. ADORATION OF THE MAJESTAS DOMINI. MAINZ, ELEVENTH CENTURY. (EACH PAGE:
5 $^{15}/_{16}$ × 4 $^{11}/_{16}$") COD. 2940, FOLIOS 26 VERSO AND 27, GRÄFLICH SCHÖNBORNSCHE BIBLIOTHEK, POMMERSFELDEN.

curiously unstable. There is a lavish use of opaque white and gold for rendering zones
of light, often making surfaces of objects seem coated with confectioners' icing.

Towards the end of Heribert's archepiscopate two monks in the monastery of
Reichenau, the twin brothers Purchardus and Chuonradus, were invited to Cologne by
a priest named Hillinus to write and illuminate a Gospel Book for the cathedral
(Domschatz, Cod. 12). Since an accurate depiction of Cologne cathedral appears on the
dedication page, it may be assumed that the work was done there; moreover some of
the initials are in the purest Cologne style and obviously the work of a local calligrapher.
The stay of the two artists in Cologne gave the art of that city a new direction, leading
to a curious blend of styles, that fusion of coloristic and linear techniques which we find
in three Gospel Books made in the second quarter of the 11th century: one in Bamberg Illustration page 206
(Staatsbibl., bibl. 94), another in Cologne (Priesterseminar, Cod. 753 b) and the third in
the Morgan Library, New York (M. 651). Two miniatures relating to the Incarnation
of the Word, as signified by the adoration of the Christchild in the manger and Christ's

transfiguration on the mountain, that figure at the beginning of St John's Gospel in the Bamberg manuscript, are charged with symbolical intimations of a wholly novel order and treated in a quite new way. But the development of this second Cologne style was (for some unknown reason) cut short abruptly. And towards the middle of the century we find the impressionist handling of color giving place to studious imitations of the style of the Master of the Registrum as found in the Manchester Gospel Book. This applies to the Stuttgart Gospels (Landesbibl., Bibl. fol. 21), a manuscript of particular interest since it gives the best idea of the miniatures which are lacking in the Manchester Gospels. In the last books produced by the Cologne school, such as the two Sacramentaries, one in Freiburg-im-Breisgau (Univ. Bibl., 360) and the other at Cracow (ex-Zamoyski Library), not only is the technique austerely linear, but both figures and decorations are lamentably devoid of life. The most that can be said for this final phase of the art of the Cologne school is that in its curious rigidity it anticipated what was soon to be a feature of the early Romanesque style.

Illustration page 209

Beside Trier and Cologne, Mainz, also the seat of an archbishopric, ranks as an important center of Ottonian art, though its achievements in the field of illumination fall short of theirs. We have already had occasion to mention Mainz, when speaking of the works of art commissioned for the palace-chapel in the reign of Otto the Great. That under Archbishop Willegis (975-1011) the Mainz atelier continued working for the royal house is evidenced by a small prayer-book made for the use of a young prince who figures in several miniatures in this manuscript, now in the library of the Castle of Pommersfelden (Cod. 2940). Though the prince's name is not stated, everything points to his being Willegis' pupil, subsequently Otto III. The Sacramentary in the Treasure of Mainz cathedral is in the same style and dates from the last decade of the 10th century. Byzantine influence is yet more in evidence in the technique of the school of Mainz than in other Ottonian schools and affects even the iconography of many of the scenes, as when we are shown Otto III kneeling before Christ. This need not surprise us when we remember that Willegis was one of the most fervent partisans of the Empress Theophano and could, thanks to her, obtain Byzantine models for the use of the local atelier.

Under Archbishop Aribo (1021-1031) the school of Mainz seems to have had an overriding influence on the art of South Germany. We have an example of the then prevailing style in a Sacramentary formerly owned by the Duke of Aremberg and now in the Bodmer Collection in Geneva. Other Mainz productions of the same period are two large Gospel Books; one of them is in Berlin (Staatsbibl., Theol. lat. fol. 18), while the other has since the middle of the 11th century remained at Fulda (Landesbibl., Aa 44). But the renown of the school of Mainz was based less on illumination than on its goldsmiths' work, and it is not too far-fetched to see in the dazzling light that plays on garments and buildings in the Mainz miniatures a reflection of the sister art. Though it has recently been proposed to attribute to the school of Fulda the Basel antependium (now in the Musée de Cluny, Paris) and some affiliated masterpieces of Ottonian metalwork, a still stronger case could be made out for their having been produced at Mainz, by comparing them with the manuscripts mentioned above.

UTA CODEX. ST ERHARD CELEBRATING MASS. REGENSBURG, ELEVENTH CENTURY. ($11 \times 8^{13}/_{16}$″)
CLM. 13601, FOLIO 4, BAYERISCHE STAATSBIBLIOTHEK, MUNICH.

CODEX AUREUS EPTERNACENSIS. THE PARABLE OF THE VINEYARD (MATTHEW, XXI, 33). ECHTERNACH, CA. 1035-1040. (4 7/16×8 5/8 ") FOLIO 78, GERMANISCHES MUSEUM, NUREMBERG.

Further east, the ancient duchy of Tassilo, Charlemagne's ill-starred rival, contributed to the new flowering of German art. Henry II, Duke of Bavaria before his accession to the imperial throne, had a natural predilection for the school of Regensburg, whose development has been traced in Georg Swarzenski's pioneer work on the subject. The convent of St Emmeram possessed an exceptionally fine Carolingian manuscript, the Codex Aureus of Charles the Bald, which the Emperor Arnulf had brought to Regensburg from France along with other precious works of art. This codex, dated to 870, acted as the starting-off point of the new style of illumination that grew up at Regensburg, and its prestige is vouched for by the fact that the eminent Abbot Ramwold (974-1001) not only saw to its restoration but had his portrait drawn on one of the blank pages.

In the early years of his reign King Henry gave a commission to the Regensburg atelier for the making of a richly ornate Sacramentary (Munich, Staatsbibl., Clm. 4456), in which he is twice portrayed as Roman emperor invested with divine right—*a deo coronatus*, crowned by the hand of God, as the official title styles it. The decorated pages of this codex show that the Regensburg artists had studied carefully their famous Carolingian model and turned its lessons to account, for almost every motif they employ is a paraphrase of decorative elements in the Golden Book of Charles the Bald. Indeed the copies tend to outclass the original; the rather dull hues and inexpressive forms of the Carolingian manuscript are replaced by crisper drawing and livelier colors.

It was also in Regensburg that Henry II had a Gospel Book made for the monastery of St Benedict after his conquest of Monte Cassino in 1022. In this manuscript, now in the Vatican (Ottobon. lat. 74), the structure of the multipartite frames still shows the influence of the Codex Aureus. A peculiar and inexplicable feature of this Gospel Book is that in it we find the emperor taking the place of St John the Evangelist. It has affinities with another Regensburg manuscript (Munich, Staatsbibl., Clm. 13601), in which an abbess of the name of Uta figures as donatrix. This manuscript may be regarded as a highly important contribution to early medieval art, since in it for the first time the miniature is put to the service of scholastic philosophy.

Let us take as an example the picture representing the ceremony of the Mass. The figurative scenes are distributed in several parts of the composition. We are shown Uta, *Domna Abbatissa*, seated in the upper righthand corner, and in the other corners women Illustration page 211

symbolizing the various religious virtues. Uta is gazing in adoration at the Lamb of God, the mystical bridegroom who is indicating a text of the Bible written in the open book before him. In the central scene St Erhard, clad in the robes of a high priest of the Old Covenant, is celebrating the divine rite, making use of the gifts donated to the convent of St Emmeram; besides the golden ciborium of King Arnulf (still in existence in Munich) we can see the Codex Aureus of Charles the Bald in its gold cover. From the fragments of text included in the composition we learn that it is an allegory of the triads of the ecclesiastical hierarchy as described by pseudo-Dionysius the Areopagite in the Latin translation of Joannes Scotus. Thus

PERICOPES OF HENRY II. JOSEPH'S DREAM. BEFORE 1014. (6¼×5¼″) BIBL. 95 (A. II. 46), FOLIO 8 VERSO, STAATLICHE BIBLIOTHEK, BAMBERG.

(1) the sacred objects used in the celebration of the Mass, (2) the officiating priest and (3) his deacon symbolize three degrees of access to the godhead. On the opposite page (not reproduced) is Christ on the Cross, depicted both in priestly raiment and as a king wearing a crown. The four successive phases of the Redemption, as revealed in Holy Writ, from Adam's sin to the divine expiation, are likened, by means of verses and *schemata*, to the four basic figures of geometry, the four elements of music, and so forth.

Thanks to Bernhard Bischoff's researches into the subject, we now know that the man who devised these intricate formulae was a learned theologian of the name of Hartwic, resident at Regensburg, and that he had studied for a time in France under Fulbert of Chartres. The name, however, of the artist who so faithfully carried out Hartwic's instructions is unknown. To his credit it must be said that he brought much esthetic feeling to the execution of a rather thankless task; the explanatory inscriptions are interwoven into the texture of the composition so skillfully that its general effect is not impaired by their presence. As a matter of fact the "paneling" of the picture surface, which we already found in the Codex Aureus, lent itself to this technique by helping the artist to fit each item of the commentary into an appropriate compartment.

With their criss-cross golden borders and the gold ribboning of the garments, these Regensburg miniatures produce the effect of a woven "cloth of gold," and it would be interesting to trace the connection, if any, between the arts of illumination and embroidery in that city. For there can be no question of the remarkable family likeness between Regensburg illumination and the sumptuous Ottonian altar-cloths and draperies preserved in Bamberg cathedral.

Though the school of Regensburg worked for Henry II, it is not to be identified with that monarch's personal atelier, which practised a somewhat different style. This is seen in a group of manuscripts owned by the library of Bamberg: the so-called Prayer Books of Henry and Cunigunda (Lit. 7 and 8) for which magnificent Byzantine ivory diptychs were used as bindings; a Pontifical with a picture of the emperor's coronation (Lit. 53); and a Book of Pericopes with scenes of the life of Christ (Bibl. 95), Illustration page 213 one of which we reproduce. In this miniature the artist has enlivened the tale of Joseph's dream with some amusing details. Before going to bed Mary's husband has been careful to deposit his shoes and other paraphernalia on a bench beside the bed, near which a servant is sound asleep wrapped in a big cloak. Are we to see in the unusually large format given this scene an allusion to the fact that the emperor's marriage to Cunigunda was reputed to be a *mariage blanc* like St Joseph's? A book of antiphons in Cassel (Landesbibl., Theol. qua. 15), paleologically affiliated to the same group, bore an inscription on its original binding to the effect that it was written by "Marcus, Chaplain of the Court"—a definite proof that it was a production of the Chapel Royal. It is believed, largely on liturgical grounds, that the place of origin of this group of manuscripts was Seeon in Bavaria, where the art of illumination is known to have been practised. An epigraph of which a copy has been preserved describes a monk named Eberhard, resident in the monastery of Seeon, as being a scribe and deacon "well versed in handling gold and pigments."

Besides the schools already named there were ateliers in other South German monasteries—for example at Tegernsee, Niederaltaich and Freising—generally known under the name of the "Bavarian monastery school" *(Bayerische Klosterschule)*. The work turned out in them was rather uninspired and its chief interest is that of illustrating the gradual transition from the Ottonian style to Romanesque round about the decade 1060-1070.

The Salzburg School, exhaustive studies of which have been made by Georg Swarzenski and (sometimes differing from him) by Paul Buberl, displayed on the whole more freedom and originality. Datable to the first half of the 11th century, the best work of this school is the handsome Book of Pericopes in the Morgan Library (M. 781), stylistically akin to the productions of the court atelier of Henry II. In another manuscript similar in type, dating to the middle of the century (Munich, Staatsbibl., Clm. 15713), we find two different stylistic tendencies, one keeping to the manner of the Morgan Library manuscript, while the other follows the Byzantine technique of using olive-green shadings in the flesh-tints and has much in common with the Regensburg Sacramentary. There is difficulty in deciding whether (as the dates of the two manuscripts suggest) this Byzantinizing tendency came to Salzburg from Regensburg or whether it took the opposite direction, as, from the geographical standpoint, would seem more likely. In any case the manuscript must be regarded as a product of the Austrian school.

The key work of the Salzburg School in the second half of the 11th century is another manuscript in the Morgan Library (M. 780), signed by a *custos* named Berthold. In it Byzantine influences are yet more pronounced. Folds of garments tend to become stiffer, as if carved in stone, and we can almost speak of a striving for architectonic form—the Romanesque style is on the threshold. Swarzenski has very justly pointed out that the school of Salzburg in its golden age during the 12th century took its lead from the "Berthold style," whose influence is particularly noticeable in the Evangelist portraits in some Romanesque Gospel Books made in the metropolis or its environs.

While Salzburg, lying as it did on the trade route to Byzantium, was the eastern outpost of Ottonian illumination, the monastery of Echternach in the Grand Duchy of Luxemburg was its most westerly point. Situated in the neighborhood of Trier, Echternach took over the legacy of the Master of the Registrum. The chief connecting link between the schools of Trier and Echternach is the Sainte-Chapelle Gospel Book in Paris (Bibl. Nat., lat. 8851) already mentioned. The *Majestas Domini*, Eusebian canons and Evangelist portraits in this manuscript were adopted as models by the Echternach school; we find them reappearing in the first great work produced by it, the Codex Aureus Epternacensis, and thereafter in almost every Echternach manuscript.

Preserved in the Ducal Museum of Gotha until the last world war, the Codex Illustration page 212 Epternacensis is now the proudest possession of the Germanisches Museum at Nuremberg. The exceptionally handsome binding of this manuscript was not made for it but pre-dates it, curiously enough, by some fifty years. Among the figures in gold relief on the front cover we see Otto III as a youth and his mother Theophano, who died in 991; thus the binding must have been made before this date, presumably in Archbishop Egbert's atelier at Trier. Albert Bœckler has advanced the ingenious hypothesis that the manuscript for which this binding was originally employed was none other than the Sainte-Chapelle Gospel Book mentioned above. The dimensions of the two books are in fact the same and it well may be that the earlier manuscript with its superb illustrations was presented to the French king on some ceremonial occasion, possibly one of the meetings between Henry II and Robert the Pious that took place at Ivois (now Carignan) in Lorraine, in 1008 and 1023; since the portraits of Otto III and Theophano on the cover would have been unsuitable for a gift to the French king, Henry II had the binding removed and kept at Echternach. Thus for a time it was left unused—an assumption which is supported by the curious fact that a pericope for a service held in connection with the consecration of a church has been written directly on the wood of the inner side of the front cover. Presumably this text was employed at the consecration of the new church of Echternach in 1031, built to replace the church destroyed by fire in 1016.

The abbot of Echternach at this time was Humbert (1028-1051), a monk of Trier whom Poppo von Stavelot, chancellor of Emperor Conrad II, had charged with the reformation of the monastery. An enlightened disciplinarian, Humbert did much not only to elevate the spiritual life of the community but also to promote its cultural activities. He had the walls of the new church adorned with frescos, the outline drawings of some of which have been uncovered in the vaulting of the crypt, and it is highly probable that these decorations stimulated the revival of the art of illumination which now took place at Echternach. For the scenes of the childhood of Christ in the crypt have close stylistic and iconographical affinities with those depicted in illuminated manuscripts made a few years later. Under the first page of the Nuremberg codex a drawing, hitherto concealed, was brought to light in 1931; it represents Christ enthroned above two cherubim whose wings are spangled with eyes. Since this motif is unique in book illumination, it is quite possible that we have here a relic of one of the preliminary studies for their frescos made by the artists working in the Church.

The school reached its apogee in the reign of Henry III (1039-1056). We can date a lavishly decorated book of pericopes (Bremen, Stadtbibl., b. 21) to the early forties of the 11th century on the strength of two remarkable miniatures on the opening pages which depict a visit made by the emperor and his mother Gisela (who died in 1043) to the monastery of Echternach. In one of the pictures the young king is accompanied by Humbert and another abbot, almost certainly Poppo von Stavelot, who at the time was abbot of St Maximin's in Trier. The close cultural relations between Echternach and Trier are further evidenced by the fact that the Codex Egberti, preserved at Trier, was used as the model for over half the New Testament miniatures in the Bremen manuscript. One of the miniatures is of special interest since it shows a scribe in a monk's frock and a lay brother in ordinary attire working side by side in the monastery of Echternach represented as a church. We have here no doubt a realistic picture of a monastic atelier at work, with a layman doing the illuminations and a monk the writing of the sacred text. This is an Ottonian counterpart of the Mozarabic miniature in the Madrid Beatus representing the atelier in the watchtower of Távara.

The Evangelist portraits in the Bremen manuscript follow those in the Nuremberg codex and we are therefore justified in assuming that Humbert showed the king that masterwork, the Codex Aureus of Nuremberg, in the same state as it is today. That this manuscript has no inscription or dedicatory picture in honor of a royal patron can be accounted for only on the assumption that the text was written at the expense of the monastery in order to restore the superb Ottonian binding to its original use. In any case there can be no doubt that Henry's visit to the monastery of Echternach had a great and lasting influence on the young king's artistic taste. With its backgrounds delicately patterned in the manner of Byzantine fabrics, its handsome initials done in gold on purple and filling entire pages, and its many biblical scenes in three rows, one above the other, as in the Bible of Tours, the newly completed Codex Aureus must have so much impressed him that he promptly decided to commission similar Gospel Books on his own account. Thus, not long after, we learn of several "golden Gospel Books" being made at Echternach for use in the great new cathedrals of his empire. Two have survived: the Codex Aureus made for Speyer cathedral in 1045-1046, now in the Escorial Library, and the Codex Caesareus at Upsala (Univ. Bibl., c. 93), which Henry III presented to the cathedral of Goslar at its dedication in 1050 or shortly after. Another sumptuously decorated book was the so-called Luxeuil Gospels (Paris, Bibl. Nat., nouv. acq. lat. 2196), which an abbot of Luxeuil named Gerhard donated to a "St Peter's church" whose precise location is uncertain. The fact that a French abbot gave the order for this manuscript to the German court atelier is a striking confirmation of the intimate relations between Burgundy and the German Empire during the reign of Henry III.

A comparative study of the miniatures in the Echternach manuscripts enables us to group them chronologically. In this respect the Evangelist portraits, whose type forms are transmitted from manuscript to manuscript, are particularly helpful. In the light of these it becomes evident that the Luxeuil Gospel Book was made later than the Codex Aureus of Nuremberg and before the Codex Aureus of Speyer and that of Goslar. Such is the wealth of illustrations and decorated pages in the Speyer manuscript that it ranks as the *opus maius* of the Echternach illuminators, and with its hundred and twenty figurative or decorative illuminations is the most ornate, most eye-filling production of the whole Ottonian period. Particularly impressive are the big dedication pages in which we see the emperor and his wife Agnes in adoration at the feet of Christ and, next, humbly offering the book to the Virgin, to whom the cathedral was dedicated. A peculiarity of these miniatures (which has never been fully explained) is that the heads of Christ and Mary and the hand, raised in benediction, of the former were painted in later by some skilled Byzantine artist. Everything goes to show that he worked at Speyer, though there is no knowing when this was. One thing is certain: he was never active at Echternach—or he would certainly have had a revolutionary influence on the local style.

Already in the Nuremberg codex we find tendencies towards an hieratic rendering of forms and a rather frigid academicism; tendencies which become more pronounced in the later works of the school. The dynamic movement to which the earlier Ottonian miniatures owe their wonderful vitality steadily diminished and despite the school's importance in the history of art its record makes depressing reading. After the death of Henry III the Echternach scriptorium ceased to be the court atelier. An immediate consequence was a reduction in the size of the books produced, while the composition continued to grow more and more schematic. Nevertheless the school died hard; under the rule of its scholarly abbot Thiofrid (1081-1108), two illuminated copies of whose *Liber floridum* are extant, Echternach still kept faith with the Ottonian art tradition, as, on the political plane, it remained loyal to the German emperor.

When, on a general survey of early medieval illumination, we compare the work of the Ottonian artists with that of previous and contemporary schools in other lands, the part it played in the evolution of Western art is plain to see. More than Carolingian or English illumination, it stood for clearly stated, plastic, monumental form. But this tendency did not develop in the school's early days; it was due, above all, to the Master of the Registrum Gregorii, that great artist who worked for Egbert of Trier and who perhaps is to be identified with the Italian court painter employed by Otto III. His works were much admired and copied in all Ottonian schools, though a reaction set in against his methods, notably in the two most independent-minded schools of the time, those of Reichenau and Cologne. However, his plastic style made good in most parts of the Empire and if we seem to find a logical, continuous development from the art of the late Ottonian monastery schools of Bavaria and Echternach to the first works of the Romanesque illuminators, this is due to the persistence of a tradition inaugurated by the Master of the Registrum. Even in the 12th century his lessons were turned to good account, as can be seen most notably in the productions of the Mosan school.

Yet it is evident that Ottonian art alone does not suffice to explain the origin of the Romanesque style; there certainly were other influences at work when it arose. In Romanesque art and particularly Romanesque illumination we can discern a new religious feeling quite other than that which found expression in the works sponsored by the German emperors. Until 1050, German art, blissfully unconscious of any conflict between Church and State, could "render to Caesar the things that are Caesar's and to God the things that are God's." Indeed this union between the spiritual and temporal powers was a prime condition of the Ottonian renaissance. But when Henry IV was excommunicated by the pope, this age-old tradition came to an abrupt end and Germany lost her place in the vanguard of European art. Yet the loss was not definitive; later, in its second flowering, German art regained triumphantly the pre-eminence it had enjoyed in the Ottonian epoch.

APPENDIX

BIBLIOGRAPHY

INDEX OF MANUSCRIPTS

INDEX OF NAMES AND PLACES

LIST OF COLORPLATES

# APPENDIX

Photo *GFN*.

THE ANGEL OF THE ANNUNCIATION.　　　　　THE REDEEMER.

## San Vincenzo
## at the source of the Volturno

Though owing to the extremely poor condition of these frescos we
have had to abandon the idea of reproducing them in color, so
exceptional is their interest that we include the two photographs
above, taken about 1925, which have been kindly placed at our
disposal by the Gabinetto Fotografico Nazionale of the Ministero
della Pubblica Istruzione in Rome.

# BIBLIOGRAPHY

## MOSAICS AND MURAL PAINTING

### GENERAL

E. W. Anthony, *Romanesque Frescoes*, Princeton 1951 (this study also covers pre-Romanesque frescos).

### AUSTRIA

J. Garber, *Die karolingische St. Benediktkirche in Mals*, in *Zeitschrift des Ferdinandeums*, vol. 59, Innsbruck 1915.

### FRANCE

H. Woodruff, *The Iconography and Date of the Mosaics of La Daurade*, in *The Art Bulletin* XIII, 1931.

J. Hubert, *L'art préroman*, Paris 1937.

P. Deschamps and Marc Thibaut, *La peinture murale en France. Le haut moyen âge et l'époque romane*, Paris 1951.

R. Louis, *Les églises d'Auxerre*, Paris 1952.

### GERMANY

Paul Clemen, *Die romanische Monumentalmalerei in den Rheinlanden*, Düsseldorf 1916.

Hans Jantzen, *Ottonische Kunst*, Munich 1947.

H. Eichler, *Peintures murales carolingiennes à Saint-Maximin de Trèves*, in *Cahiers Archéologiques* VI, 1952.

### ITALY

J. Wilpert, *Die Malereien der Katakomben Roms*, Freiburg-im-Breisgau 1903. — Idem, *Die römischen Mosaiken und Malereien der kirchlichen Bauten vom 4. bis 13. Jahrhundert*, vol. I-IV, Freiburg-im-Breisgau 1916.

E. Bertaux, *L'art dans l'Italie méridionale*, Paris 1904.

W. de Grüneisen, *Sainte-Marie-Antique*, Rome 1911.

P. Toesca, *La pittura e la miniatura nella Lombardia*, Milan 1912. — Idem, *Storia dell'arte italiana* I, Turin 1927.

J. Garber, in *Mitt. der K. K. Zentral-Kommission* XIV, 1915 (on Naturno).

M. van Berchem and E. Clouzot, *Mosaïques chrétiennes du IVe au Xe siècle*, Geneva 1924.

A. Calderini, G. Chierici, C. Cecchelli, *La basilica di S. Lorenzo Maggiore in Milano*, Milan 1951.

R. Oertel, *Die Frühzeit der italienischen Malerei*, Stuttgart 1953.

C. Cecchelli, *I Mosaici della basilica di S. Maria Maggiore*, Rome 1956.

### SPAIN

F. de Selgas, *La basilica de San Julián de los Prados*, in *B.S.E.E.* XXIV.

J. Puig y Cadafalch, *Novas descobertas en la catedral de Egara, Ars Hispaniae, Historia universal del arte hispánico* II, Madrid 1947.

H. Schlunk, *Las pinturas de Santullano*, in *Archivo Español de Arqueología*, Madrid 1952, 1.

### SWITZERLAND

J. Zemp and R. Durrer, *Das Kloster St. Johann zu Münster in Graubünden*, in *Mitt. der schweiz. Ges. zur Erhaltung hist. Kunstdenkmäler*, Geneva 1906-1910.

L. Birchler, *Zur karolingischen Architektur und Malerei in Münster-Müstair*, in *Art du haut moyen âge dans la région alpine*, Olten-Lausanne 1954.

G. de Francovich, *Il ciclo pittorico della chiesa di S. Giovanni a Münster (Müstair) nei Grigioni*, in *Arte Lombarda* II, 1956.

## BOOK ILLUMINATION

### 1. GENERAL

A. Boeckler, *Abendländische Miniaturen (Tabulae ad usum scholarum*, ed. J. Lietzmann, vol. 10), Berlin 1930.

A. Boeckler, *Deutsche Buchmalerei vorgotischer Zeit (Die blauen Bücher)*, Königstein a. Taunus 1942; 2nd edition, 1952.

A. Boeckler and A. Schmid, *Die Buchmalerei (Handbuch der Bibliothekswissenschaft*, founded by F. Milkau. New edition, vol. I, 4), Stuttgart 1950.

J. A. Herbert, *Illuminated Manuscripts*, London 1911.

E. Kitzinger, *Early Medieval Art in the British Museum*, London 1955 (2nd edition).

G. L. Micheli, *L'Enluminure du haut moyen âge et les influences irlandaises*, Brussels 1939.

E. A. van Moé, *La lettre ornée dans les manuscrits du VIIIe au XIIe siècle*, Paris 1943; English edition 1950.

L. Réau, *Histoire de la Peinture au Moyen-Age. La Miniature*, Melun 1946.

H. Swarzenski, *Vorgotische Miniaturen (Die blauen Bücher)*, Königstein a. Taunus, 1927; 2nd edition 1931.

H. Swarzenski, *Miniaturen des frühen Mittelalters*, Bern 1951.

J. J. Tikkanen, *Studien über die Farbengebung in der mittelalterlichen Buchmalerei* (Societas Scientiarum Fennica, Comment. Human. Litter., Vol. V, 1), Helsinki 1933.

### 2. LATE ROMAN ILLUMINATION

B. Bischoff and W. Koehler, *Eine illustrierte Ausgabe der spätantiken Ravennater Annalen* (Medieval Studies in Memory of A. Kingsley Porter I, Cambridge, Mass. 1939, pp. 125-138; reprinted in Studi Romagnoli III, 1952, pp. 1-17).

A. Byvanck, *Antike Buchmalerei (Mnemosyne*, vol. 3a, series 6-8, Leyden 1938-40).

*Codices e Vaticanis selecti*, vol. 1 (Vergilius Vaticanus) and vol. 2 (Vergilius Romanus), Rome 1943 (3rd ed.) and 1902.

H. Degering and A. Boeckler, *Die Quedlinburger Itala-Fragmente* (Veröffentlichungen der Cassiodor-Gesellschaft), Berlin 1932.

O. v. Gebhardt, *The Miniatures of the Ashburnham Pentateuch*, London 1883.

C. Nordenfalk, *Die spätantiken Kanontafeln*, Göteborg 1938.

C. Nordenfalk, *The Beginning of Book Decoration* (Beiträge für Georg Swarzenski), Berlin-Chicago 1951, pp. 9-20.

F. Saxl and H. Meier, *Verzeichnis astrologischer und mythologischer illustrierter Handschriften des lateinischen Mittelalters. III, Handschriften in englischen Bibliotheken*, ed. H. Bober, London 1953.

H. STERN, *Le Calendrier de 354* (Institut français d'archéologie de Beyrouth. Bibliothèque archéologique et historique, vol. LV), Paris 1953.

K. WEITZMANN, *Illustrations in Roll and Codex* (Studies in Manuscript Illumination, 2), Princeton 1947.

F. WORMALD, *The Miniatures in the Gospels of St Augustine*, Cambridge 1954.

## 3. PRE-CAROLINGIAN ILLUMINATION

*Codices latini antiquiores. A Paleographical Guide to Latin Manuscripts prior to the 9th Century*, ed. E. A. Lowe, vols. I-VII, Oxford 1934-1956.

E. H. ZIMMERMANN, *Vorkarolingische Miniaturen*, Berlin 1916. (See also the critique of this book by A. HASELOFF in *Repertorium für Kunstwissenschaft*, vol. XLII, 1920, pp. 164-220).

### a) IRELAND AND ENGLAND

Facsimiles in color of the *Book of Kells* (Introduction E. H. ALTON and P. MEYER), of the Irish manuscripts at St Gall (Introduction J. DUFT and P. MEYER) and of the *Book of Lindisfarne* (Introduction J. BROWN, BRUCE-MITFORD and others), published by Urs Graf Verlag, Bern 1951-1957.

F. HENRY, *Irish Art in the Early Christian Period*, London 1947 (2nd edition).

F. HENRY, *Art Irlandais*, Dublin 1954.

T. D. KENDRICK, *Anglo-Saxon Art to A. D. 900*, London 1938.

F. MASAI, *Essai sur les Origines de la Miniature dite irlandaise* (Publications de Scriptorium, vol. I), Brussels 1947.

C. NORDENFALK, *Before the Book of Durrow* (Acta archaeologica XVIII, 1947, pp. 141-174).

C. NORDENFALK, *A Note on the Stockholm Codex Aureus* (*Libri Aurei*. Nordisk Tidskrift för Bok- och Biblioteksväsen XXXVIII, 1951, pp. 145-156).

M. RICKERT, *Painting in Britain. The Middle Ages* (The Pelican History of Art), London 1954.

### b) MEROVINGIAN ILLUMINATION

B. BISCHOFF, *Die Kölner Nonnenhandschriften und das Skriptorium von Chelles* (*Karolingische und ottonische Kunst*, Wiesbaden 1957, pp. 395-411).

R. BRANNER, *The Art of the Scriptorium at Luxeuil* (Speculum XXIX, 1954, pp. 678-690).

O. DOBIACHE-ROZDESTVENSKAIA, *Codices Corbeienses Leninopolitani* (Academy of the Sciences of the U.S.S.R. Proceedings of the Institute for the History of Science and Technics, series II, fasc. 3), Leningrad 1934.

E. A. LOWE, *The "Script of Luxeuil" - A Title Vindicated* (Revue Bénédictine 1953, pp. 132-142).

C. MOHLBERG, *Missale Gothicum* (Codices liturgici I), Augsburg 1929.

P. SALOMON, *Le Lectionnaire de Luxeuil* (Collectanea biblica latina IX), Rome 1953.

## 4. CAROLINGIAN ILLUMINATION

A. BOINET, *La miniature carolingienne*, Paris 1913.

A. BOUTEMY, *Le style franco-saxon, style de St-Amand* (Scriptorium III, 1949, pp. 260-264).

E. T. DE WALD, *The Stuttgart Psalter*, Princeton 1930.

E. T. DE WALD, *The Illustrations of the Utrecht Psalter*, Princeton 1933.

A. M. FRIEND, *The Carolingian Art in the Abbey of St Denis* (Art Studies I, 1923, pp. 132-148). — Idem, *Two Manuscripts of the School of St Denis* (Speculum I, 1926, pp. 59-70).

A. GOLDSCHMIDT, *Die deutsche Buchmalerei*, vol. I, Munich and Florence 1928.

O. HOMBURGER, *Eine unveröffentlichte Evangelienhandschrift aus der Zeit Karls des Grossen* (Zeitschrift für schweizerische Archäologie und Kunstgeschichte V, 1943, pp. 149-163).

O. HOMBURGER, *Eine spätkarolingische Schule von Corbie* (Karolingische und ottonische Kunst. Wesen, Werden, Wirken, Wiesbaden 1957, pp. 412-426).

E. KANTOROWICZ, *The Carolingian King in the Bible of San Paolo fuori le mura* (Late Classical and Mediaeval Studies in honor of A. M. Friend, Princeton 1955, pp. 287-300).

W. KOEHLER, *Die karolingischen Miniaturen*. I, *Die Schule von Tours*, Berlin 1930-1933.

F. LANDSBERGER, *Der St. Galler Folchard-Psalter*, St Gall 1912.

G. LEIDINGER, *Der Codex aureus der Bayerischen Staatsbibliothek in München*, Munich 1921-1925.

K. MENZEL, P. CORSSEN, H. JANITSCHEK etc., *Die Trierer Ada-Handschrift* (Publikationen der Gesellschaft für Rhein Geschichtskunde, VI), Trier 1889.

A. MERTON, *Die Buchmalerei in St. Gallen*, Leipzig 1923 (2nd edition).

C. NIVER, *A Study of certain of the more important Manuscripts of the Franco-Saxon School*, Harvard University, Cambridge, Mass. 1941.

C. NORDENFALK, *Ein karolingisches Sakramentar aus Echternach und seine Vorläufer* (Acta archaeologica II, 1931, pp. 207-244).

D. PANOFSKY, *The Textual Basis of the Utrecht Psalter Illustrations* (Art Bulletin XXV, 1943, pp. 50-58).

P. E. SCHRAMM, *Die deutschen Kaiser und Könige in Bildern ihrer Zeit* (*Die Entwicklung des menschlichen Bildnisses*, ed. W. Götz, vol. II), Leipzig 1929.

G. SWARZENSKI, *Die karolingische Malerei und Plastik in Reims* (Jahrbuch der Kgl. Preuss. Kunstsammlungen XXIII, 1902, pp. 81-104).

H. J. TORP, *Note sugli affreschi più antichi dell'oratorio di S. Maria in Valle in Cividale* (Atti del 2º Congresso Internazionale di Studi sull'Alto Medioevo), Spoleto 1953.

P. UNDERWOOD, *The Fountain of Life in Manuscripts of the Gospels* (Dumbarton Oaks Papers V, 1950, pp. 41 and f.).

L. WEBER, *Einbanddecken, Elfenbeintafeln, Miniaturen, Schriftproben aus Metzer liturgischen Handschriften*. I, *Jetzige Pariser Handschriften*, Metz and Frankfort on Main 1912.

F. WORMALD, *The Utrecht Psalter*, Utrecht 1953.

## 5. MOZARABIC ILLUMINATION

J. DOMINGUEZ BORDONA, *Die spanische Buchmalerei vom 7. bis 17. Jahrhundert*, Munich and Florence 1930.

*Exposición de códices miniados españoles*. Catalogue by J. DOMINGUEZ BORDONA, Madrid 1929.

A. GARCIA FUENTE, *La miniatura española primitiva, siglo VIII-XI*, Madrid 1936.

W. NEUSS, *Die Apokalypse des hl. Johannes in der altspanischen und altchristlichen Bibel-Illustration* (Spanische Forschungen der Görresgesellschaft 2-3), Münster (Westphalia) 1951.

W. Neuss, *Probleme der christlichen Kunst im maurischen Spanien des 10. Jahrhunderts* (Frühmittelalterliche Kunst I. Neue Beiträge zur Kunstgeschichte des ersten Jahrtausends, Mainz 1954, pp. 249-284).

M. Schapiro, *From Mozarabic to Romanesque in Silos* (Art Bulletin XXI, 1939, pp. 313-374).

H. Schlunk, *Observaciones en torno al problema de la miniatura visigoda* (Archivo español de Arte XVII, 1945, pp. 241-265).

6. ANGLO-SAXON ILLUMINATION
IN THE TENTH AND ELEVENTH CENTURIES

M. Harrsen, *The Countess Judith and the Library of Weingarten* (Papers of the Bibliographical Society of America XXIV, 1930, pp. 1-13).

O. Homburger, *Die Anfänge der Malerschule von Winchester im 10. Jahrhundert* (Studien über christliche Denkmäler XIII), Leipzig 1912.

T. D. Kendrick, *Late-Saxon and Viking Art*, London 1949.

E. G. Millar, *English Illuminated Manuscripts from the 10th to the 13th Century*, Paris and Brussels 1926.

C. Niver, *The Psalter in British Museum Harl. 2904* (Medieval Studies in Memory of A. Kingsley Porter II, Cambridge, Mass. 1939, pp. 681-687).

Sir Francis Oppenheimer, *The Legend of the Sainte Ampoule*, London 1954.

D. T. Rice, *English Art 871-1100* (The Oxford History of English Art, vol. II), Oxford 1952.

M. Rickert, *Painting in Britain. The Middle Ages*, London 1954.

M. Schapiro, *The Image of the Disappearing Christ, The Ascension in English Art around the Year 1000* (Gazette des Beaux-Arts XXII, 1943, pp. 135-152).

*The Caedmon Manuscript of Anglo-Saxon Biblical Poetry.* Introduction by Sir Israel Gollancz, London 1927.

J. B. L. Tolhurst, *An Examination of Two Anglo-Saxon MSS of the Winchester School* (Archaeologia LXXXIII, 1933, pp. 27-74).

F. G. Warner and H. A. Wilson, *The Benedictional of Aethelwold* (Roxburghe Club), London 1910.

H. A. Wilson, *The Missal of Robert of Jumièges* (Henry Bradshaw Society, vol. XI), London 1896.

F. Wormald, *Decorated Initials in English Manuscripts from A. D. 900 to 1100* (Archaeologia XCI, 1945, pp. 107-135).

F. Wormald, *English Drawings of the 10th and 11th Centuries*, London 1952.

W. Worringer, *Über den Einfluss der angelsächsischen Buchmalerei auf die frühmittelalterliche Monumentalplastik des Kontinents* (Schriften der Königsberger Gelehrten Gesellschaft, Geisteswiss. Kl. VIII, 1), Halle 1931.

7. OTTONIAN ILLUMINATION

E. F. Bange, *Eine Bayerische Malerschule des 11. und 12. Jahrhunderts*, Munich 1923.

S. Beissel, *Die Bilder der Handschrift des Kaisers Otto im Münster zu Aachen*, Aachen 1886.

B. Bischoff, *Literarisches und künstlerisches Leben in St. Emmeram während des frühen und hohen Mittelalters* (Studien und Mitt. zur Geschichte des Benediktiner-Ordens LI, 1933, pp. 102-142).

A. Boeckler, *Der Codex Wittekindeus*, Leipzig 1938.

A. Boeckler, *Die Reichenauer Buchmalerei* (*Die Kultur der Reichenau*. Eine Erinnerungsschrift, Munich 1925, pp. 956-998).

A. Boeckler, *Das goldene Evangelienbuch Heinrichs III.*, Berlin 1934.

A. Boeckler, *Das Erhardbild im Uta-Kodex* (Studies in Art and Literature for Belle da Costa Greene, Princeton 1954, pp. 219-230).

A. Boeckler, *Kölner ottonische Buchmalerei* (Beiträge zur Kunst des Mittelalters, Berlin 1950, pp. 144-149).

P. Buberl, *Über einige Werke der Salzburger Buchmalerei des 11. Jahrhunderts* (Kunstgeschichtliches Jahrbuch der K. K. Zentralkommission II), Vienna 1907.

H. Ehl, *Die ottonische Kölner Buchmalerei* (Forschungen zur Kunstgeschichte Westeuropas IV), Bonn and Leipzig 1922.

G. Fischer, *Die sog. Gebetbücher Heinrichs und Kunigundas* (*Heinrich der Heilige*. Festschrift zur Neunjahrhundertfeier des Todestages des hl. Heinrichs), Bamberg 1924, No 10, pp. 7-12.

W. Gernsheim, *Die Buchmalerei der Reichenau*, Munich 1934 (Diss.).

A. Goldschmidt, *Die deutsche Buchmalerei* II, Munich and Florence 1928.

A. Haseloff and H. V. Sauerland, *Der Psalter Erzbischof Egberts v. Trier* (Festschrift der Gesellschaft f. nützliche Forschungen), Trier 1901.

H. Jantzen, *Ottonische Kunst*, Munich 1946.

F. X. Kraus, *Die Miniaturen des Codex Egberti*, Freiburg-im-Breisgau 1884.

W. Koehler, *Die Tradition der Ada-Gruppe und die Anfänge des ottonischen Stiles in der Buchmalerei* (Festschrift zum 60. Geburtstage von Paul Clemen, Bonn 1926, pp. 255-272).

G. Leidinger, *Das sog. Evangeliarium Kaiser Ottos III. (Miniaturen aus Handschriften der Kgl. Hof- und Staatsbibliothek I)*, Munich 1912.

P. Metz, *Das goldene Evangelienbuch von Echternach im Germanischen Nationalmuseum zu Nürnberg*, Munich 1956.

C. Nordenfalk, *Neue Dokumente zur Datierung des Echternacher Evangeliars in Gotha* (Zeitschrift für Kunstgeschichte I, 1932, pp. 153-157).

C. Nordenfalk, *Der Meister des Registrum Gregorii* (Münchener Jahrbuch der Bildenden Kunst III, Folge Bd. 1, 1950, pp. 61-77).

E. Schipperges, *Der Hitda-Kodex, ein Werk ottonischer Kölner Buchmalerei*, Bonn 1938.

A. Schmidt, *Die Miniaturen des Gero-Kodex*, Leipzig 1924.

W. Schöne, *Über das Licht in der Malerei*, Berlin 1954.

G. Swarzenski, *Die Regensburger Buchmalerei des 10. und 11. Jahrhunderts*, Leipzig 1901.

G. Swarzenski, *Die Salzburger Malerei von den ersten Anfängen bis zur Blütezeit des romanischen Stils*, Leipzig 1913.

W. Vöge, *Eine deutsche Malerschule um die Wende des ersten Jahrtausends* (Westdeutsche Zeitschrift für Geschichte und Kunst, Erg. Heft 7), Trier 1891.

H. Wölfflin, *Die Bamberger Apokalypse*, Munich 1921, 2nd edition.

E. H. Zimmermann, *Die Fuldaer Buchmalerei in karolingischer und ottonischer Zeit* (Kunstgeschichtliches Jahrbuch der K. K. Zentralkommission IV, Vienna 1910, pp. 1-104).

# INDEX OF MANUSCRIPTS

Page numbers in italics refer to miniatures illustrated in the text

FLORENCE, Biblioteca Laurenziana:
Amiatinus 1 *Codex Amiatinus*, Jarrow-Wearmouth, early 8th century *119*, 121.

FREIBURG-IM-BREISGAU, Universitätsbibliothek:
Cod. 360 *Sacramentary*, Cologne, 3rd quarter of 11th century 210.

FULDA, Landesbibliothek:
Cod. Bonif. 2 *Codex Ragyntrudis*, deriving from Luxeuil, 7th-8th century (on loan to the Cathedral) 133.
Aa 44 *Gospel Book*, Mainz (?), 11th century 210.

GENEVA, Bodmer Collection:
*Sacramentary* (formerly Duke of Aremberg Collection), Mainz, 11th century 210.

GERONA, Cathedral Library:
*Beatus Apocalypse*, Távara (?), 975 166, *170*, *171*.

GHENT, Treasure of St Bavo's:
*Gospels of St Livinus*, France, early 9th century 162.

GIESSEN, Universitätsbibliothek:
Cod. 660 *Gospel Book*, Cologne, 1st quarter of 11th century 208.

GÖTTINGEN, Universitätsbibliothek:
Theol. fol. 231 *Sacramentary*, Fulda, 10th century 195.

GYULA-FEHÉRVÁR (now Alba Julia, Rumania), Cathedral Library:
*Codex Aureus* (see also Vatican, Pal. lat. 50), Palace School of Charlemagne, early 9th century 137, 199.

HEIDELBERG, Universitätsbibliothek:
Sal. IX b. *Sacramentary*, Reichenau, late 10th century 199.

HELMINGHAM HALL, Collection of Lord Tollemache:
*Orosius*, Winchester (?), 10th century 177.

HILDESHEIM, Cathedral Treasure:
Cod. 61 *Bible of St Bernward of Hildesheim*, Hildesheim, early 11th century 193, 199.

LA CAVA (Cava dei Tirreni), Archives of the Abbey:
*Danila Bible*, Spain, 9th century 162.

LAON, Bibliothèque Municipale:
MS 137 *Paulus Orosius, Historiae*, Laon, 8th century 134;
MS 423 *Isidore, De natura rerum*, Laon, 8th century 134.

LENINGRAD, Public Library:
Q.V.I.14 *Gregorius Homeliae*, Corbie, 7th century 134.

LEÓN, Cathedral:
Cod. 6 *Bible of the Year 920*, Spain 163, *164*, 165.

LEÓN, San Isidoro:
Cod. 2 *Bible of the Year 960*, Spain 165, 166, *167*.

LE PUY, Cathedral Treasure:
*Bible of Theodulf*, Fleury, 9th century 162.

LEYDEN, University Library:
Periz. 17 *Liber Machabeorum*, Reichenau (?), 9th-10th century 158.
Voss. lat. 79 *Aratus Manuscript*, France, 9th century 91, 92.

LIÉGE, Musée Archéologique:
*Notker Gospel Book* 203.

LONDON, British Museum:
Add. 5111 *Greek Gospel Book* (fragment), Byzantium, 7th century 106;
Add. 10546 *Grandval Bible*, Tours, ca. 840 148, *152*;
Add. 11695 *Beatus Apocalypse*, Silos, before 1109 168;
Add. 34890 *Grimbald Gospels*, Winchester, early 11th century *181*, 185;
Add. 37517 *Bosworth Psalter*, Canterbury (?), 10th century 185;
Add. 37768 *Psalter of Lothair*, Lorraine, 9th century 147;
Arundel 155 *Psalter*, Canterbury, 11th century 179;

LONDON, British Museum:
Cotton Caligula A.XV *Psalter*, Canterbury, 11th century 179;
Cotton Claudius B.IV *Aelfric's Paraphrase of the Pentateuch and Joshua*, England, 11th century 186, *189*;
Cotton Galba A.XVIII *Psalter of King Aethelstan*, France, 9th century, and Winchester, 10th century 178, 188, 195;
Cotton Julius A.VI *Anglo-Saxon Calendar*, 11th century 191;
Cotton Nero D.IV *Book of Lindisfarne*, late 7th century 109, *116*, *117*, 121, 122, 126;
Cotton Tiberius B.V *Anglo-Saxon Calendar*, 11th century 191;
Cotton Tiberius C.VI *Cotton Psalter*, Winchester, ca. 1050 *184*, 186, 190;
Cotton Vespasianus A.I. *Psalter*, Canterbury, 8th century *124*;
Harl. 603 *Copy of the Utrecht Psalter*, Canterbury, ca. 1000 186;
Harl. 647 *Aratus Manuscript*, France, 9th century *91*, 92;
Harl. 1775 *Gospel Book*, Italy, 6th century 98;
Harl. 2788 *Gospel Book*, Palace School of Charlemagne, ca. 800 137, 140;
Harl. 2904 *Ramsey Psalter*, South England, late 10th century 188;
Royal I.E.VI *Gospels* (perhaps fragment of a Bible), Canterbury, 8th century 125.

MADRID, Archivo Histórico Nacional:
Cod. 1240 *Beatus Apocalypse*, Távara, 970 166, 168, *173*, 174.

MADRID, Biblioteca Nacional:
B. 31 (Vit. 13.I) *Beatus Apocalypse*, León, 1047 168.

MAESEYCK, St Catherine's Church:
*Gospel Book* (fragment), York (?), 7th-8th century *120*, 122.

MAINZ, Cathedral Treasure:
*Sacramentary*, Mainz, late 10th century 210.

MANCHESTER, John Rylands Library:
MS 98 *Coronation Gospel Book of Otto III*, Master of the Registrum Gregorii, Trier, 996 202, 203, 210.

MERSEBURG, Cathedral Library:
Cod. 202 *Annals of Ravenna* (fragment), 9th-century copy 89.

MILAN, Biblioteca Ambrosiana:
C. 53 sup. *Gospel Book*, Cologne, early 11th century 208.

MONTPELLIER, Bibliothèque de l'Ecole de Médecine:
Cod. 409 *"Charlemagne" Psalter*, South Germany, 8th century 142.

MOUNT ATHOS, Stavronikita Monastery:
Cod. 43 *Greek Gospel*, Constantinople, 10th century 121.

MUNICH, Schatzkammer der Münchener Residenz:
*Book of Hours of Charles the Bald*, Palace School, 9th century 151.

MUNICH, Bayerische Staatsbibliothek:
Clm. 4452 *Book of Pericopes of Henry II*, Reichenau, early 11th century *204*, 205, 206;
Clm. 4453 *Gospel Book of Otto III*, Reichenau, ca. 1000 *198*, 205/207;
Clm. 4456 *Sacramentary of King Henry II*, Regensburg, early 11th century 212, 215;
Clm. 13601 *Uta Codex*, Regensburg, ca. 1025 *211*, 213;
Clm. 14000 *Codex Aureus of Charles the Bald*, Palace School, 870 151, 157, 212, 213;
Clm. 15713 *Book of Pericopes*, Salzburg, mid-11th century 215.

NEW YORK, The Pierpont Morgan Library;
M. 1 *Lindau Gospels*, St Gall, 9th century 109, 157;
M. 334 *Augustinus*, Luxeuil, 669 133;

234

# LIST OF COLORPLATES

## NINTH CENTURY

MINIATURES AND DRAWING:

## ELEVENTH CENTURY

FRESCOS:

MINIATURES AND DRAWING: